Changes in Decision-Making Capacity in Older Adults

Wiley Series in Clinical Geropsychology
Series Editor, Sara Honn Qualls

Psychotherapy for Depression in Older Adults
Sara Honn Qualls and Bob G. Knight, Eds.

Changes in Decision-Making Capacity in Older Adults
Sara Honn Qualls and Michael A. Smyer, Eds.

Forthcoming: *Aging Families and Caregiving*
Sara Honn Qualls and Steven H. Zarit, Eds.

Changes in Decision-Making Capacity in Older Adults

Assessment and Intervention

Edited by

Sara Honn Qualls

Michael A. Smyer

BICENTENNIAL
1807
WILEY
2007
BICENTENNIAL

John Wiley & Sons, Inc.

This book is printed on acid-free paper. ∞

Copyright © 2007 by John Wiley & Sons, Inc. All rights reserved.

Published by John Wiley & Sons, Inc., Hoboken, New Jersey.
Published simultaneously in Canada.

Wiley Bicentennial Logo: Richard J. Pacifico

Library of Congress Cataloging-in-Publication Data:

Changes in decision-making capacity in older adults : assessment and
intervention / edited by Sara Honn Qualls, Michael A. Smyer.
    p.   cm.—(Wiley series in clinical geropsychology)
  ISBN 978-0-470-03798-0 (cloth)
  1. Decision making in old age.   I. Qualls, Sara Honn.   II. Smyer, Michael A.
  BF724.85D44C48   2008
  155.67′1383—dc22   7017667
                                                      2007028125

Printed in the United States of America..

10 9 8 7 6 5 4 3 2 1

Contents

PART III: Clinical Evaluation and Intervention

Preface

The epidemic of cognitive impairment among very old adults has begun to permeate our awareness as a society, generating a sense of urgency in addressing the implications of limits on decision-making capacity in clinical, family, and legal settings. The contributors to this book are outstanding scholars and practitioners whose work is paving the way to new understanding and new practices. It may be only a slight overstatement to say that their work could revolutionize the policies and practices used throughout society to ensure that individual rights are protected while providing a safety net that prevents fraud, abuse, exploitation, and self-neglect.

Changes in several disciplines contribute to this revolution in policy and practice. Neuropsychologists are moving beyond their traditional role in diagnostic assessment to embrace a key role in assessing specific domains of decision-making capacity. Attorneys are engaging in the traditional counselor role with families who are confused about how to work with an aging member whose lack of insight into cognitive deficits is generating high safety risks. Health providers recognize that they cannot identify cognitive impairment accurately enough in brief screenings to make clear statements about capacity in particular domains. New legal and procedural standards are being invoked in courts with guardianships and conservatorships that require richer, more specific assessments of decision-making capacity.

What a great time to create a conference to train mental health professionals about assessments and interventions for decision-making capacity! The conference that forms the basis of this book was a remarkably creative event. Although the conference was intended to benefit mental health professionals who want to build skill in geropsychology, this particular event was as intellectually challenging to the presenters as it was to the attendees. Discussions among the presenters and attendees generated controversy, paradigm shifts, and collegial banter about the frameworks that would be most useful as well as tools that might benefit courts, health providers, or families. In short, the conference itself was a creative adventure.

In the middle of the conference, presenters escaped for a lovely dinner (in a wine room designed to facilitate the flow of creativity!) over which they debated and created the structure of this book. Some of the chapters represent material that was not part of the conference but was recognized for its importance in guiding mental health clinicians in their work around these issues. The presenters were remarkably generous with their time and scholarly skill as they agreed to work together to create what we hope is a coherent guidebook for clinicians. One principle the authors readily embraced was to provide regular and rich case illustrations throughout the book. Real-life, complex cases illustrate the importance of absorbing the material in all chapters in the book in order to be prepared for clinical practice in this complex arena of work.

The authors organized their contributions around the three cornerstones of information needed by clinicians working with older adults: normative age changes, distinctive contexts of clinical work with older adults, and aging-specific approaches to assessment and intervention. Therefore, the book is organized into three parts that address the effects of aging on decision-making capacity, the social and legal contexts of capacity decisions, and clinical evaluations and interventions related to decision-making capacity. Part I reviews research literature on aging against which all assessments of functioning must be compared. Part II introduces the social and legal systems in which clinicians must work. Finally, clinical frameworks, guidelines, and strategies for assessment and intervention are detailed in Part III. We encourage you to resist the temptation to begin in Part III with the hope of learning the clinical "how-tos." Like all cornerstones, all parts are necessary but not sufficient on their own.

Part I opens with Smyer's framework for conceptualizing decision-making capacity focusing on issues related to the person, the process, and the context. In the second chapter, Foster, Cornwell, Kisley, and Davis integrate research from neuroscience, cognitive psychology, and neuropsychology to provide a very thorough overview of the research literature on changes in cognition across the life span in healthy, community-dwelling older adults. The impact of common age-related medical conditions on cognitive functioning is reviewed by Kaye and Grigsby in Chapter 3, a particularly critical topic for geriatric mental health professionals trying to sort out the causes of decision-making impairments. Chapter 4, the last in this section, contains an excellent review by Woods and Tanius of the many ways in which dementia deleteriously impacts decision-making ability as well as aspects of decision making that are often spared.

Part II examines social and legal contexts of capacity decisions. Often, clinicians are taught to practice their skills without regard to context. The skills are often taught as if they have universal utility although research confirms that context shapes the behavior of both client and clinician. Qualls begins with an overview of the many players whose roles influence the lives of persons with compromised decision-making capacity, including people in almost all sectors of society. As experts in the practice of elder law, Marshall, Seal, and Vanatta-Perry tutor mental health professionals on the legal system in their readable, succinct chapter. Finally, Karel explores the effects of culture on decision making in her review of one particular domain, medical decision making. The chapters in Part II outline material many seasoned geropsychologists wish they could have read before learning it while practicing.

The clinical meat of the book is in the third and final part. The guidance and strategies presented in these chapters are outstanding, provided by leaders in the field of the psychology of decision-making capacity in older adults. Moye opens this part with an overview of a clinical framework for assessment that represents the culmination of years of work by the American Psychological Association and American Bar Association Working Group. Wood then reviews the role of neuropsychological assessment of decision-making capacity. The following two chapters review assessment approaches and tools relevant to specific domains of decision-making capacity. Moye and Braun review the capacity to consent to medical treatment and to make independent living choices. Hebert and Marson review findings from their elegant research program that examines multiple layers of complexity in the financial domain. Qualls argues that intervention is also a relevant focus for mental health professionals who are ideally positioned to determine whether environmental, technological, or social interventions can preserve autonomy while ensuring safety in persons with cognitive impairments. Finally, Kaye and Kenny address the bottom line that clinicians desperately want—strategies and principles for managing finances and business practices with impeccable ethical standards.

Smyer closes the book as he opened it, by raising the big picture issues so critical to clinical work in this rapidly evolving area of clinical practice. His epilogue highlights the interaction between the older person and his or her environment in shaping decision-making behavior and capacity.

Several metaphors might be suggested to capture the usefulness of this book: a road map; travel guide; or photo album of clinical images. The common thread is our hope that it will contribute to setting an exceptionally high bar for clinical practice in this practice domain at the intersection of legal and clinical practice. We also hope the book is supportive of clinicians who are willing to tackle the complexity and, often, the ambiguity of practice with some of the most vulnerable members of society.

SARA HONN QUALLS

Acknowledgments

We want to acknowledge the outstanding contributions of the authors who exceeded our expectations with their creative, insightful, and detailed analysis of this rapidly emerging field. Very few scientists write well for practitioners—and our authors more than met the challenge. We also appreciate the excellent editorial guidance of Patricia Rossi and her colleagues at John Wiley & Sons, who made it possible for this clinical geropsychology series to supply information to mental health professionals whose original clinical training may not have included skills needed to work with older adults. Providing learning resources targeted at seasoned professionals will help to build a much-needed workforce in geriatric mental health.

This book owes much to the people and funding who supported the Clinical Geropsychology Conference series. The financial sponsors of the conference can consider this book to be another benefit of their investment in the training resources in the field of Geropsychology. Special thanks to John Santos, trustee, and Marilyn Hennessey, executive director of the Retirement Research Foundation who have generously supported this effort. Many staff at the University of Colorado at Colorado Springs (UCCS) contributed hard work that made the conference possible, including Brian Glach, Lynette Van Eaton, Andrea Williams, Gwen Gennaro, David DuBois, and Lori Kisley. Raphael Sassower, professor of Philosophy at UCCS and restaurant proprietor par excellence, contributes generously to our working dinner each year at The Warehouse. Finally, the graduate students in the Geropsychology doctoral program at UCCS work behind the scenes primarily to make the details work. Thanks to Shannon Foster, Kimberly Hiroto, Heidi Layton, Molly Maxfield, Tara Noecker, Mary Stephens, and Ashley Williams—your enthusiasm for the conference series adds magic to the weekend.

Finally, Sara Qualls cannot complete these acknowledgments without noting that Mick Smyer has served not only as co-editor of this volume and conference co-chair, but more importantly has served as her primary career mentor since graduate school. She is most grateful for the myriad opportunities, tidbits of guidance and wisdom, and moral support over the years (especially in Toronto when she realized she will never catch up to him, not even when she grows up!).

Contributors

Michelle Braun, PhD
Department of Neurology
Wheaton Franciscan
    Healthcare—All Saints
Racine, Wisconsin

R. Elisabeth Cornwell, PhD
Department of Psychology
University of Colorado—Colorado
    Springs
Colorado Springs, Colorado

Hasker P. Davis, PhD
Department of Psychology
University of Colorado—Colorado
    Springs
Colorado Springs, Colorado

Shannon M. Foster, MA
Department of Psychology
University of Colorado—Colorado
    Springs
Colorado Springs, Colorado

Jim Grigsby, PhD
University of Colorado—Denver
Denver, Colorado
and
Health Sciences Center
Aurora, Colorado

Katina R. Hebert, MS
Department of Psychology
University of Alabama
Tuscaloosa, Alabama

Kathryn Kaye, PsyD
University of Colorado—Denver
Denver, Colorado
and
Health Sciences Center
Aurora, Colorado

Michele J. Karel, PhD
Department of Psychiatry
Harvard Medical School
Brockton Roxbury VA Medical
    Center
Brockton, Massachusetts

Michael Kenny, PsyD
Colorado University Aging Center
University of Colorado—Colorado
    Springs
Colorado Springs, Colorado

Michael A. Kisley, PhD
Department of Psychology
University of Colorado—Colorado
    Springs
Colorado Springs, Colorado

Wayna M. Marshall, JD, PC
Colorado Springs, Colorado

Daniel C. Marson, JD, PhD
Department of Neurology
University of Alabama—
   Birmingham
Birmingham, Alabama

Jennifer Moye, PhD
Department of Psychiatry
Harvard Medical School
VA Boston Healthcare System
Brockton, Massachusetts

Sara Honn Qualls, PhD
Department of Psychology
University of Colorado—
   Colorado Springs
Colorado Springs, Colorado

Catherine Seal, JD
Kirtland & Seal LLC
Colorado Springs, Colorado

Michael A. Smyer, PhD
Center on Aging and Work
Boston College
Chestnut Hill, Massachusetts

Betty E. Tanius, BA
Claremont Graduate University
Claremont, California

Lynn Vanatta-Perry, JD
Colorado Springs, Colorado

Stacey Wood, PhD
Scripps College
Claremont, California

Aging Effects on Decision-Making Capacity

CHAPTER

1

Aging and Decision-Making Capacity: An Overview

Michael A. Smyer

The following three examples introduce the complexities and challenges of assessing decision-making capacity in older adults.

Case Example: One Katrina Case

As Hurricane Katrina headed for New Orleans, residents were faced with difficult decisions. Should they stay? Should they leave? How should they decide? Michelle had lived in New Orleans her entire life. She had heard her parents tell stories of Hurricane Betsy and Camille. The lessons were simple: If you were on high ground in the city, you could survive a very strong hurricane. But Katrina was different. Forecasters were warning that it might be a category 5 storm when it hit New Orleans. Her parents were urging Michelle to evacuate, but Michelle was hesitating. Finally, her dad called: "It's time to go. We need to get out now while we can." Michelle was still not sure: "Our apartment is on high ground near the river. We will be okay." Her dad, now worried that she would stay behind, finally said what he was most worried about: "You're pregnant, and you have to be thinking about what the next few days will be like

3

not only for you but for that baby." Does Michelle have the capacity to make this life or death decision for herself and her baby?

 ## Case Example: The Day after Thanksgiving

Claire was tired after Thanksgiving dinner; tired and she had a headache. She took a quick nap and felt better. The next day, early in the morning, she awoke with the same headache. She went into the bathroom and sat down. The next thing she knew, she was in a brightly lit room, with a nurse standing by her bed. "Do you know where you are? Do you know what day it is?" "I have no idea where I am," she thought. "November something?" she answered. "It's February 6," the nurse answered. And that was the first sign Claire had that things had changed.

Over the next several months, she slowly put together the pieces of the puzzle that was now her life. Her dog had alerted her husband, Charles, when Claire collapsed. Charles called 911 and the rescue squad stabilized Claire and got her to the local hospital. The doctors there correctly diagnosed a brain aneurysm and transferred her to another hospital, with neurosurgery facilities. After surgery to repair the aneurysm, she was in a coma for almost 3 weeks. Then she slowly regained consciousness, but had little sense of where she was, little sense of herself, and only small islands of memory, but no way to connect the dots. By late spring, she was aware of how much her life had changed: She could barely walk now, could not drive, had periodic unpredictable mood swings, and was facing daily home health aide visits when she was released from the hospital. She would never be able to work again. She was depressed and angry: "They should have let me die!" she shouted. The doctors wanted to perform one more surgery, to insert a shunt to allow them to relieve pressure on her brain. Claire was adamant: "No more surgery." Does Claire have the capacity to make this decision?

Case Example: Hospice Request

David had been diagnosed with melanoma 2 years ago. At first, it looked like the surgery had been successful. But then the cancer reemerged and the news was sobering: stage 4. His doctor was direct and deliberate: "You have at most a year to live. You should put your affairs in order."

The doctor had been an optimist. Now 9 months later David was receiving hospice care at home. He knew that the end was near. As a religious person, he was not afraid of death. In fact, his religious devotion gave him a great deal of comfort. But he was worried about those whom he would leave behind, in particular Jane. David had been part of Jane's life for 19 years, ever since he married Jane's mother, Barbara. Although David and Barbara were now divorced, David had been a fatherly presence for Jane, a consistent source of support and encouragement. David had two biological children—Jane's half-brother, Dan, and another daughter, Pat. Pat and David had been estranged for several years; he refused to see her during his time in hospice.

During the week before his death, David called his lawyer. "I need your help. I want to adopt Jane, and I want to change my will. I want to write Jane into the will and I want to eliminate Pat from any inheritance." Does David have the capacity to make this set of decisions?

Each of these cases represents the dilemmas of decision making: How do we assess people's capacity to make decisions regarding themselves, their medical care, or their property? Does age matter in these deliberations? Our answers lie at the intersection of legal doctrine, behavioral science research, and clinical practice (Ganzini, Volicer, Nelson, & Deese, 2003). In crafting our answers, we try to balance two essential ethical principles: autonomy (or self-determination) and beneficence (protection) (Berg, Appelbaum, Lidz, & Parker, 2001; Moye & Marson, 2006).

Our answers reflect assumptions regarding three interacting elements: the person, the process, and the context (Smyer, 1996). Bronfenbrenner (1989), Lewin (1935, 1951), and Lawton (1998, 2000) remind us that these elements shape behavior and development across the life span. The other chapters in this volume will provide detailed discussions of each of these elements. The purpose of this chapter, however, is to provide a framework for thinking about decision-making capacity, using the person, process, and context as a focus.

THE PERSON

Definitions of decision-making capacity and incapacity have changed over time, developing a "legal fiction" of competency among older adults. Legal fictions are often developed in times of transition within the law (Sabatino, 1996). In the absence of national consensus on the defining elements of decision-making incapacity, there is a natural development of case-by-case and state-by-state legal fictions of capacity and incapacity and of the person.

Anderer (1990) noted that there has been an evolution in states' definitions of incapacity and, by extension, of decision-making capacity as well. Early on, many states equated advanced age (e.g., age 65) with disability. In essence, reaching an advanced age led to a presumption of possible disability.

This equation of age and disability was supplanted with the expectation that the presence of a disabling condition would have to be shown in order to secure a ruling of incapacity. Over time, however, this standard also changed, as the legal fiction caught up with gerontological research. It was no longer sufficient to carry a diagnosis of a disabling condition. Instead, the focus shifted to the functional impairment that accompanied the disabling condition (Grisso, 2003). In many ways, this development paralleled increased attention to activities of daily living (ADLs) and instrumental activities of daily living (IADLs) in clinical and research practice (e.g., Lawton, 1988).

The most recent developments of state definitions of incapacity have included a necessity for action by the state. This aspect emphasizes the

Table 1.1   District of Columbia Incapacity Tests

Aspect	Statute
Cognitive test	"Incapacitated individual" means an adult whose ability to receive and evaluate information effectively or to communicate decisions is impaired without court assistance or the appointment of a guardian or conservator, . . .
Behavioral test	. . . to such an extent that he or she lacks capacity to manage all or some of his or her financial resources or to meet all or some essential requirements for his or her physical health, safety, habilitation, or therapeutic needs . . .
Necessity test	. . . without court assistance or the appointment of a guardian or conservator."

Source: DC Code Annotated §21–2011(11) 2005.

conditions under which the state must intervene, the situations in which the duty of beneficence (protection) supersedes the assumption of the individual's autonomy.

The current best practice of legal fiction regarding incapacity among older adults requires three tests: cognitive, behavioral, and necessity. In Table 1.1, the District of Columbia statute is outlined as an example.

The absence of a national consensus on the legal fiction of capacity and incapacity requires clinicians and researchers to understand the relevant statutes in their own locale. As we see in the next section, states can vary not only on the legal fiction of the person, but also on their underlying assumptions regarding the process of decision making.

THE PROCESS

U.S. case law suggests four core abilities are essential in decision-making capacity: expressing a choice, understanding, appreciation, and reasoning (Appelbaum & Grisso, 1988; Moye & Marson, 2006). Expressing a choice implies the ability to take in information and the ability to convey a preference that is relatively consistent. Understanding implies the ability to comprehend information, including the risks and benefits of various actions. Age-related changes in cognitive functioning (see Foster, Cornwell, Kisley, & Davis, Chapter 2, this volume) and diseases of later life (see Moye, Karel, Azar, & Gurrera, 2004; Wood & Tanius, Chapter 4, this volume) affect these two abilities.

Jurisdictions will vary in the extent to which they emphasize the last two elements: appreciation and reasoning. Frank and Smyer (1998) suggested that "rationality dependent" standards have been excluded from more recent statutes that emphasize "appreciation dependent" processes. Rationality dependent definitions, as outlined by Roth, Meisel, and Lidz (1977) followed four standards: evidencing a choice; the reasonableness of the choice; the rationality of the reasons for the choice; and actual understanding. Stanley, Guido, Stanley, and Shortell (1984) emphasize rationality of the choice as well as the quality of the reasoning, as evidenced by weighing risks and benefits. Some have argued, however, that rationality and reasonableness are too subjective to be used as criteria for assessing an individual's decision-making capacity. Moreover, cultural influences may affect significantly the definition of rationality or reasonableness (see Karel, Chapter 7, this volume).

For example, consider one aspect of the California Probate Code:

> For purposes of a judicial determination, a person has the capacity to give informed consent to a proposed medical treatment if the person is able to do all of the following: (1) Respond knowingly and intelligently to queries about that medical treatment. (2) Participate in that treatment decision by means of a rational thought process. (California Probate Code §813)

In contrast, appreciation-dependent approaches emphasize the person's ability to appreciate the consequences of her or his actions or decisions. Appelbaum and Grisso's work (1988) represents this approach. They emphasized assessing the individual's understanding of information presented, including its relevance for the person and the person's ability to weigh the consequences of action or inaction.

Again, the California Probate Code offers an example:

> A deficit in the mental functions listed above may be considered only if the deficit, by itself or in combination with one or more other mental function deficits, significantly impairs the person's

ability to understand and appreciate the consequences of his or her actions with regard to the type of act or decision in question. (California Probate Code §811)

Marson and his colleagues provide an excellent example of clinically useful research that illustrates both a rational standard and an appreciation of the consequences of actions or decisions, even in the face of cognitive impairment (e.g., Marson, Cody, Ingram, & Harrell, 1995; Marson, Ingram, Cody, & Harrell, 1995). They use a treatment scenario to assess decision making by older adults with mild Alzheimer's disease (AD), older adults with moderate AD, and older adults in a control group:

Let us suppose that last night you awoke with sharp pains in your chest. You woke up hot and sweaty. You had problems breathing, and you felt dizzy. Today you have seen me, your doctor. I run some tests and I find out that you have two blocked blood vessels in your heart. (Marson, Ingram, et al., 1995)

Marson and his colleagues point out in Table 1.2 that there are several legal standards for the capacity to consent to treatment.

As Figure 1.1 summarizes, the performance of the groups varied by the legal standard applied. Under the most basic standards, evidencing a choice and making a reasonable choice, the majority of all three groups were deemed competent. However, as the cognitive demands of

Table 1.2   Legal Standards for Capacity to Consent

Standard	Capacity
S1	To evidence a treatment choice
S2	To make the reasonable choice (when the alternative is manifestly unreasonable)
S3	To appreciate the consequences of the choice
S4	To provide rational reasons for choice
S5	To understand treatment situation, choices, and respective risks/benefits

Source: "Assessing the Competency of Patients with Alzheimer's Disease under Different Legal Standards," by D. C. Marson, K. K. Ingram, H. A. Cody, and L. E. Harrell, 1995, *Archives of Neurology, 52,* pp. 949–954.

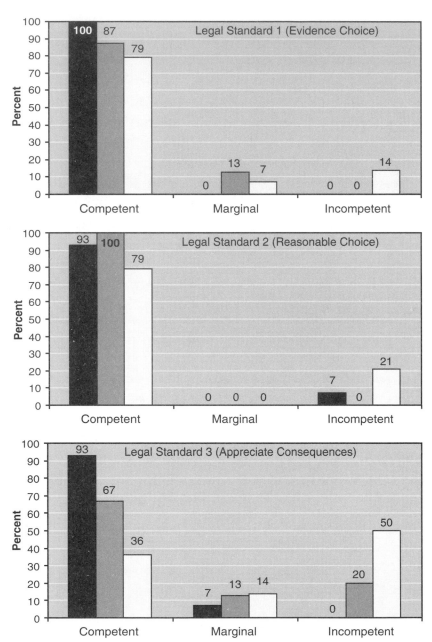

Figure 1.1 Competency Outcomes. Black represents older controls, grey represents patients with mild AD, and white represents patients with moderate AD. From "Assessing the Competency of Patients with Alzheimer's Disease under Different Legal Standards," by D. C. Marson, K. K. Ingram, H. A. Cody, & L. E. Harrell, 1995, *Archives of Neurology, 52*, pp. 949–954. Adapted with permission.

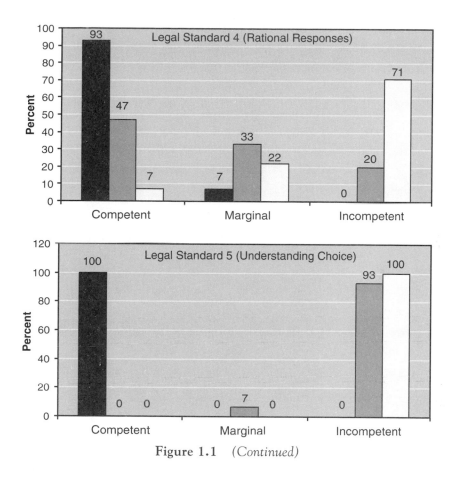

Figure 1.1   *(Continued)*

the standard increase (e.g., appreciating the consequences, providing rational responses, or understanding the consequences of their choices), larger percentages of those with mild and moderate AD were deemed incompetent.

Marson and his colleagues have also examined the capacity of older adults with mild and moderate AD in financial domains (Marson et al., 2000; see Hebert & Marson, Chapter 11, this volume). Here, too, they outlined several different standards of capacity, ranging from having basic monetary skills (Standard 1) to evidencing financial judgment (Standard 6). In these domains, the majority of patients with moderate AD were deemed incapable on the most basic standard (basic monetary skills), while over half of those with mild AD were deemed capable on this standard. On the most stringent criterion, however, only 13% of those with mild AD were deemed capable.

Others in this volume (e.g., Moye, Chapter 8, this volume) and elsewhere (e.g., Moye & Marson, 2006) map psychological functioning onto these elements of expressing a choice, understanding, appreciation, and reasoning. For now, however, there is a simple message: You must understand the emphasis—rationality dependent or appreciation dependent—of the jurisdictions you are practicing in. This emphasis will shape your assessment and reporting approaches.

THE CONTEXT

Legal and public policy developments provide a context for the increasing salience of issues of decision-making capacity. In this section, two examples highlight how these issues will become increasingly important: consumer-directed, community-based long-term care; and driving. In both domains, mental health professionals will be called on to balance autonomy and beneficence. In both domains, mental health professionals' practice will be shaped by demographics and by state-level legal and policy emphases. In both domains, state legislatures and executive offices play a key role in defining who has the capacity to be involved in key processes of self-maintenance in later life: planning for their own long-term care and continuing to be a licensed driver. In both domains, states will focus increased attention on functional capacities as the press of an aging population makes long-term care and personal mobility increasingly important issues at the intersection of public policy and personal life.

Consumer-Directed, Community-Based Long-Term Care

Over the past 20 years, legal, policy, and familial concerns have assured the growing reliance on consumer-directed, community-based long-term care. Legally, the 1999 U.S. Supreme Court *Olmstead* decision found that under the Americans with Disabilities Act undue institutionalization qualifies as discrimination when three conditions hold: treatment professionals have determined that community placement is appropriate; the individual does not oppose transfer to a less restrictive setting; and placement can be "reasonably accommodated" (National Council on Disabilities, 2003).

The National Council on Disabilities (NCD) recently reviewed the federal and state responses to the *Olmstead* decision. On the federal level, there were two major developments. In 2001, the president signed an executive order to provide technical assistance to the states for implementing responses to the decisions. In 2004, there was a commitment to a money-follows-the-person rebalancing demonstration, allowing states to seek home- and community-based waivers for long-term care services. The states have underscored the need to address systemic and fiscal barriers to responding to the *Olmstead* decision. Not surprisingly, NCD (2003) concluded that there is no consistency in approach across the states. There is, however, increasing pressure for states to develop community-based alternatives to institutional care, particularly in the area of mental health and long-term care (Cook & Jonikas, 2002; Dougherty, 2003). The federal government will award $1.75 billion of money-follows-the-person (MFP) grants over the next 5 years, beginning in January, 2007 (Fox-Grage, Coleman, & Freiman, 2006). This assures that states will be increasingly focused on home- and community-based long-term care options, and older adults' capacity for being maintained in the community.

The *Olmstead* decision occurred during a period of increased fiscal pressure on state budgets, caused, in part, by the increasing burden of Medicaid. For example, from 1991 to 2001, Medicaid spending grew at an annual rate of 11% nationwide. From 2001 to 2004, the annual growth rate for spending declined to 9% and the 2004 to 2005 growth rate was 6%, reflecting the increasing state and federal pressure on cost containment. Nationally, the Medicaid program spent more than $305 billion in fiscal year 2005, with approximately 35% spent on long-term care (Kaiser Family Foundation, 2007). The impact on state budgets has been clear: in fiscal year 2003, 21% of state budgets was spent on Medicaid expenditures (American Association for Retired Persons, 2004), adding pressure and increasing calls for cost containment at the state and federal levels. At the same time, policy makers and advocates are increasingly exploring less restrictive and less expensive community-based long-term care alternatives to institutional care. Their explorations require, however, a clear sense of who has the capacity to direct consumer-directed care in the community.

As Moye and Marson (2006) note, assessing the capacity for independent living requires straddling a "somewhat fuzzy line" among the family, clinical, and judicial roles in responding to adults' changing capacities. Family members have an important, direct stake in these issues: estimates suggest that there are more than 44 million caregivers in the United States; 21% of U.S. households include a caregiver. The majority of family caregivers (59%) provide care without calling on paid caregivers. For a sizeable minority (41%), however, paid help shares the challenges of caregiving (National Alliance for Caregiving, 2005).

Fiscal and family concerns have coalesced as states have pursued various options for home- and community-based long-term care, especially in their emphasis on consumer-directed care. Wiener (2006) summarized the key aspects of consumer-directed home care programs: "These programs give consumers control over who provides services, when they are provided, and how these services are delivered" (p. 29).

One example of consumer-directed, community-based long-term care is the Cash and Counseling Demonstration and Evaluation (CCDE) program (Brown et al., 2005). The CCDE program operates under waivers from the Centers for Medicare and Medicaid services and is now under way in a total of 15 states. Under CCDE, the consumer is able to flexibly manage a budget equivalent in value to what an agency would spend on personal care attendants for that individual under the traditional system. The participant can use that budget to hire workers (even relatives) and/or purchase a whole range of goods and services, assistive devices, or home renovations. CCDE also allows consumers to designate representatives, such as relatives or friends, to help make decisions about managing care. The CCDE program offers counseling regarding hiring and managing caregivers and fiscal management services to help consumers/participants handle their program responsibilities. The CCDE program was originally implemented in three states: Arkansas, New Jersey, and Florida. Evaluations of the CCDE implementation found that the program improved the health and well-being of care recipients and their caregivers, while costing no more than traditional services (Dale & Brown, 2005;

Foster, Brown, Phillips, & Carlson, 2005). Recent analyses of the CCDE data have focused on an important issue: Does mental illness affect consumer direction of community-based care? Researchers have found that the CCDE program worked just as well for older clients with mental illness as for those with other health problems but without mental illness (Shen, Smyer, Mahoney, Loughline, & Mahoney, in press).

This experience with CCDE is an important harbinger of issues that will become increasingly important for mental health professionals, older consumers, family caregivers, and policy makers. There are increasing legal, fiscal, and familial pressures to provide community-based, consumer-directed long-term care. Since care recipients typically have a combination of physical and mental health challenges, mental health professionals will be called on to assess the capacity of older adults to participate in care decisions. Much of this volume provides tools to make these assessments.

Assessing Driving Capacity

Our society is a mobile society, placing a premium on driving. Driving is a complex activity that requires both physical and cognitive skills. However, medical conditions, medications, and functional limitations may pose significant challenges for older drivers (Carr, Duchek, Meuser, & Morris, 2006; Cohen, Wells, Kimball, & Owsley, 2003). As a result, many older adults fear a variation on a once-familiar question: "Mom, may I have the car keys?"

By 2030, adults 65 and older will represent 25% of licensed drivers (Insurance Information Institute, 2006). As our driving population ages, policy makers, family members and older adults themselves are appropriately concerned: The rate of risk for an accident for adults over age 75 is nearly equal to the risk for younger drivers, ages 16 to 24 (Hartford Financial Services, 2005a). We are also facing a major challenge balancing autonomy and beneficence.

Knapp and VandeCreek (2005) have outlined the ethical, legal, and practice issues that arise for mental health professionals working with older, impaired drivers. They note that state laws regarding driving vary in several important ways: Requiring vision testing for license renewal; requiring a test of road knowledge; varying these requirements by ages; requiring health-care providers to alert the state if they have diagnosed a medical condition that will affect driving. Table 1.3 summarizes the significant variation state by state. It is a reminder that mental health professionals must be aware of the jurisdictional requirements that frame their own practice and the driving habits of their older clients.

Knapp and VandeCreek (2005) suggest a three-step model for mental health professionals to follow in working with older adults and their families around driving issues: (1) Be alert to triggers indicating a potential driving problem; (2) consider compensatory strategies; and (3) monitor the older adult's functioning in order to intervene as necessary.

Fortunately, there are informal and formal assessment approaches that can indicate potential driving problems. For example, there are self-assessment instruments that older adults can use to assess whether they should be concerned about their driving (e.g., American Association for Retired Persons, 2007). Similarly, there are checklists for family members to use in observing older drivers for patterns of driving limitations or impairments (e.g., Hartford Financial Services, 2005b). There are also structured interview formats for interviewing older drivers who are coping with cataracts (Owsley, Stalvey, Wells, & Sloane, 1999) or dizziness (Cohen et al., 2003), and these formats may be of broader interest, for use with both older drivers and their family members (comparing and contrasting their perspectives).

In addition to these informal assessments, mental health professionals may want to consider two more formal approaches: a driving simulation test and neuropsychological testing. Driving simulations are a useful proxy for actual road tests with older adults. The American Association for Retired Persons (AARP) now offers an online driving simulation at their web site (for a fee) and the Association for Driver Rehabilitation also has an online directory of member sites that can offer either a driving simulation test or a road test for older drivers (see www.aded.net).

Mental health professionals have been concerned with assessing older adults' driving performance for many years (e.g., Fitten, Perryman, & Wilkinson, 1995; Logsdon, Teri, & Larson, 1992). Recently, Szlyk Myers, Zhang, Wetzel, and Shapiro (2002) assessed the utility of a

Table 1.3 State Drivers License Renewal Laws Including Requirements for Older Drivers

State	Require Retest for Renewals at All Ages (1)				Age at Which States Require Older Drivers to Pass Tests				Require Doctors to Report Medical Conditions (2)	Age Limits on Mail Renewal
	Vision	Road	Knowledge	Medical	Vision	Road	Knowledge	Medical		
Alabama										
Alaska	X	(3)	X							69
Arizona	X	(3)			65					70
Arkansas	X									
California	X	(3)	X	(3)					X (4)	70
Colorado	X	(3)	(3)	X						66
Connecticut					65					65
Delaware		(3)	(3)	(3)	(3)	(3)	(3)	(3)	X	
D.C.					70	75	75	70		
Florida	X	(3)	(3)		80					
Georgia	X	(3)		(3)					X	
Hawaii	X	(3)		(3)		(3)	(3)			
Idaho	X	(3)		(3)		(3)	(3)	(3)		
Illinois	(5)		X	(3)		75				
Indiana				(3)				(3)		
Iowa		(3)	(3)	(3)						
Kansas	X	(3)	X							
Kentucky		(3)		(3)						
Louisiana	X	(3)	X							70
Maine					40, 62 (6)					
Maryland	X	(3)	(3)		40			(3)		
Massachusetts										
Michigan	X	(3)	X	(3)						

(continued)

17

Table 1.3 (Continued)

State	Require Retest for Renewals at All Ages (1)				Age at Which States Require Older Drivers to Pass Tests				Require Doctors to Report Medical Conditions (2)	Age Limits on Mail Renewal
	Vision	Road	Knowledge	Medical	Vision	Road	Knowledge	Medical		
Minnesota			X							
Mississippi		(3)	(3)							
Missouri	X									
Montana	X	(3)								
Nebraska	X	(3)	(3)							
Nevada	X (7)	(3)	(3)		65			70 (8)	X	
New Hampshire	X					75				
New Jersey	(9)								X	
New Mexico										
New York		(3)	(3)	(3)						
North Carolina	X	(3)	X	(3)						
North Dakota	X	(3)	(3)							
Ohio	X	(3)	(3)	(3)						
Oklahoma	(9)									
Oregon					50				X	
Pennsylvania	(10)			(8)	45 (11)			45 (11)	X	
Rhode Island	X	(3)		(3)						
South Carolina	X	(3)	(3)	(3)	65					
South Dakota	X									
Tennessee	(12)			(3)						
Texas	X			X						
Utah		(3)	(3)		65				X	

Vermont					
Virginia	X		(3)		
Washington	(3)	(3)	(3)	X	
West Virginia					X
Wisconsin		(3)	(3)		
Wyoming	X	(3)	(3)		80

(1) Periodic retests. Some states will waive vision retests for mail renewal or clean-record drivers.
(2) Physicians must report physical conditions that might impair driving skills.
(3) Retesting only for cause (e.g., after specific number of accidents or other points and infractions, for specific physical conditions) sometimes at examiner's discretion.
(4) Specifically requires doctors to report a diagnosis of dementia.
(5) 8-year vision re-examination.
(6) Vision tests are required at first renewal at age 40; at every second renewal after age 40; at every renewal after age 62.
(7) Except for in-state renewals by mail, unless applicant is over 70.
(8) Renewing by mail.
(9) 10 percent of all renewals are screened.
(10) 10 percent of drivers at or over 45 randomly chosen for medical and/or vision test.
(11) Random re-examination at specified age.
(12) Will retest at renewal for nonspecified cause.

Source: "Older Drivers," by Insurance Information Institute, October 2006. Retrieved January 15, 2007, from http://www.iii.org/media/hottopics/insurance/olderdrivers.

battery of neuropsychological tests in predicting older adults' driving performance. Their work involved two steps: (1) they surveyed neuropsychologists to assess what types of measures are currently used in assessing driving capacity; and (2) they assessed a sample of older drivers using the consensus battery of 12 measures, comparing their performance on the neuropsychological measures with their performance on a driving simulation task. The testing results were successful in differentiating older drivers with suspected dementia from unaffected older drivers. The psychological testing results were also correlated with the driving simulation results. In particular Trails A, Trails B, and Logical Memory (immediate) correlated with the largest number of driving measures (see Wood, Chapter 9, this volume, for more detail on neuropsychological testing).

The implications for psychological practice are clear and compelling. In the near future, many older adults and their family members will be asking for help in assessing older drivers' capacity for continued driving. Mental health professionals can draw on both informal and formal assessment approaches to assist in these difficult decisions. As they do so, they must be aware of their state's regulatory and statutory requirements regarding assessing driving risks.

CONCLUSION

This chapter provides a framework for considering the intersection of legal, social, and psychological approaches to assessing older adults' decision-making capacity. Mental health professionals are often called on to help older adults and their family members balance concerns for autonomy, beneficence, and risk. Older adults routinely seek assistance in making health-care decisions, decisions about their property and finances, and, eventually, decisions about their independence and interdependence. Mental health professionals bring to these exchanges an appreciation of the role of inter-individual differences in intra-individual change. Increasingly, our practice will require an ability to communicate our expertise to lawyers, judges, physicians, and family members. Three elements will shape psychological practice in these important areas: the changing legal fiction of the competent person; the legal and psychological assessment process; and the political, legal, and social context.

REFERENCES

American Association for Retired Persons. (2004). *Across the states: Profiles of long-term care* (6th ed.). Washington, DC: AARP Public Policy Institute.

American Association for Retired Persons. (2007). *Close call quiz.* Retrieved January 15, 2007, from www.aarp.org/families/driver_safety/driver_safetyissues/a2004-06-07-closecall.html.

Anderer, S. J. (1990). *Determining competency in guardianship proceedings.* Washington, DC: American Bar Association.

Appelbaum, P. S., & Grisso, T. (1988). Assessing patients' capacities to consent to treatment. *New England Journal of Medicine, 319,* 1635–1638.

Berg, J. W., Appelbaum, P. S., Lidz, C. W., & Parker, L. S. (2001). *Informed consent: Legal theory and clinical practice.* New York: Oxford University Press.

Bronfenbrenner, U. (1989). Ecological systems theory. In R. Vasta (Ed.), *Six theories of child development* (pp. 185–246). Greenwich, CT: JAI Press.

Brown, R., Carlson, B. L., Dale, S., Foster, L., Phillips, B., & Schore, J. (2005). *Cash and counseling: Improving the lives of Medicaid beneficiaries who need personal care or home- and community-based services* [Draft report]. Princeton, NJ: Mathematica Policy Research.

California Probate Code §811 (2007).

California Probate Code §813 (2007).

Carr, D. B., Duchek, J. M., Meuser, T. M., & Morris, J. C. (2006). Older adult drivers with cognitive impairment. *American Family Physician, 73*(6), 1029–1036.

Cohen, H. S., Wells, J., Kimball, K. T., & Owsley, C. (2003). Driving disability and dizziness. *Journal of Safety Research, 34,* 361–369.

Cook, J. A., & Jonikas, J. A. (2002). Self-determination among mental health consumers/survivors: Using lessons from the past to guide the future. *Journal of Disability Policy Studies, 13*(2), 87–95.

Dale, S., & Brown, R. (2005). *The effect of cash and counseling on Medicaid and Medicare costs: Findings for adults in three states.* Princeton, NJ: Mathematica Policy Research.

DC Code Ann. §21–2011(11) (2005).

Dougherty, R. H. (2003, June). Consumer-directed health care: The next trend? *Behavioral Healthcare Tomorrow, 21–27.*

Fitten, J., Perryman, K. M., & Wilkinson, C. J. (1995). Alzheimer and vascular dementia and driving: A prospective road and laboratory study. *Journal of the American Medical Association, 273*(17), 1360–1365.

Foster, L., Brown, R., Phillips, B., & Carlson, B. L. (2005). Easing the burden of caregiving: The impact of consumer direction on primary informal caregivers in Arkansas. *Gerontologist, 45,* 474–485.

Fox-Grage, W., Coleman, B., & Freiman, M. (2006). *Rebalancing: Ensuring greater access to home- and community-based services.* Retrieved March 22, 2007, from http://www.aarp.org/research/longtermcare/trends/ib79_mmltc.html.

Frank, L., & Smyer, M. A. (1998). Understanding decisional capacity of older adults. In A. S. Bellack & M. Hersen (Series Eds.) & B. Edelstein (Vol. Ed.), *Comprehensive Clinical Psychology: Vol. 7. Clinical Geropsychology* (pp. 113–131). Amsterdam: Elsevier Science.

Ganzini, L., Volicer, L., Nelson, W., & Deese, A. (2003). Pitfalls in the assessment of decision-making capacity. *Psychosomatics, 44,* 237–243.

Grisso, T. (2003). *Evaluating competencies* (2nd ed.). New York: Plenum Press.

The Hartford Financial Services. (2005a). *Are older drivers at risk?* Retrieved January 15, 2007, from www.thehartford.com/talkwitholderdrivers/driversatrisk.htm.

The Hartford Financial Services. (2005b). *Warning signs for older drivers.* Retrieved January 15, 2007, from www.thehartford.com/talkwitholderdrivers/worksheets/warningsigns2.pdf.

Insurance Information Institute. (2006). *Older drivers.* Retrieved January 15, 2007, from www.iii.org/media/hottopics/insurance/olderdrivers/on.

Kaiser Family Foundation. (2007). *State health facts.* Retrieved January 15, 2007, from www.statehealthfacts.org.

Knapp, S., & VandeCreek, L. (2005). Ethical and patient management issues with older impaired drivers. *Professional Psychology: Research and Practice, 36*(2), 197–202.

Lawton, M. P. (1988). Scales to measure competence in everyday activities. *Psychopharmacology Bulletin, 24*(4), 609–614.

Lawton, M. P. (1998). Environment and aging: Theory revisited. In R. J. Scheidt & P. G. Windley (Eds.), *Environment and aging theory: A focus on housing* (pp. 1–31). Westport, CT: Greenwood Press.

Lawton, M. P. (Ed.). (2000). *Annual review of gerontology and geriatrics: Focus on the end of life—Scientific and social issues.* New York: Springer.

Lewin, K. (1935). *A dynamic theory of personality.* New York: McGraw-Hill.

Lewin, K. (1951). *Field theory in social science.* New York: Harper & Brothers.

Logsdon, R. G., Teri, L., & Larson, E. B. (1992). Driving and Alzheimer's disease. *Journal of General Internal Medicine, 7,* 583–588.

Marson, D. C., Cody, H. A., Ingram, K. K., & Harrell, L. E. (1995). Neuropsychological predictors of competency in Alzheimer's disease using a rational reasons legal standard. *Archives of Neurology, 52,* 955–959.

Marson, D. C., Ingram, K. K., Cody, H. A., & Harrell, L. E. (1995). Assessing the competency of patients with Alzheimer's disease under different legal standards. *Archives of Neurology, 52,* 949–954.

Marson, D. C., Sawrie, S., Snyder, S., McInturff, B., Stalvey, T., Boothe, A., et al. (2000). Assessing financial capacity in patients with Alzheimer's disease: A conceptual model and prototype instrument. *Archives of Neurology, 57,* 877–884.

Moye, J., Karel, M., Azar, A. R., & Gurrera, R. J. (2004). Capacity to consent to treatment: Empirical comparison of three instruments in older adults with and without dementia. *Gerontologist, 44,* 166–175.

Moye, J., & Marson, D. C. (2006). Assessment of decision-making capacity in older adults: An emerging area of practice and research. *Journals of Gerontology, 62B*(1), P3–P11.

National Alliance for Caregiving. (2005). *Caregiving in the U.S.* Bethesda, MD: National Alliance for Caregiving. Retrieved January 15, 2007, from www.caregiving.org.

National Council on Disabilities. (2003). *Olmstead: Reclaiming institutionalized lives.* Washington, DC: Retrieved January 15, 2007, from www.ncd.gov /newsroom/publications/2003/pdf/relaimabridged.pdf.

Owsley, C., Stalvey, B., Wells, J., & Sloane, M. E. (1999). Older drivers and cataract: Driving habits and crash risk. *Journal of Gerontology: Medical Sciences, 54A,* M203–M211.

Roth, L. H., Meisel, A., & Lidz, C. W. (1977). Tests of competency to consent to treatment. *American Journal of Psychiatry, 134*(3), 279–284.

Sabatino, C. (1996). Competency: Refining our legal fictions. In M. A. Smyer, K. W. Schaie, & M. B. Kapp (Eds.), *Older adults' decision-making and the law* (pp. 1–28). New York: Springer.

Shen, C., Smyer, M. A., Mahoney, K. J., Loughline, D. M., & Mahoney, D. M. (in press). Does mental illness affect consumer direction of community-based care? Lessons from the Arkansas Cash and Counseling Program. *Gerontologist*.

Smyer, M. A. (1996). Decision-making capacity among older adults: Person, process and context. In M. A. Smyer, K. W. Schaie, & M. B. Kapp (Eds.), *Older adults' decision-making and the law* (pp. 283–287). New York: Springer.

Stanley, B., Guido, J., Stanley, M., & Shortell, D. (1984). The elderly patient and informed consent: Empirical findings. *Journal of the American Medical Association, 252*(10), 1302–1306.

Szylk, J. P., Myers, L., Zhang, Y., Wetzel, L., & Shapiro, R. (2002). Development and assessment of a neuropsychological battery to aid in predicting driving performance. *Journal of Rehabilitation Research and Development, 39*(4), 483–496.

Wiener, J. M. (2006). It's not your grandmother's long-term care anymore! *Public Policy and Aging Report, 16*(3), 28–35.

CHAPTER

2

Cognitive Changes across the Life Span

SHANNON M. FOSTER, R. ELISABETH CORNWELL,
MICHAEL A. KISLEY, AND HASKER P. DAVIS

In Western countries, the dynamic of age distribution across the population has changed dramatically in the past half century. In the early 1970s, the population age distribution was represented by a pyramid shape with a large base of young, by the year 2000, the population pyramid started to square off with a midlevel bulge of baby boomers, and by 2030, there will be approximately equal numbers of individuals in each decade of life with a total worldwide population of 1.4 billion individuals over 60 years of age. Medical science has greatly extended life expectancy, a positive event; yet, one that brings with it the potentially negative effects associated with declines in cognition, memory, and mental agility in a growing population of elderly.

Individuals entering midlife or later indicate frequent concern about changes in cognition, presenting a major assessment challenge for the clinical psychologist or primary physician. Few psychologists and even fewer physicians are properly trained in administering assessment tools to evaluate a patient's subjective or objective cognitive decline. With a growing elderly population, there are increasing demands for a quick and economical evaluation method that can correctly assess cognition and distinguish between normal age-related and pathological changes.

In this chapter, we describe the current view of normal cognitive changes across the adult life span in conjunction with findings from our data set comprised of approximately 4,000 individuals. Next, we note the distinction between normative and pathological changes in cognition, as well as declines in cognition including Cognitive Impairment, No Dementia (CIND); Age-Associated Memory Impairment (AAMI); Aging-Associated Cognitive Decline (AACD); and Mild Cognitive Impairment (MCI). This is followed by a discussion of neuropsychological, informant, and computerized screens for detecting early cognitive decline. Finally, we note recent findings on the effects of cognitive activity and physical exercise on cognitive functioning.

VERBAL RECALL AND SPATIAL MEMORY

Verbal recall and spatial memory have received extensive attention in the literature on age-related cognitive changes. Similar rates of decline occur in verbal and visuospatial memory, beginning as early as the 20s and continuing as a general linear decline across the life span (Park et al., 2002). Park and colleagues suggest that these defects may be first detectable in the 40s, but changes in abilities will not begin to affect everyday activities until the 80s.

Testing over 1,100 individuals between 15 and 89 years of age, we examine verbal recall and visuospatial memory using the Rey Auditory Verbal Learning Test (RAVLT) and a memory card task respectively. The RAVLT consists of five immediate trials followed by a delay trial. The memory card task is a variation of the television game show *Concentration* where participants must turn over cards in a 4 × 6 matrix and obtain matching pairs. The participant turns over two cards and, if they are not a match, the cards are turned back over to remain in play, whereas matches are removed from play. The memory card task also consists of five immediate trials followed by a delay trial that varies from 20 minutes to 1 year. For the purposes of this chapter, where we simply want to show changes across the life span, we present only the first trial of each. The results in the form of standard z-scores are shown in Figure 2.1.

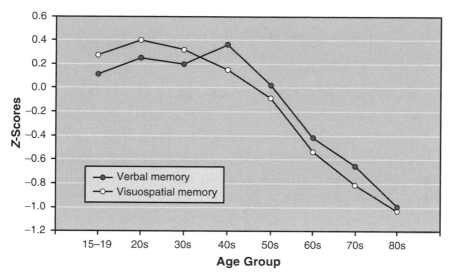

Figure 2.1   Standard Z-Scores for Performance on the First Trials of the RAVLT and Memory Card Task for Participants from 15 to 89 Years of Age (N = 1,138)

For the verbal material, individuals aged 15 to 19 and over 50 are impaired relative to participants in their 40s, and a linear decline is notable, beginning in the 40s. Similarly, a linear decline is present in visuospatial memory, which begins in the 20s and becomes significant in the 40s.

WORKING MEMORY

There is considerable ambiguity concerning the definition of *working memory*. It has been attributed various meanings, as well as being used interchangeably with short-term memory. For the purposes of this chapter, a practical sense of working memory versus short-term memory is given by multiplying 16 × 18 in your head versus attempting to remember a telephone number long enough to dial it. The former uses working memory and the latter short-term memory. Thus, a key attribute of working memory is the active manipulation of information, not just holding information in consciousness via rehearsal as occurs in short-term memory.

Among older individuals, working memory has received considerable attention, in part, because the process may underlie many of our higher order cognitive skills (e.g., memory, reasoning, problem solving). Age-related decline in working memory ability may manifest its effects in numerous aspects of everyday life. For example, the ability to make complex decisions in realms such as the selection of a health insurance policy may be compromised when multiple attributes are not easily held in consciousness. Salthouse (1993) has shown that the effects of age-related decline in performance of reasoning tasks are markedly reduced when controlling for working memory. Consistent with other research (Park et al., 2002; Salthouse, Kausler, & Saults, 1988), our data shows a predictable decline in working memory across the life span.

In our laboratory, we focus on two forms of the n-back task to examine both spatial and verbal working memory. For the n-back task, participants are shown a series of stimuli at the rate of one every 4 seconds and asked to indicate if the stimulus is identical to the stimulus n back in the series of stimuli. The n ranges from 1 to 3. The verbal working memory task uses letters for stimuli, while the spatial task uses location on a computer screen of red dots as stimuli. We tested over 400 individuals between 15 and 89 years of age. Individuals' scores were converted to z-scores and the mean performance across the life span is shown in Figure 2.2. The raw vocabulary score was also converted to a z-score and indicates that cognitive decline is not global (i.e., vocabulary does not show a decline). There was no significant difference between the spatial and verbal tasks; and a significant decline was detected in the 50s. These results are consistent with earlier reports (Park et al., 2002; Salthouse et al., 1988) and suggest similar rates of decline in verbal and spatial working memory with little difference in the extent of impairment.

EXECUTIVE FUNCTION

Executive functions are a conglomeration of complex processes (e.g., organizing, planning, initiating, inhibiting, and decision making), which

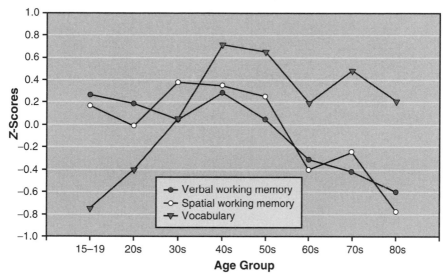

Figure 2.2   Standard Z-Scores for Performance on the 3-Back Component of a Verbal and Spatial Working Memory Task for Participants between 15 and 89 Years of Age (N = 404)

are loosely defined as the functions that guide higher-order complex be-havior. This entity of higher-order processes is believed to be dependent on neural activity of the frontal lobes. West (1996) has identified early morphological and physiological changes in the frontal cortex and pro-posed a prefrontal cortex theory of cognitive aging, which predicts that cognitive functions supported by the prefrontal cortex will show early age-related decline. As such, impaired performance on tasks measuring executive functions would be expected.

Problem Solving

To assess problem-solving ability, a specific executive function, per-formance on the Tower of Hanoi (TOH) transformation puzzle has been widely used. The TOH consists of three pegs with a number of disks varying in size. At the start, disks are typically arranged on the left peg with the largest disk on the bottom and the smallest on the top to form a pyramidal shape. The goal is to achieve the same arrangement on the goal peg with the constraints of moving one disk at a time and never placing a larger disk on top of a smaller disk. The minimal number of moves to achieve the goal is $2^n - 1$ moves where n represents the number of disks.

This task has long attracted the interest of investigators in the fields of cognitive psychology and artificial intelligence because of its application in the areas of problem solving and development of solution strategies (Simon, 1975). The TOH task is particularly useful in studying the effects of aging on executive function, and in the following section we show that the onset of significant impairment begins by the 6th decade of life.

We tested over 800 individuals in their 20s through 80s as part of an ongoing study and found impairment in performance consistent with previous findings (Rönnlund, Lövdén, & Nilsson, 2001). Using a computerized version, we administered five trials of a 3-ring TOH puzzle followed by five trials of a 4-ring puzzle. Participants unfamiliar or uncomfortable with using a computer mouse were administered the test on a touch screen. The standard TOH procedure was followed, and after each solution attempt the computer screen displayed the number of moves made for that attempt. If the number of moves made was greater than the optimal solution number, the participant was told the optimal solution number of moves (7 moves for 3-rings and 15 moves for 4-rings) and that they should try for this best solution. The task was administered in a single session of 10 trials.

Our analysis revealed that only the participants in their 80s were impaired on the 3-ring TOH puzzle. For the 4-ring puzzle, individuals 60 years of age or older made significantly more moves than individuals in their 20s, 30s, and 40s. The z-scores for number of moves on the TOH by the different age groups are shown in Figure 2.3.

Decision Making

Decision making is perhaps one of the most essential aspects of human behavior, and the decisions we make every day can range from inconsequential to critical. While all of us struggle with difficult decisions, as we age these struggles may become unmanageable. The elderly

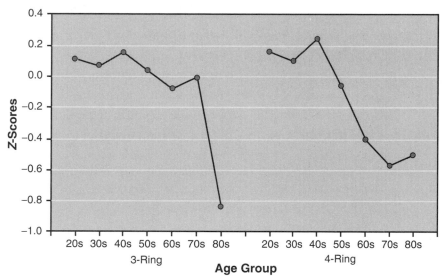

Figure 2.3   Standard Z-Scores for Performance on the Average of Five Trials for a 3-Ring and 4-Ring Tower of Hanoi Puzzle for Participants between 20 and 89 Years of Age (N = 755)

are often faced with an array of complex decisions, from health care to finances, all of which can dramatically affect their quality of life. Thus, it is of great importance to researchers, social workers, lawmakers, and the public at large to understand the effects of aging on decision making.

Researchers have largely focused on three basic types of decisions:

1. *Judgment and decision making:* Participants are generally asked to make a decision about some event based on several items of information. For example, if asked to make a decision about who should be admitted into graduate school, you would consider letters of recommendation, grade-point average, graduate record exam scores, self-statement of purpose, and research and/or clinical experience.

2. *Choice:* This type of decision making is sometimes referred to as "choice with certainty." Having been admitted to several graduate programs in psychology, you might establish a grid with the

programs arranged in rows and the attributes of interest in columns to provide a visual aid for your decision.

3. *Risky choice:* A risky choice is defined as choosing between two or more choices associated with uncertain consequences. In the laboratory, risky choice is frequently studied with simulated gambling games where the outcome is uncertain. Gambling tasks are particularly useful as they mimic similar behavior in the real world and have been used with an aging population.

Risky Choices (Choice with Uncertainty)

To explore the relationship between aging and decision making, we examined data collected using the Iowa Gambling Task (IGT). This task has been proposed as a laboratory analogue of everyday decision making under conditions of reward and punishment uncertainty (Bechara, Damasio, Damasio, & Anderson, 1994). We tested individuals between 20 and 89 years of age using a computerized version of the IGT, with four decks (A, B, C, and D), to assess decision-making skills across the life span. Participants were asked to select from any of the four decks and told they were free to switch decks at any time. The goal of the game was to win as much play money as possible and to avoid losing. Additionally, participants were told the game was fair, but that some decks were worse than others and they could avoid losing if they stayed away from the worst decks. After each choice, participants received feedback as to whether they won or lost money. Two decks (A and B) are associated with high reward but even higher loss, resulting in a net loss. The other two decks (C and D) are associated with low reward but lower loss, resulting in a net gain. Participants began with a $2,000 credit and were told they had to continue playing until the end of the game. The game consisted of 100 trials and took approximately 20 minutes to complete.

In two studies, we used the IGT to examine the effects of aging on risk taking and decision making. In Study 1, participants ($N = 155$) were divided into a young group ranging in age from 18 to 34 years (M = 22.14) and an older group ranging in age from 65 to 88 years (M = 77.3; Wood, Busemeyer, Koling, Cox, & Davis, 2005). Both young and elderly participants showed improved performance at similar rates over trials (i.e., increased the number of choices from good decks relative to bad decks) and did not differ in the number of choices to good versus bad decks. However, decision processes were analyzed using a theoretical mathematical model developed by Busemeyer and Stout (2002), showing that young and older participants used different strategies for successful performance on the IGT. The model referred to as the *expectancy-valence model* assesses several different performance parameters. One significant difference detected between the two groups was a stronger recency effect and more rapid forgetting of the response consequences by the elderly. Additionally, the older group gave equal weight to wins and losses in contrast to the younger participants who gave more weight to losses. In other words, the younger group used recollection of losses across more trials and the elderly more accurately represented the wins and losses.

In Study 2, we expanded our age range, adding participants to form 10 groups: 5 to 9 years ($n = 46$), 10 to 14 years ($n = 65$), 15 to 19 years ($n = 98$), 20 to 29 years ($n = 99$), 30 to 39 years ($n = 25$), 40 to 49 years ($n = 42$), 50 to 59 years ($n = 31$), 60 to 69 years ($n = 26$), 70 to 79 years ($n = 70$), and 80 to 89 years ($n = 29$). The outcome of interest was the net number of advantageous choices (Deck C + Deck D) − (Deck A + Deck B) made in blocks of 25 trials by the different age groups. For our purposes, we only note that the 5- to 14-year-old participants made fewer advantageous choices overall than age groups from 15 to 79 years of age, $p < .025$, and fewer advantageous choices on blocks two to four than all other age groups between 20 and 59 years of age, $p < .05$. Older adults in their 70s chose the advantageous decks significantly less often than adults in their 30s, $p < .05$; and adults in their 80s chose the advantageous decks significantly less often than the adults in their 30s or 50s, $p < .05$. On the fourth block of trials, the participants in their 70s continued to make fewer advantageous choices than adults in their 30s; and the participants in their 80s made significantly fewer advantageous choices relative to participants between 15 and 59 years of age, $p = .05$. The performance of age groups from the 20s through the 80s is shown in Figure 2.4.

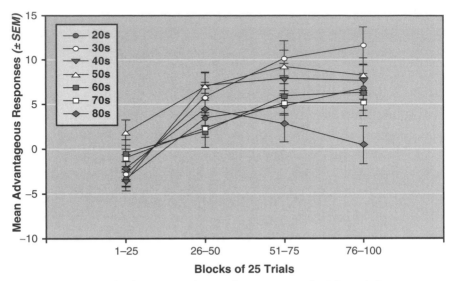

Figure 2.4 Standard Z-Scores for Performance on the Mean Advantageous Decision on the Iowa Gambling Task for Participants between 20 and 89 Years of Age (N = 222)

Poorer performance by individuals in their 70s and 80s in Study 2, but not Study 1 may be attributed to an increased sample size that provides more statistical power and allows for a finer grained analysis between age groups. Normal performance on the IGT is thought to be dependent on the ventromedial sector of the prefrontal cortex, and individuals with damage to this area demonstrate impairment (Bechara, 2004). This brain region is particularly sensitive to the negative effects of aging and may contribute to the deficit observed in our participants over 70 years of age (West, 1996). Accordingly, researchers have detected predicted deficits on the IGT among the elderly (Denburg, Recknor, Bechara, & Tranel, 2006).

EMOTION RECOGNITION

Recognizing emotions from facial displays is of great social importance, but research indicates differences between younger and older adults. In comparing older participants to younger ones, the former show significantly poorer recognition of fear and sadness, while being more sensitive to facial signals of disgust (Calder et al., 2003). However, findings from other studies, while indicating age-related differences in reading emotion in faces, have been inconsistent concerning age of onset. These differences could be due to inconsistent use of methods across studies.

In an attempt to clarify some of the inconsistencies found in previous studies, we presented all six of Ekman's basic emotions to participants across an age range of 20 to 89 years, with sample sizes adequate to examine subgroups of the elderly population (60 to 74 years and 75 to 89 years; Ekman & Friesen, 1976). To assess face-emotion recognition, we used a computer animation technique that better simulated actual emotional interactions than did previous studies. Participants were initially presented with a neutral expression, which incrementally increased, frame by frame, toward the full emotional expression (Animated Full Facial Expression Comprehension Test, AFFECT; Gagliardi et al., 2003; based on Ekman & Friesen, 1976). More specifically, we used four (two male; two female) of the standard Ekman photographs of the six basic emotions (i.e., fear, anger, sad, disgust, happy, and surprise). A morphing technique was used to generate 21 frames depicting a beginning neutral face expressing no emotion (0%) to a final face expressing either 25%, 50%, 75%, or 100% of the full expression for each emotion (with an additional 10% for happy). That is, on each trial an emotionally neutral face was initially presented and then morphed into one of the four intensity levels depicting the target emotion. To the left of each image presented were labels for the six basic emotions. After presentation, participants were asked to select the label corresponding to the emotion displayed in the final frame. Using this method, we can identify which, if any, of the six basic emotion-recognition tasks show age-related impairment, as well as identify the degree of impairment for each emotion.

Young adults (20 to 39 years old; $M = .77$, $SE = .01$) and middle-age adults (40 to 59 years old; $M = .77$, $SE = .01$) demonstrated the highest proportion of correct recognition for the six emotions combined. Young-old adults (60 to 74 years old; $M = .71$, $SE = .02$, $p < .05$) showed a significant decrease in correct recognition as compared to both the young and middle-age adults. The old-old adults (75 to 89 years old; $M = .66$,

$SE = .02$, $p < .05$) demonstrated significant impairment compared to all three younger groups.

Participants consistently and correctly identified the happy expression, followed by accurate identification of surprise, and then disgust. Individuals were most impaired in recognition of the three negative emotional expressions of fear, anger, and sadness. Figure 2.5 illustrates the changes in recognition accuracy rates for each emotion across age groups.

The two older adult groups were significantly impaired for the recognition of fear, anger, and sadness compared to the younger two adult groups ($p < .05$). Moreover, the old-old group exhibited significant impairment in recognizing anger and sad expressions compared to the young-old group ($p < .05$). The effect of sex was examined in the two elderly groups because of adequate representation of both male and female participants (60 to 74: 33% male; 75 to 89: 52% male) within these groups. Females ($n = 45$; $M = .71$, $SE = .02$) were significantly better than males ($n = 19$; $M = .63$, $SE = .02$) at correctly identifying all six emotions combined.

The method we used to assess age-related decline in emotion-expression recognition, allowed us to avoid the confound of initial primary emotional processing observed in other studies; giving us a clearer picture of how and

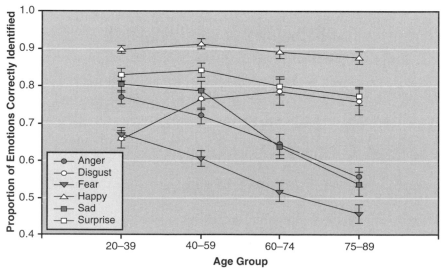

Figure 2.5   Proportion of Six Emotions Correctly Recognized by Research Participants between the Ages of 20 and 89 Years (N = 182)

when these changes occur across the adult life span. Consistent with previous studies, our findings support the view that age-related changes in emotion recognition occur across the adult life span.

EARLY PATHOLOGICAL COGNITIVE DECLINE

By understanding normative changes in cognition across the life span, abnormal variation can be recognized; this is the key to early detection of pathological changes. Individuals who experience normative cognitive decline may be able to adapt in ways that allow them to continue making decisions for themselves as well as maintaining an active, meaningful lifestyle. However, there may come a point when individuals experiencing pathological decline will find their decision making is compromised and negatively affecting day-to-day living. With this in mind, it is particularly important to detect pathological decline early so that individuals prepare and make important decisions about their future care before they have lost the ability to do so. To discuss the issues surrounding age-related cognitive decline, researchers have employed various terms to describe the particular pathologies associated with aging. These include: Cognitive Impairment, No Dementia (CIND); Age-Associated Memory Impairment (AAMI); Aging-Associated Cognitive Decline (AACD); and Mild Cognitive Impairment (MCI).

Cognitive Impairment, No Dementia

Of the descriptive categories noted above, CIND has the most general criteria; individuals display cognitive impairment (based on clinical judgment) but do not meet the criteria for dementia (Peters, Graf, Hayden, & Feldman, 2005). The criteria for CIND are vague because the category is meant to capture *all* individuals at risk for *any* type of dementia, not just Alzheimer's disease (AD).

Prevalence and Conversion

Data from two Canadian samples (Ebly, Hogan, & Parhad, 1995; Graham et al., 1997) suggest 16.8% to 29.5% of the population over age 65 could be classified as CIND. The Graham et al. study found that individuals living in the community showed a 15.8% prevalence, compared to 30.0% among institutionalized individuals. Other studies have found similar rates of prevalence ranging between 15% and 30% for individuals over 60 years of age (Feldman et al., 2003).

Longitudinal studies ranging between 18 months and 5 years have found conversion rates from CIND to dementia between 30% and 50% (Hsiung et al., 2006; Tuokko et al., 2003). Peters et al. (2005) examined five sub-groups of individuals with CIND: verbal dysfunction; verbal-visuospatial dysfunction; memory/verbal dysfunction; memory dysfunction; and, visuospatial dysfunction. Individuals in the memory dysfunction group were more likely to convert to dementia than those in other groups.

Age-Associated Memory Impairment

Criteria for AAMI, originally proposed in 1986 by a National Institute of Mental Health Work Group, include a subjective memory complaint and an objective memory impairment (measured by any memory test) at least one standard deviation (SD) below that of young adults, with otherwise normal general cognition and no dementia (Crook et al., 1986). Because impairment is measured against performance of young adults and episodic memory has been shown to decline with age, the utility of this concept for differentiating between normal and abnormal aging has been controversial.

Prevalence and Conversion

Hänninen et al. (1995) found that between the ages of 60 and 67 there is a 43.5% prevalence rate, which then drops to 37.7% for individuals between 68 and 78 years of age. Additionally, Pioggiosi, Berardi, Ferrari, Quartesan, and De Ronchi (2006) found that among 90-year-old individuals prevalence was 17.6%. The decline with age is likely due to individuals exhibiting increased signs of dementia and/or additional impairments across multiple domains.

Findings concerning conversion rates have been mixed (Crook et al., 1986). Whereas Nielson, Lolk, and Kragh-Sørensen (1998) found no differences in cognitive decline between controls and individuals diagnosed with AAMI (aged 60 to 80) over a 3.5-year period, Goldman and Morris (2001) found that individuals (older than 50 years of age) diagnosed with AAMI had a three-fold greater risk of developing AD over a 3-year period than age- and education-matched individuals. Likewise, although Hänninen et al. (1995) found AAMI to be a heterogeneous classification, 9.1% of AAMI individuals converted to dementia over a 3.6-year period, a higher rate than typically observed for controls. Taken together, studies of AAMI suggest prevalence is around 40% in individuals over the age of 60, with a conversion rate (~3% per year) only slightly higher than that of individuals without objective memory impairment.

Aging-Associated Cognitive Decline

Whereas the criteria for AAMI are limited to impairment in memory relative to that of young adults, the criteria for AACD include impairments in cognitive domains other than memory. These include attention and concentration, thinking, language, and visuospatial skills (Levy et al., 1994). To be classified within the AACD category, an individual must display objective impairment (>1 *SD*) in memory, as well as in at least one other cognitive domain relative to age- and education-matched peers. Additionally, the individual must have a subjective complaint of memory impairment (preferably corroborated by an informant) and must not meet the criteria for dementia.

Prevalence and Conversion

Ritchie, Artero, and Touchon (2001) estimate prevalence of AACD as 20.9% in the general population over the age of 60, but 48.7% to 56.8% among individuals with subjective cognitive complaints. In contrast, Busse, Bischkopf, Riedel-Heller, and Angermeyer (2003) examined the prevalence of cognitive impairment as defined by four conceptual criteria in a population-based sample (over the age of 75): (1) AACD, (2) a modified AACD that included individuals who did not have a subjective memory complaint, (3) amnestic-MCI, and (4) an impairment based on a Mini Mental State Examination (MMSE) score below 27. They found that original and modified AACD groups comprised 9% and 20% of their sample, respectively. Although it is unclear whether it is more common in those with or without subjective complaints, AACD is prevalent in approximately 10% to 20% of the population.

Ritchie et al. (2001) found that individuals (above age 60) classified as AACD had a conversion rate of 28.6% over a 3-year period. Busse et al. (2003) found conversion rates of 47% and 36% for their original and modified AACD groups, respectively, and concluded that the modified AACD had the best predictive power (over the other three concepts examined) for development of dementia. Over a 10-year period, Visser, Kester, Jolles, and Verhey (2006) calculated the risk of dementia in a memory-clinic sample (aged 39 years and above) as 0.28 and found that the risk increased with age. Overall, the prevalence of AACD is around 10% to 20% for individuals over 60 years of age, and annual conversion rates are also estimated at 10% to 20%, increasing with age.

Mild Cognitive Impairment

Originally the MCI concept was loosely defined as meeting the following criteria: (a) memory complaint, (b) normal activities of daily living, (c) normal general cognitive function, (d) abnormal memory for age, and (e) not demented. In 1999, Petersen et al. quantified the abnormal memory and general cognitive function criteria, such that an individual generally needed to perform 1.5 SD below age- and education-matched peers on memory tasks and be within 0.5 SD of age- and education-matched peers on a measure of general cognitive function (e.g., verbal and performance IQ). Following the Current Concepts in Mild Cognitive Impairment Conference in 1999, this definition became recognized as the definition for amnestic-MCI (a-MCI) because it is characterized solely by memory loss (Petersen et al., 2001). During this conference, two other sets of criteria were proposed to represent other possible presentations of MCI: multiple domain (slight impairments in multiple domains of cognition—language, attention, executive function, visuospatial skills—not necessarily requiring a memory deficit) and single nonmemory domain (impairment in a single cognitive domain other than memory).

In 2004, Petersen refined these concepts, such that individuals with multiple domain MCI could be classified as either having a memory impairment (a-MCI-multiple domain) or not (na-MCI-multiple domain), and individuals having a single impairment could likewise be classified with (a-MCI-single domain) or without (na-MCI-single domain) memory impairment. Petersen suggested that, regardless of categorization, it was important that the individual had minimal functional impairments and could not be diagnosed with dementia. Perneczky and Kurz (2006) assessed impairments in activities of daily living (ADLs) and instrumental activities of daily living (IADLs) for individuals diagnosed with MCI in an attempt to clarify "minimal functional impairment." Individuals met the criteria for MCI if they were impaired in at least one cognitive domain (in other words, they could fall into any of the four subgroups). These researchers found that all individuals were impaired in performing at least one IADL. The majority of IADL impairments were related either to activities that involved memory (e.g., finding things at home, keeping appointments, remembering conversations) or complex reasoning (e.g., finances, preparing meals/shopping). Results from this study suggest that most individuals who can be classified in an MCI category have deficits in IADLs, but not ADLs (e.g., bathing, transferring, eating). Researchers and clinicians should use this finding to clarify the nature of Petersen's "minimal functional impairment."

The importance of using the different classification schemes is related to differential dementia outcomes. Individuals classified as a-MCI-single domain or a-MCI-multiple domain are expected to be most likely to progress to AD, whereas those in the na-MCI-single domain and na-MCI-multiple domain groups are considered more likely to progress to other dementias, such as dementia with Lewy bodies or frontotemporal dementia. However, examination of the outcome for various MCI subgroups has produced conflicting results. Zanetti et al. (2006) found that individuals diagnosed with a-MCI-single domain consistently progressed to AD, whereas those diagnosed with MCI-multiple domain (amnestic status unknown) reliably progressed to vascular dementia. In contrast, Loewenstein et al. (2006) found no statistical differences in MCI subtype presentation between individuals exhibiting a gradually progressive decline (MCI-AD) versus an abrupt onset/stepwise decline (MCI-vascular). In other words, individuals with a-MCI-single or multiple domain and those with na-MCI-multiple domain were just as likely to be classified into the MCI-AD group as the MCI-vascular group.

Prevalence

Fisk, Merry, and Rockwood (2003) used the Canadian Study of Health and Aging (CSHA) sample of individuals over the age of 65 to examine prevalence rates of a-MCI. In doing so, they varied the definition of a-MCI to create four overlapping groups. The prevalence of a-MCI in the first group, which was required to have a subjective complaint of memory problems and intact IADLs, as well as an objective memory impairment, was 1.03%. The second group did not require intact IADLs; prevalence for this group was 1.48%. When individuals were included that did not express a subjective complaint, prevalence rose to 2.40%. Finally, prevalence was estimated as 3.02% when individuals were not required to express a subjective memory complaint or have intact IADLs. Ganguli, Dodge, Shen, and DeKosky (2004) found slightly higher prevalence rates of 3.2% (using 1.0 SD) or 1.1% (using 1.5 SD) when individuals ($M_{age} = 74.6$, $SD = 5.3$) were required to have intact IADLs and a subjective memory complaint, 6.3% when a memory complaint was not required (1.0 SD), and 9.9% when neither the memory complaint nor intact IADLs were required (1.0 SD). Using the strictest criteria for a-MCI (single domain), Ritchie et al. (2001) estimated the prevalence of this group as 3.2% in individuals over the age of 60. Likewise, Busse et al. (2003) found an a-MCI prevalence rate of 3% in a population-based sample of individuals over the age of 75. Among a group of individuals over 90 years of age, Pioggiosi et al. (2006) found the prevalence of a-MCI (multiple domain) to be 32.4%. Ribeiro, de Mendonça, and Guerreiro (2006) found that the majority of individuals ($M_{age} = 68.7$, $SD = 7.7$) diagnosed with a-MCI have impairments in at least one other domain, with 52.6% having impairment in another domain that is at least as severe as the memory impairment.

Alladi, Arnold, Mitchell, Nestor, and Hodges (2006) found that a-MCI prevalence rates in a memory clinic, serving individuals over that age of 50, varied according to the tests used to assess memory impairment. If only a verbal memory deficit was required prevalence was 43%, visual only resulted in 42% prevalence, either verbal or visual produced a prevalence rate of 54%, and requiring both a verbal and a visual impairment produced a prevalence of 31%. Additionally, similar to the findings of Ribeiro et al., Alladi et al. found that the majority of individuals with memory deficits also had deficits in other domains.

Overall, estimates suggest that prevalence of MCI is largely dependent on the definition used to describe the condition, with lower estimates (1% to 3%) in individuals with a-MCI-single domain and higher estimates (approximately 5% to 10%) in individuals with a-MCI-multiple domain. In specialized populations (e.g., memory clinic), prevalence estimates are higher (30% to 55%) and are dependent on the memory domain used to establish the diagnosis. Additionally, the number of cognitive domains assessed plays an active role in the diagnostic process, in that it is more likely that an individual will be diagnosed with a-MCI-single domain if assessment is limited in multiple domains.

Conversion

Using the 1999 criteria, Petersen et al. found that individuals with MCI converted to AD at a rate of 12% per year (over a 4-year period), whereas the conversion rate for controls was 1% to 2% per year. Ganguli et al. (2004) found similar results (10% to 17% versus 2% to 3%) over 2-year periods. Over 6 years, approximately 80% of individuals classified using the 1999 criteria converted to AD (Petersen, 2004). In contrast, Ritchie et al. (2001) found the conversion rate for a-MCI to be 11.1% over a 3-year period. Although Busse et al. (2003) found a conversion rate of 33% over a 2.6-year period; inspection of receiver operating characteristics suggested that the a-MCI criteria lacked ability to predict dementia. In an Asian sample, Wang, Lirng, Lin, Chang, and Liu (2006) reported an annual conversion rate of 18.2%.

Several studies and reviews have been conducted in an attempt to describe and understand differences in estimated conversion rates. Reviewing 19 longitudinal studies assessing conversion rates in MCI (unspecified criteria), Bruscoli and Lovestone (2004) found that annual conversion rates varied from 2% to 31%, with a mean rate of 10.24%. Individuals recruited from clinic settings had higher conversion rates than those recruited from community settings. In the Fisk et al. (2003) study examining differences in prevalence rates based on the criteria used to define a-MCI, the investigators did not find a significant difference in relative risk of conversion to dementia (44.2 to 46.7). However, Fisk and Rockwood (2005) found that among incident cases of a-MCI, individuals who had cognitive complaints had a greater relative risk of converting to dementia than those without cognitive complaints (26.4 to 38.7 versus 6.2 to 6.6). To determine if conversion rate varies by MCI subtype, Alexopoulos, Grimmer, Perneczky, Domes, and Kurz (2006) examined 81 individuals for approximately 3.5 years. Over this period, 25% of individuals with a-MCI, 54% of individuals with MCI-multiple domain (amnestic status unidentified), and 37.5% of individuals with na-MCI-single domain converted to dementia. Similarly, Tabert et al. (2006) found that over a 3-year period, individuals with a-MCI-multiple domain converted to dementia more frequently than individuals with a-MCI-single domain (50% versus 10%). Hodges, Erzinçlioğlu, and Patterson (2006) followed 10 individuals initially diagnosed with a-MCI-single domain for a minimum of 6 years. All individuals converted to dementia and the majority (7 of 10) progressed through a-MCI-multiple domain before converting. Storandt, Grant, Miller, and Morris (2006) compared rate of decline and survival rates for (1) individuals classified as *a-MCI-single domain*, (2) individuals categorized as *revised MCI* (i.e., individuals who met the criteria for a-MCI-multiple domain, na-MCI-single domain, and na-MCI-multiple domain), (3) individuals regarded as *pre-MCI* (i.e., a group of individuals who met informant-based subjective, but not objective, criteria for early dementia), and (4) a group of *controls* who did not meet any criteria for decline. They found a steeper rate of decline for the a-MCI-single domain group than for the other groups. The revised-MCI group declined at a steeper rate than the pre-MCI group and controls, and the pre-MCI group declined at a steeper rate than the controls. The a-MCI-single domain and revised-MCI groups progressed to dementia at similar rates (3.93 years versus 4.35 years), whereas the pre-MCI group took twice as long (7.82 years). At autopsy, 100% of individuals with a-MCI-single domain, 90% of those with revised-MCI, and 91% of those with pre-MCI had a neuropathologic diagnosis of AD. Over a 10-year period, Visser et al.

(2006) calculated the risk of developing dementia for individuals with a-MCI presenting at a memory-clinic (single or multiple domain) as .48 (i.e., individuals with a-MCI were 48% more likely to develop dementia than individuals without MCI) and found that the risk increased with age (.06 in ages 40 to 54, .52 in ages 55 to 69, 1.0 in ages 70 to 85). In general, prevalence of MCI ranges from 1% to 10% of the general population over the age of 60, with annual conversion rates of approximately 10% to 20%. Overall, these results suggest that a-MCI (single- or multiple-domain) may be a descriptor for early AD.

Across classification categories, it appears that early pathological cognitive decline is prevalent, but heterogeneous. Indeed, it appears to us that as many as 10% to 30% of the population over 60 years of age may have some form of cognitive impairment. Many individuals will convert to dementia, but others will remain stable or even improve. Much research is still needed to determine which characteristics of the current classification schemes are most useful in predicting which individuals will progress to what type of dementia and at what rate.

EARLY COGNITIVE DECLINE AND SCREENING

Our review of normal aging and pre-AD classifications reveals a predictable decline of cognitive functioning with age. Currently, there is no single simple test that can be administered to determine if an age related decline is normal or pathological. Given our increasing population of individuals over age 60, the demand for a quick, reliable and easily administered screening tool is growing. In the next section, we discuss how neuropsychological variables and informant reports can be used to detect cognitive decline, followed by a description of a few of the screening tests currently in use.

Neuropsychological Variables

Episodic memory has received the most attention in research on cognitive abilities that decline early in the dementia process. Greenaway et al. (2006) examined differences in performance on the California verbal learning test (CVLT) between controls, individuals with MCI, and individuals with AD. Results indicated that individuals with MCI perform between controls and individuals with AD across learning and memory measures. Specifically, individuals with MCI exhibit reduced learning, rapid forgetting, increased recency effects, more intrusions, and poor recognition displayed as increased false-positives. Although this pattern of deficits is present, the combination of delayed recall and total learning is the most efficient at differentiating between individuals classified as normal, MCI, and AD (68.7% correct classification).

Beyond deficits in episodic memory, many researchers have examined the utility of different test combinations in predicting conversion to dementia. Several researchers have suggested that the combination of memory and language deficits is best at identifying predementia. Hänninen et al. (1995) examined the ability of various neuropsychological tests to predict conversion from AAMI to AD over a 3.6-year period. These investigators found that even though tests of memory (verbal and visual) were the most efficient predictors of conversion, a combination of these measures along with measures of language ability (category and semantic fluency) resulted in the most accurate prediction of conversion from AAMI to AD. Likewise, Chételat et al. (2005) found that change in global cognitive ability measured by the total score of the Mattis Dementia Rating scale correlated with baseline performance in delayed episodic memory, as well as semantic autobiographical and category word fluencies. Hodges et al. (2006) also found that the most consistent early deficits in 10 individuals with MCI, who eventually converted to AD, were in episodic memory and category fluency. Howieson et al. (2003) investigated which neuropsychological variables predicted conversion to mild impairment and then dementia in a group of old-old individuals (72 years and older, M_{age} = 81.4, SD = 6.2). Several memory measures were associated with development of mild impairment, but only confrontational naming was associated with conversion from mild impairment to dementia. Tabert et al. (2006) examined the predictive utility of neuropsychological variables in the conversion from MCI to AD. Measures that significantly predicted time to conversion included those of learning/memory (immediate recall, delayed recall, and percentage savings), language (category fluency and confrontational naming), and attention.

Using stepwise regression techniques, Tabert et al. concluded that the combination of immediate verbal recall and attention was the most predictive of time to conversion.

The combination of memory and executive function measures has also been shown to accurately predict conversion to AD from MCI. For example, Chen et al. (2001) examined differences in preclinical performance changes for several measures of orientation, language, visuospatial skills, memory, and executive function in a prospective community-based study. They found that the best predictors were in executive functions (Trail-Making Tests A and B) and episodic memory (Word List: delayed recognition and third learning trial).

Comprehensive reviews of the literature have revealed similar conclusions. In a review of the various concepts of early cognitive decline, including AAMI, AACD, CIND, and MCI, Feldman and Jacova (2005) found that episodic memory is one of the best predictors of dementia, while semantic memory/language may add to the discriminative ability of a screen. Reviewing the literature on MCI, researchers at the Current Concepts in Mild Cognitive Impairment conference (1999) suggested that neuropsychological testing batteries should include measures of new learning, delayed recall, attention, and executive function (Petersen et al., 2001). Rosenberg, Johnston, and Lyketsos (2006) made similar recommendations for clinicians assessing individuals for early cognitive decline; suggesting the inclusion of tests of delayed episodic verbal and logical recall, verbal category and semantic fluency, attention, processing speed, visuospatial functions, and executive functions.

Overall, studies of neuropsychological indicators of early decline suggest that testing batteries should include measures of episodic memory (learning and recall), as well as measures assessing attention, language skills, visuospatial abilities, and executive functions (Feldman & Jacova, 2005).

Informant Reports

Tierney, Herrmann, Geslani, and Szalai (2003) found that the predictive validity of the MMSE (69% sensitivity, 78% specificity) could be improved when used in combination with an informant rating of cognitive decline from the 19-item scale in Section H of the Cambridge Mental Disorders Examination (CAMDEX; 83% sensitivity, 79% specificity). Ready, Ott, and Grace (2003) evaluated the utility of asking informants two questions, one related to repetitive questioning (i.e., does he or she ask the same question repeatedly) and the other related to repetitive behaviors (i.e., does he or she repeat the same behavior continuously). Repetitive questioning, but not repetitive behaviors, was sensitive in identifying early dementia cases in the absence of any other measure (88% sensitivity, 72% specificity, 82% classification accuracy).

More generally, the Clinical Dementia Rating (CDR) scale has been used to identify changes in previously established cognitive functioning. Frequently, use of this scale allows researchers and clinicians to identify changes in an individual's cognitive functioning (based on informant report), before the individual meets the criteria for MCI (Storandt et al., 2006). The CDR assesses whether cognitive abilities in a variety of domains (e.g., memory, orientation, executive function) have begun to decline and interfere (to some extent) with daily functioning. A score of 0 represents no decline and normal functioning; 0.5 suggests some decline, but not enough to be classified as demented; and 1.0 signifies mild dementia.

Using a single-case study design, Godbolt et al. (2005) followed an individual at risk for familial AD for 11 years and came to the same conclusion; the earliest signs of pathological decline may be reports of intra-individual change that are made before an individual meets the criteria for MCI. When the individual entered the study, he was functioning normally and showing no signs of cognitive decline. Five years after he entered the study, he and his wife reported that his memory had declined slightly over the previous year; however, they did not seek medical attention for his memory problems until 5 years after they first noticed changes in his memory (10 years into the study). He was diagnosed with AD the following year. Neuropsychological assessment results showed practice effects over the first few years of the study, with gradual decline beginning (on some tests) as early as 6 years before his diagnosis (5 years into the study). This individual did not meet the criteria for MCI until 3 years before diagnosis (8 years into the study).

Taken together these studies suggest that informant reports of intra-individual change may be highly sensitive measures of early cognitive decline, especially in the absence of sequential measures of cognitive ability.

Neuropsychological Screening Tools
Variations of the Mini Mental State Examination

Loewenstein et al. (2000) created and examined a modified Mini Mental State Examination (MMSE) with extended delayed recall. In addition to the standard administration of the MMSE, three additional recall measures were added. After each recall of the three words, the participant was reminded of the words. The first recall was given approximately 2 minutes after initial presentation of the words (standard administration), and subsequent recalls were given at approximately 5 minute intervals, with other tasks filling the intervals. Discriminant function and optimal sensitivity analyses revealed that a cumulative recall score of the first three delay recall trials was the best measure at discriminating between controls and individuals with MCI (83.3% sensitivity, 90.4% specificity, 80% positive predictive value). This was a large improvement over the MMSE alone, which yielded 70.8% sensitivity, 84.6% specificity, and 68% positive predictive value.

Using the full-length versions of the MMSE and the patient and informant ratings of Section H of the CAMDEX, Tienery et al. (2003) found that only six items from the three measures were necessary to produce the greatest predictive validity in detection of AD (90% sensitivity, 94% specificity). The six questions included the day of the week and delayed-word recall items from the MMSE, informant questions about the patient's ability to manage money and remember short lists of items, and patient questions about any changes in his or her mood or ability to find the right word. Affirmations to the questions addressing money management, memory for a short list, and changes in mood all increase the likelihood that the patient will develop dementia within 2 years, whereas affirming that the patient has difficulty finding the right word decreases the chance that the patient will develop dementia.

Computerized Screens

There are now a number of commercially available computerized screens for detecting cognitive decline. We note two commercially available examples:

1. *Mindstreams* is a computerized battery designed to detect MCI. Testing lasts approximately 45 minutes and covers the domains of memory, executive functions, visuospatial ability, language, attention, information processing, and motor skills. The tests are adaptive, such that level of difficulty is adjusted depending on performance to minimize ceiling effects. Dwolatzsky et al. (2004) found that the memory, executive function, visuospatial, language, and information-processing outcome parameters were effective in discriminating between individuals with no impairment and those with MCI. These measures were at least as effective as traditional neuropsychological tests of the same domains. In addition, the memory, visuospatial, and language outcome parameters were effective in discriminating between individuals with MCI and those with mild AD. Mindstreams has also been shown effective at discriminating between normally aging individuals and those with MCI or AD, even in the presence of depressive symptoms (Doniger et al., 2006). All domains, except motor skills, were shown to be unaffected by level of depression.

2. *The Computer-Administered Neuropsychological Screen for Mild Cognitive Impairment (CANS-MCI)* measures memory, executive function, and language performance. Initial analyses suggest that this screen has high internal and test-retest reliabilities, as well as concurrent validity (Tornatore, Hill, Laboff, & McGann, 2005). Further, all tests of the CANS-MCI were able to differentiate between a sample of memory impaired and normally functioning older adults. Further analyses in individuals with early cognitive

decline are necessary to determine the discriminative and predictive abilities of this screen.

ALLEVIATING COGNITIVE DECLINE

Given the pervasiveness of cognitive decline with aging (both normal and pathological), it is reasonable to question whether anything can be done to delay or alleviate this decline. Researchers have investigated the effects of cognitive activity and physical exercise on cognitive performance. Generally, the results from both sets of studies are inconclusive, but suggest that neither can hurt you and either or both may be helpful.

Cognitive Activity

Cognitive Outcomes

Salthouse (2006) reviewed research related to the mental-exercise hypothesis, more commonly known as the use-it-or-lose-it hypothesis. Included in this review were studies on training interventions and comparisons of preexisting groups. To examine the causal relationship between mental activity and cognitive ability, Salthouse argued that it was necessary to examine differences in the rate of change in cognitive abilities, rather than differences in level of cognitive ability. More specifically, examining rate of change in cognitive abilities was necessary to differentiate between the differential-preservation hypothesis, which suggests that mental activity protects against cognitive decline, and the preserved-differentiation hypothesis, which holds that an individual's current level of cognitive activity is at least partially dependent on his or her cognitive abilities. In this review, Salthouse argues that engagement in cognitive activity may enhance cognitive ability, but this enhancement is typically circumscribed to a specific ability and the process does not decelerate the rate of cognitive decline. Although he concluded that there is little empirical support for the mental-exercise hypothesis, he suggested that individuals engage in mentally stimulating activity; after all, such activities are certainly not harmful, could possibly be helpful, and at a minimum increase positive activity for the participant.

Functional Outcomes

A recent large-scale longitudinal study of cognitive training on retention of mental abilities provides a different perspective. The Advanced Cognitive Training for Independent and Vital Elderly (ACTIVE) study sought to examine whether improvements in cognition translated to benefits in everyday functioning (Willis et al., 2006). Individuals (N = 2,802) were randomly assigned to one of four groups: (1) reasoning training, (2) memory training, (3) speed training, or (4) control. Training consisted of 10 sessions that lasted 60 to 75 minutes. A subset of individuals in each of the training groups also received booster training during the 1st and 3rd years post training. Booster training consisted of four sessions lasting 75 minutes. Assessment included cognitive measures of reasoning, memory, and attentional speed, as well as functional measures of everyday problem solving, ADL and IADL abilities, and everyday speed of processing. Individuals were assessed at baseline, immediately after training, and then 1, 2, 3, and 5 years post training. Each training condition produced improved cognitive performance (circumscribed to the ability trained). Individuals who participated in the reasoning and speed of processing booster groups improved significantly more than those who did not receive training. These results remained significant at year 5. Concerning the effects of training on daily functioning, all three training groups reported fewer IADL difficulties; however, this result was only significant for the reasoning training group. No effects of training were found on the everyday measure of problem solving; however, individuals who received booster training in the speed of processing group performed significantly better on the everyday measure of processing speed than those who did not receive the booster training. Although the evidence is limited, findings from this study suggest that improvements in cognitive function attained through cognitive training can have a positive effect on daily functioning.

Physical Exercise

Several studies have examined the effects of physical activity on cognitive functioning. Reviews of these studies provide conflicting results about the beneficial effects of physical activity on cognitive functioning. In 2003, Colcombe and Kramer conducted a meta-analysis of longitudinal studies examining the effects of physical fitness on the cognitive functioning of older adults. Their results suggested that physical activity can have a profoundly beneficial effect on the cognitive abilities of older adults. Generally, fitness training (aerobic or a combination of aerobic plus strength) improved cognitive performance by .5 *SD*. The effect was strongest for executive processes, but was also significant for controlled, spatial, and speeded processes. Combined training produced significantly better results than aerobic training alone. Additionally, training programs lasting more than 6 months produced significantly better results than short or moderate programs. Duration of the session needed to be greater than 30 minutes to obtain a significant effect. Finally, women benefited more than men, and mid- to old-old adults seemed to benefit more than young-old adults. The observational studies reviewed by Lautenschlager and Almeida (2006) provide similar support for the beneficial effects of physical activity on cognition and seem to suggest that physical activity reduces the risk of developing dementia. Together these reviews suggest a beneficial effect of physical activity on cognition; however, randomized clinical trials have not been conducted to offer conclusive evidence that physical activity reduces the risk of cognitive decline or dementia.

Although the Colcombe and Kramer (2003) and Lautenschlager and Almeida (2006) reviews supported the beneficial effect of physical activity on cognition, a meta-regression analysis conducted by Etnier, Nowell, Landers, and Sibley (2006) suggested that the relationship between physical activity and cognition cannot be explained by the cardiovascular fitness hypothesis. This hypothesis posits that cardiovascular fitness (resulting in more oxygen to the brain) mediates the relationship between physical activity and cognition. Therefore, although a positive relationship appears to exist between physical activity and cognition, it cannot be explained by cardiovascular fitness. Further, an unexpected finding of the Etnier et al. analysis suggested that physical activity might actually be negatively associated with cognition in older adults.

The results from studies on the effects of physical activity on cognition are inconclusive. Generally, the findings suggest that there is a positive relationship between physical activity and cognition, although as of yet an unequivocal explanation for this relationship does not exist. Overall, there seem to be more reasons for engaging in physical activity than not. At the very least, physical fitness will enable an individual to perform physically challenging IADLs and ADLs longer.

CONCLUSION

Decline in most cognitive domains, with the exception of crystallized intelligence, begins in adulthood and demonstrates a progressive decline across the life span.

Approximately 10% to 30% of individuals 60 years of age and older can be classified into a category indicative of early cognitive decline. Indeed, the numbers of elderly experiencing cognitive difficulties suggest a hidden epidemic.

There is no agreed on screen for detection of preclinical Alzheimer's disease, but success has been achieved with screens using neuropsychological variables, informant reports, standardized screens such as the MMSE, and more recently, computerized screens using neuropsychological variables.

Physical exercise appears to ameliorate cognitive decline in the elderly. Evidence for cognitive training as a means of reducing cognitive decline is equivocal, but does no harm and may be helpful.

REFERENCES

Alexopoulos, P., Grimmer, T., Perneczky, R., Domes, G., & Kurz, A. (2006). Progression to dementia in clinical subtypes of mild cognitive impairment. *Dementia and Geriatric Cognitive Disorders, 22*(1), 27–34.

Alladi, S., Arnold, R., Mitchell, J., Nestor, P. J., & Hodges, J. R. (2006). Mild cognitive impairment: Applicability of research criteria in a memory clinic and characterization of cognitive profile. *Psychological Medicine,* 1–9.

Bechara, A. (2004). The role of emotion in decision-making: Evidence from neurological patients with orbitofrontal damage. *Brain and Cognition, 55,* 30–40.

Bechara, A., Damasio, A. R., Damasio, H., & Anderson, S. W. (1994). Insensitivity of future consequences following damage to human prefrontal cortex. *Cognition, 50,* 7–15.

Bruscoli, M., & Lovestone, S. (2004). Is MCI really just early dementia? A systematic review of conversion studies. *International Psychogeriatrics, 16,* 129–140.

Busemeyer, J. R., & Stout, J. C. (2002). A contribution of cognitive decision models to clinical assessment: Decomposing performance on the Bechara gambling task. *Psychological Assessment, 14,* 253–262.

Busse, A., Bischkopf, J., Riedel-Heller, S. G., & Angermeyer, M. C. (2003). Mild cognitive impairment: Prevalence and predictive validity according to current approaches. *Acta Neurologica Scandinavica, 108,* 71–81.

Calder, A. J., Keane, J., Manly, T., Sprengelmeyer, R., Scott, S., Nimmo-Smith, I., et al. (2003). Facial expression recognition across the adult life span. *Neuropsychologia, 41,* 195–202.

Chen, P., Ratcliff, G., Belle, S. H., Cauley, J. A., DeKosky, S. T., & Ganguli, M. (2001). Patterns of cognitive decline in presymptomatic Alzheimer's disease: A prospective community study. *Archives of General Psychiatry, 58,* 853–858.

Chételat, G., Eustache, F., Viader, F., de la Sayette, V., Pélerin, A., Mézenge, F., et al. (2005). FDG-PET measurement is more accurate than neuropsychological assessments to predict global cognitive deterioration in patients with mild cognitive impairment. *Neurocase, 11,* 14–25.

Colcombe, S., & Kramer, A. F. (2003). Fitness effects on the cognitive function of older adults: A meta-analytic study. *Psychological Science, 14*(2), 125–130.

Crook, T., Bartus, R. T., Ferris, S. H., Whitehouse, P., Coehn, G. D., & Gershon, S. (1986). Age-associated memory impairment: Proposed diagnostic criteria and measures of clinical change: Report of a National Institute of Mental Health work group. *Developmental Neuropsychology, 2,* 261–276.

Denburg, N. L., Recknor, E. C., Bechara, A., & Tranel, D. (2006). Psychophysiological anticipation of positive outcomes promotes advantageous decision-making in normal older persons. *International Journal of Psychophysiology, 61,* 19–25.

Doniger, G. M., Dwolatzky, T., Zucker, D. M., Chertkow, H., Crystal, H., Schweiger, A., et al. (2006). Computerized cognitive testing battery identifies mild cognitive impairment and mild dementia even in the presence of depressive symptoms. *American Journal of Alzheimer's Disease and Other Dementias, 21*, 28–36.

Dwolatzky, T., Whitehead, V., Doniger, G. M., Simon, E. S., Schweiger, A., Jaffe, D., et al. (2004). Validity of the Mindstream™ Computerized Cognitive Battery for Mild Cognitive Impairment. *Journal of Molecular Neuroscience, 24*, 33–44.

Ebly, E. M., Hogan, D. B., & Parhad, I. M. (1995). Cognitive impairment in the nondemented elderly: Results from the Canadian Study of Health and Aging. *Archives of Neurology, 52*, 612–619.

Ekman, P., & Friesen, W. V. (1976). Measuring facial movement. *Environmental Psychology and Nonverbal Behavior, 1*, 56–75.

Etnier, J. L., Nowell, P. M., Landers, D. M., & Sibley, B. A. (2006). A meta-regression to examine the relationship between aerobic fitness and cognitive performance. *Brain Research Reviews, 52*, 119–130.

Feldman, H. H., & Jacova, C. (2005). Mild cognitive impairment. *American Journal of Geriatric Psychiatry, 13*, 645–655.

Feldman, H. H., Levy, A. R., Hsiung, G.-Y., Peters, K. R., Donald, A., Black, S. E., et al. (2003). A Canadian Cohort Study of Cognitive Impairment and Related Dementias (ACCORD): Study methods and baseline results. *Neuroepidemiology, 22*, 265–274.

Fisk, J. D., Merry, H. R., & Rockwood, K. (2003). Variations in case definition affect prevalence but not outcomes of mild cognitive impairment. *Neurology, 61*, 1179–1184.

Fisk, J. D., & Rockwood, K. (2005). Outcomes of incident mild cognitive impairment in relation to case definition. *Journal of Neurology, Neurosurgery, and Psychiatry, 76*, 1175–1177.

Gagliardi, C., Frigerio, E., Burt, D. M., Cazzaniga, I., Perrett, D. I., & Borgatti, R. (2003). Facial expression recognition in William's syndrome. *Neuropsychologia, 41*, 733–738.

Ganguli, M., Dodge, H. H., Shen, C., & DeKosky, S. T. (2004). Mild cognitive impairment, amnestic type: An epidemiologic study. *Neurology, 63*, 115–121.

Godbolt, A. K., Cipolotti, L., Anderson, V. M., Archer, H., Janssen, J. C., Price, S., et al. (2005). A decade of pre-diagnostic assessment in a case of familial Alzheimer's disease: Tracking progression from asymptomatic to MCI and dementia. *Neurocase, 11*, 56–64.

Goldman, W. P., & Morris, J. C. (2001). Evidence that age-associated memory impairment is not a normal variant of aging. *Alzheimer Disease and Associated Disorders, 15*, 72–79.

Graham, J. E., Rockwood, K., Beattie, B. L., Eastwood, R., Gauthier, S., Tuokko, H., et al. (1997). Prevalance and severity of cognitive impairment with and without dementia in an elderly population. *Lancet, 349*, 1793–1796.

Greenaway, M. C., Lacritz, L. H., Binegar, D., Weiner, M. F., Lipton, A., & Cullum, C. M. (2006). Patterns of verbal memory performance in mild cognitive impairment, Alzheimer's disease, and normal aging. *Cognitive Behavioral Neurology, 19*(2), 79–84.

Hänninen, T., Hallikainen, M., Koivisto, K., Helkala, E.-L., Reinikainen, K. J., Soininen, H., et al. (1995). A follow-up study of age-associated memory impairment: Neuropsychological predictors of dementia. *Journal of the American Geriatrics Society, 43*, 1007–1015.

Hodges, J. R., Erzinçlioğlu, S., & Patterson, K. (2006). Evolution of cognitive deficits and conversion to dementia in patients with mild cognitive impairment: A very-long-term follow-up study. *Dementia and Geriatric Cognitive Disorders, 21*, 380–391.

Howieson, D. B., Camicioli, R., Quinn, J., Silbert, L. C., Care, B., Moore, M. M., et al. (2003). Natural history of cognitive decline in the old old. *Neurology, 60*, 1489–1494.

Hsiung, G.-Y., Donald, A., Grand, J., Black, S. E., Bouchard, R. W., Gauthier, S. G., et al. (2006). Outcomes of cognitively impaired not demented at 2 years in the Canadian Cohort Study of Cognitive Impairment and Related Dementias. *Dementia and Geriatric Cognitive Disorders, 22*, 413–420.

Lautenschlager, N. T., & Almeida, O. P. (2006). Physical activity and cognition in old age. *Current Opinions in Psychiatry, 19*, 190–193.

Levy, R., Howard, R. J., Richards, M., Amaducci, L. A., Derouesne, C., Hafman, A., et al. (1994). Aging-associated cognitive decline. *International Psychogeriatrics, 6*(1), 63–68.

Loewenstein, D. A., Acevedo, A., Agron, J., Issacson, R., Strauman, S., Crocco, E., et al. (2006). Cognitive profiles in Alzheimer's disease and in mild cognitive impairment of different etiologies. *Dementia and Geriatric Cognitive Disorders, 21*, 309–315.

Loewenstein, D. A., Barker, W. W., Harwood, D. G., Luis, C., Acevedo, A., Rodriguez, I., et al. (2000). Utility of a modified mini-mental state examination with extended delayed recall in screening for mild cognitive impairment and dementia among community dwelling elders. *International Journal of Geriatric Psychiatry, 15*, 434–440.

Nielson, H., Lolk, A., & Kragh-Sørensen, P. (1998). Age-associated memory impairment: Pathological memory decline or normal aging? *Scandinavian Journal of Psychology, 39*(1), 33–37.

Park, D. C., Lautenschlager, G., Hedden, T., Davidson, N. S., Smith, A. D., & Smith, P. K. (2002). Models of visuospatial and verbal memory across the adult lifespan. *Psychology and Aging, 17*, 299–320.

Perneczky, R., & Kurz, A. (2006). The role of activities of daily living in the MCI syndrome. *Research and Practice in Alzheimer's Disease, 11*, 174–178.

Peters, K. R., Graf, P., Hayden, S., & Feldman, H. (2005). Neuropsychological subgroups of cognitively-impaired-not-demented (CIND) individuals: Delineation, reliability, and predictive validity. *Journal of Clinical and Experimental Neuropsychology, 27*, 164–188.

Petersen, R. C. (2004). Mild cognitive impairment as a diagnostic entity. *Journal of Internal Medicine, 256*, 183–194.

Petersen, R. C., Doody, R., Kurz, A., Mohs, R. C., Morris, J. C., Rabins, P. V., et al. (2001). Current concepts in mild cognitive impairment. *Archives of Neurology, 58*, 1985–1992.

Petersen, R. C., Smith, G. E., Waring, S. C., Ivnik, R. J., Tangalos, E. G., & Kokmen, E. (1999). Mild cognitive impairment: Clinical characterization and outcome. *Archives of Neurology, 56*, 303–308.

Pioggiosi, P. P., Berardi, D., Ferrari, B., Quartesan, R., & De Ronchi, D. (2006). Occurrence of cognitive impairment after age 90: MCI and other broadly used concepts. *Brain Research Bulletin, 68*, 227–232.

Ready, R. E., Ott, B. R., & Grace, J. (2003). Amnestic behavior in dementia: Symptoms to assist in early detection and diagnosis. *Journal of the American Geriatrics Society, 51*, 32–37.

Ribeiro, F., de Mendonça, A., & Guerreiro, M. (2006). Mild cognitive impairment: Deficits in cognitive domains other than memory. *Dementia and Geriatric Cognitive Disorders, 21*, 284–290.

Ritchie, K., Artero, S., & Touchon, J. (2001). Classification criteria for mild cognitive impairment: A population-based validation study. *Neurology, 56*, 37–42.

Rönnlund, M., Lövdén, M., & Nilsson, L.-G. (2001). Adult age differences in Tower of Hanoi performance: Influence from demographic and cognitive variables. *Aging, Neuropsychology, and Cognition, 8,* 269–283.

Rosenberg, P. B., Johnston, D., & Lyketsos, C. G. (2006). A clinical approach to mild cognitive impairment. *American Journal of Psychiatry, 163,* 1884–1890.

Salthouse, T. A. (1993). Influence of working memory on adult age differences in matrix reasoning. *British Journal of Psychology, 84,* 171–199.

Salthouse, T. A. (2006). Mental exercise and mental aging: Evaluating the validity of the "Use It or Lose It" hypothesis. *Perspectives on Psychological Science, 1*(1), 68–87.

Salthouse, T. A., Kausler, D. H., & Saults, J. S. (1988). Investigation of student status, background variables, and the feasibility of standard tasks in cognitive aging research. *Psychology and Aging, 3,* 29–37.

Simon, H. A. (1975). The functional equivalence of problem solving skill. *Cognitive Psychology, 7,* 268–288.

Storandt, M., Grant, E. A., Miller, P., & Morris, J. C. (2006). Longitudinal course and neuropathologic outcomes in original vs. revised MCI and in pre-MCI. *Neurology, 67,* 467–473.

Tabert, M. H., Manly, J. J., Liu, X., Pelton, G. H., Rosenblum, S., Jacobs, M., et al. (2006). Neuropsychological prediction of conversion to Alzheimer's disease in patients with mild cognitive impairment. *Archives of General Psychiatry, 63,* 916–924.

Tierney, M. C., Herrmann, N., Geslani, D. M., & Szalai, J. P. (2003). Contribution of informant and patient ratings to the accuracy of the mini-mental state examination in predicting probable Alzheimer's disease. *Journal of the American Geriatrics Society, 51,* 813–818.

Tornatore, J. V., Hill, E., Laboff, J. A., & McGann, M. E. (2005). Self-administered screening for mild cognitive impairment: Initial validation of a computerized battery. *Journal of Neuropsychiatry and Clinical Neuroscience, 17*(1), 98–105.

Tuokko, H., Frerichs, R., Graham, J., Rockwood, K., Kristjansson, B., Fisk, J., et al. (2003). Five-year follow-up of cognitive impairment with no dementia. *Archives of Neurology, 60,* 577–582.

Visser, P. J., Kester, A., Jolles, J., & Verhey, F. (2006). Ten-year risk of dementia in subjects with mild cognitive impairment. *Neurology, 67,* 1201–1207.

Wang, P. N., Lirng, J. F., Lin, K. N., Chang, F. C., & Liu, H. C. (2006). Prediction of Alzheimer's disease in mild cognitive impairment: A prospective study in Taiwan. *Neurobiology of Aging, 27,* 1797–1806.

West, R. L. (1996). An application of prefrontal cortex function theory to cognitive aging. *Psychological Bulletin, 120,* 272–292.

Willis, S. L., Tennstedt, S. L., Marsiske, M., Ball, K., Elias, J., Koepke, K. M., et al. (2006). Long-term effects of cognitive training on everyday functional outcomes in older adults. *Journal of the American Medical Association, 263,* 2805–2814.

Wood, S., Busemeyer, J., Koling, A., Cox, C., & Davis, H. (2005). Older adults as adaptive decision makers: Evidence from the Iowa Gambling Task. *Psychology and Aging, 20,* 220–225.

Zanetti, M., Ballabio, C., Abbate, C., Cutaia, C., Vergani, C., & Bergamaschini, L. (2006). Mild cognitive impairment subtypes and vascular dementia in community-dwelling elderly people: A 3-year follow-up study. *Journal of the American Geriatrics Society, 54,* 580–586.

CHAPTER

3

⏤⏵◆⏴⏤

Medical Factors Affecting Mental Capacity

KATHRYN KAYE AND JIM GRIGSBY

Changes in cognition may be associated with a wide range of variables, including both chronic and acute medical conditions, alterations in brain dynamics (Arbib, Érdi, & Szentágothai, 1998), and changes in physiologic state due to physiologic and/or environmental factors (e.g., Bodnar, Commons, & Pfaff, 2002). Geropsychologists and geriatric neuropsychologists generally are attuned to the possibility that their patients have disorders involving structural brain lesions. These may be neurodegenerative in nature (e.g., Alzheimer's disease, Parkinson's disease, corticobasal degeneration), or they may result from focal or general insults to the central nervous system (e.g., stroke, exposure to neurotoxins). The impact of medical factors on cognition can be difficult to determine as well as to quantify; consequently, such factors may be disregarded or de-emphasized during assessment of mental capacity. It is increasingly apparent, however, that one or more medical conditions, in many cases combined with adverse effects of medication, can cause temporary or even permanent changes in mental functioning. The examiner must be aware of the presence of medically related cognitive decline and document it clearly in the evaluation report. In some cases, it will be necessary to discontinue or postpone an examination if there are suggestions of a potentially reversible disorder requiring medical attention. In other cases, in which conditions are chronic and irreversible, test results must be interpreted cautiously, so as not to attribute the patient's impairment exclusively to a more common type of neurodegenerative or focal dementia.

Variables affecting physiologic state include mood, pain, fatigue, febrile illness, inflammatory conditions, nutritional status, neuroendocrine disorders, electrolyte balance/hydration, effects of medication, time of day and circadian rhythms, and motivational state. For example, with respect to circadian rhythms, performance on certain cognitive tests has been shown to vary based on time of day (Blake, 1967). As a rule, people tend to perform some tasks better in midmorning than in late afternoon; on the digit span test, there is nearly a full digit difference between early and late in the day, and this variability should be kept in mind when patients are tested or retested at different times on separate days.

At any given moment, overall physiologic state exerts a significant effect on how an individual behaves at that time. State affects the person's responses to an interviewer's questions as well as his or her performance on various cognitive and neuropsychological measures. As Bodnar and colleagues (2002) note, "most behavioral responses above the level of the reflex do not happen instantaneously. They result from coordinated relationships among neuronal subsystems that produce states favoring their occurrence on presentation of the adequate stimulus" (p. 2). Much of the focus of this chapter is on various states, or physiologic concomitants of states, that can influence the cognitive functioning of older individuals.

The range of factors affecting physiologic state and brain dynamics is vast (Grigsby & Osuch, 2007), and a comprehensive discussion of the topic extends well beyond the scope of this chapter, the aim of which is to address some of the important biomedical issues with which the geropsychologist should be familiar when assessing capacity. Our main objective is to alert readers to the necessity of considering medical and physiologic variables that could influence their patients' cognitive status, in many cases only transiently if timely intervention is provided.

INFECTION

Aging is accompanied by a relative immunodeficiency, or immune dis-regulation, that increases susceptibility to infection (Roos, 2002). Neuroendocrine changes cause a progressive increase in the concentration of glucocorticoids and catecholamines and a decrease in the production of growth and sex hormones that is similar to a pattern associated with chronic stress (Kevorkian, 2006). Reactivation of latent infection, chronic illnesses such as diabetes, cardiopulmonary disease, cancer, or treatment with immunosuppressants or coricosteroid therapy all may contribute to decreased cell-mediated immunity. Confusion is a frequent initial indicator of an infectious process in an older adult, and the sudden development of a confusional state in a cognitively intact elder, or an abrupt decline in cognition in a person with underlying dementia, suggests an acute medical problem and always should be taken seriously.

Pneumonia

Pneumonia, an inflammatory reaction to microbes or microbial products in the pulmonary parenchyma, is the leading infectious cause of death and the fourth leading cause of mortality overall in the elderly. The underlying cause can be bacterial or viral, but in 30% to 50% of cases, no specific pathogen can be identified (Beers & Berkow, 2000). Oropharyngeal colonization and silent aspiration are two predisposing factors, but the primary risk factor for contracting and dying from pneumonia is the presence of other serious medical illnesses. Confusion is common in patients of all ages who are developing or suffering from pneumonia, but elderly pneumonia patients are particularly likely to become confused, often before other symptoms are evident.

Urinary Tract Infections

The prevalence of urinary tract infections (UTIs) increases with age in both females and males; however, such infections may go unnoticed because many patients are asymptomatic. Although the overall incidence of UTIs and urinary incontinence is higher in females, the ratio of incidence narrows with advancing age due to bladder outlet obstruction associated with benign prostatic hyperplasia (BPH) in older men (Beers & Berkow, 2000). Confusion and delirium often accompany UTIs in the elderly and can be the initial signals of an infection, especially in demented individuals (Martin & Whitehouse, 1990). Antibiotics, which unfortunately may cause side effects of gastrointestinal distress and diarrhea sometimes leading to dehydration, are the most frequently prescribed medications for treating UTIs. Some antibiotic medications, as well as drugs often used for management of urinary incontinence, also have an adverse effect on mental status in the elderly, particularly if an underlying dementia is present.

Influenza

Influenza A or B is associated with acute, severe respiratory tract illness with early symptoms of fever and myalgias. Older persons typically have a lower-than-normal body temperature (Stehman, Strachan, Glenner, Glenner, & Neubauer, 1996); therefore, the presence of fever is more difficult to detect. Elderly individuals, particularly frail nursing home residents, are more likely to experience influenza complications such as respiratory distress syndrome or septic shock, both of which can be deadly (Fornek & Henning, 2004). If the psychologist becomes aware of signs of respiratory illness in an older person who is being evaluated in an assisted living facility or nursing home, medical professionals should be informed of these concerns. In most cases, the evaluation should be postponed until medical issues have been resolved because test results are likely to represent only the transient effects of infection on the central nervous system.

Herpes Zoster

Herpes zoster, or shingles, is a common condition in older adults involving the activation of a latent herpes virus in the peripheral nervous system (Donahue, Choo, Manson, & Platt, 1995). It can be extremely painful, and following the onset of a rash consisting of vesicular eruptions, the pain may continue over a long period of time. The prolonged pain of shingles is called *postherpetic neuralgia*, and it often is accompanied by depression and sickness behavior (to be discussed later in the chapter). Treatment of herpes zoster consists of oral antiviral medications, tricyclic antidepressants, oral narcotics, or intrathecal methylprednisolone (Schabbing & Corboy, 2002). Unfortunately, sedation and cognitive impairment are common with most of these pharmacologic agents.

Poliomyelitis and Postpolio Syndrome

Acute paralytic poliomyelitis and postpolio syndrome are caused by a virus transmitted through respiratory and gastrointestinal secretions. Since acute polio infection has been eradicated in the United States, postpolio syndrome occurs almost exclusively in elderly survivors of polio acquired in childhood (Schabbing & Corboy, 2002). Weakness and fatigue are common symptoms; and dysphagia, respiratory insufficiency, and sleep apnea also may occur. Many postpolio syndrome patients experience high levels of anxiety and/or depression related to their fatigue and increasing weakness. There is no effective pharmacologic treatment for the progressive weakness, and medications such as amantadine, acetylcholinesterase inhibitors, and prednisone, which once were believed to be efficacious, now rarely are used for this purpose (Stein, Dambrosia, & Dalakas, 1995; Trojan, Colet, & Shapiro, 1999).

Nonviral Infectious Diseases

The most common nonviral diseases of the nervous system are bacterial or fungal, but tuberculous meningitis and brain abscess associated with conditions such as paranasal sinusitis, urinary sepsis, otitis media, or pyogenic lung are additional dangerous conditions in the elderly (Roos, 2002). Patients with most of these nonviral diseases appear drowsy and confused and often complain of an unrelenting headache. Medical attention should be sought immediately for individuals with these symptoms and complaints.

ENDOCRINE DISORDERS

A number of endocrine disturbances such as hypothyroidism, hyperthyroidism, diabetes, and estrogen-related changes in postmenopausal women have an adverse effect on cognition (Osterwell et al., 1992). The endocrine system also affects physiologic state, and neuroendocrine changes may have definite, though sometimes subtle, effects on cognition that should be considered in many circumstances.

Hypothyroidism

With normal functioning, thyroid-stimulating hormone (TSH) secreted by the pituitary gland causes the thyroid gland to release thyroxine and other necessary hormones. In hypothyroidism the system malfunctions, leading to depression, lethargy, and cognitive deficits that include memory problems, reduced verbal fluency, impaired visuospatial and constructional skills, and slowed visuomotor processing (Dugbartey, 1998; Mennemeier, Garner, & Heilman, 1993). Whether cognitive impairment is reversible with thyroxine replacement is unclear (Walstra, Teunisse, van Gool, & van Crevel, 1997), but much of the literature suggests that complete recovery of cognitive functioning actually is rare (Baldini et al., 1997). Problems are more likely to resolve when the disorder is subclinical (i.e., elevated thyroid stimulating hormone in the presence of normal thyroxine concentrations), although subclinical hypothryodism has been associated with an increased risk of future cognitive deterioration and depression (Davis, Stern, & Flashman, 2003; Volpato et al., 2002). Comprehensive medical dementia workups should include laboratory screening for hypothyroidism, with measurement of TSH, free T_4, and T_3U (Barzel, 1995). Elevated levels of TSH, combined with depressed T_4 values, signal the presence of the hypothyroidism.

Hyperthyroidism

Though less common in the elderly, hyperthyroidism can occur, secondary to decreased metabolic clearance, in patients receiving thyroid hormone supplementation over an extended period of time (Bagchi, Brown, & Parish, 1990). Chronic fatigue, emotional lability, depression, lethargy, agitation, dementia, and confusion are common manifestations of hyperthyroidism (Shanker, 2002). Associated laboratory results show an elevated T_4, or T_3 when T_4 is normal, and decreased TSH. Medication for hyperthyroidism usually is avoided because of the danger of toxicity and difficulty maintaining the complicated regimen that is required.

Diabetes

Diabetes mellitus (DM) is a group of metabolic disorders in which chronically high blood glucose levels (hyperglycemia) result from defects in insulin secretion or insulin action. Type 1 diabetes has an onset in childhood or adolescence and is associated with an inability to produce insulin due to autoimmune destruction of pancreatic islet beta cells. Type 2 diabetes typically begins in middle-aged or older adults and often is diagnosed only after certain medical complications have occurred. In type 2 diabetes, the development of insulin resistance, followed by progressive impairment of beta cell function, reduces the bioavailability of insulin and ultimately leads to chronic hyperglycemia and associated micro- and macrovascular complications (Pickup & Williams, 1997). Obesity, sedentary lifestyle, and smoking seem to trigger insulin resistance in genetically susceptible adults. With poor metabolic control, patients with type 2 diabetes have an increased risk of stroke, heart attack, kidney disease, blindness, and neuropathy. Older adults with the disease show clinically significant cognitive impairment, especially on measures of learning and memory (Asimakopoulou, Hampson, & Morrish, 2002; McCall & Figlewicz, 1997; Ryan & Geckle, 2000). Although the risk of cognitive impairment in persons with diabetes rises when multiple biomedical variables are present (hypoglycemia, chronic hyperglycemia, hyperinsulinemia, hypertension, and cardiovascular disease), researchers have not yet clearly identified the underlying metabolic and hormonal pathophysiologic causes for cognitive dysfunction (R. J. Stewart & Liolitsa, 1999).

Effects of Estrogen

Among women in general, higher estrogen levels have been associated with better performance on measures of verbal functioning, motor speed, and verbal and visual memory (Hampson, 1990a, 1990b; Kimura, 1999; Phillips & Sherwin, 1992b). This has been found to be the case both at the midluteal phase of the menstrual cycle in younger women and among postmenopausal women on hormone replacement therapy (HRT) compared with those who are not taking estrogen (e.g., Hampson & Kimura, 1988; Hogervorst, Boshuisen, Riedel, Willeken, & Jolles, 1999; Phillips & Sherwin, 1992a, 1992b).

Hypertension

Hypertension (HTN) is a condition of persistently elevated systolic and/or diastolic arterial pressure. Hypertension occurs frequently in older adults, predisposing them to stroke, heart failure and myocardial infarction, coronary artery disease, peripheral vascular disease, and renal disease. Patients with the most common form, uncomplicated essential hypertension, usually are asymptomatic from a medical standpoint, but patients with less common secondary hypertension often develop medical problems such as atherosclerosis and renal disease. Hypertension has been associated with impaired attention, learning, memory, and executive functioning (Waldstein et al., 1996). Troublesome side effects from antihypertensive medications (in particular, diuretics and beta-blockers) include hypokalemia, hyponatremia, sedation, and confusion (Muldoon, Waldstein, & Jennings, 1995), and the risk of associated delirium increases with advancing age (Gray, Lai, & Larson, 1999).

In addition to damage to the heart, kidneys, and eyes, white matter disease and lowered cerebral profusion have been detected in the brains of older persons with chronic HTN (Papademetriou, 2005; Waldstein et al., 1997). Areas of cognition frequently affected by the associated small vessel disease in these patients include attention, learning and memory, executive functions, visuospatial skills, and psychomotor and perceptual abilities. Low blood pressure, or hypotension, also is associated with decreased performance on cognitive assessment tasks as a consequence of cerebral ischemia (Guo, Winblad, & Vitanen, 1997; Swan, Carmelli, & LaRue, 1998).

CARDIOVASCULAR DISEASE

Arteriosclerosis is a generic term referring to any type of structural change resulting in the hardening and thickening of arterial walls. Atherosclerosis occurs when the lumen of the arteries narrows due to the accumulation of fatty deposits and fibrous tissue on the intimal layer of vessel walls (Everson, Helkala, Kaplan, & Salonen, 2001). The major negative effects of atherosclerosis are stenosis and thrombosis, both of which can result in ischemia to an organ or tissue (Lie, 1994). Particularly if severe, atherosclerosis is associated with cognitive impairment, functional decline, and greater morbidity (Haan, Shemanski, Jagust, Manolio, & Kuuler, 1999; Hofman et al., 1997).

ISCHEMIC HEART DISEASE AND CORONARY ARTERY BYPASS SURGERY

Ischemic heart disease results most often from coronary artery disease (CAD), a process in which one or more of the heart's major arteries is progressively occluded by atherosclerotic plaque, causing an imbalance of myocardial blood supply and demand. Total arterial occlusion rapidly leads to ischemia and myocardial infarction or death of heart muscle. Occlusion typically is treated by coronary artery bypass graft (CABG), a major 3- to 5-hour surgical procedure performed under general anesthesia. Study results are inconsistent, but correlational analyses have shown that immediately following CABG, elderly patients are at increased risk of cognitive decline (primarily memory loss, visuospatial impairment, and mild executive deficits), as well as depression and stroke (Ho et al., 2004; Newman et al., 1994; O'Brien et al., 1992; Vibha, Kalita, Agarwal, & Misra, 2006). In addition, cognitive deficits are evident in some patients as long as 5 years after surgery (Newman, Blumenthal, & Mark, 2004). Although the presence of preexisting severe cardiac disease increases the risk of post surgical cognitive impairment, older patients generate more micro emboli during the procedure and are less able to maintain adequate cerebral blood flow autoregulation. On-pump CABG surgery patients reportedly experience more decline immediately afterward than do patients receiving off-pump surgery (Oudenaarde et al., 2000; Runge & Runge, 2004).

CHRONIC OBSTRUCTIVE PULMONARY DISEASE

Chronic Obstructive Pulmonary Disease (COPD) is a nonspecific term referring to a medical condition that in almost all cases includes a reduction in expiratory airflow accompanied by chronic cough, chronic expectoration, and shortness of breath (Cugell, 1988). The major subtypes of COPD are chronic bronchitis and emphysema, the primary cause of which is smoking. COPD is not reversible, and as the disease progresses, supplemental oxygen usually becomes necessary. Cognitive deficits in patients with COPD typically are related to the degree of hypoxemia (Antonelli et al., 2003; Lishman, 1997); however, some studies have detected impairment in patients who are nonhypoxemic (Liesker et al., 2004). In mild to moderate cases, information processing, perceptual learning, problem-solving abilities, and memory are affected (Stuss, Perkin, & Guzman, 1997). A 2006 study by Ozge, Oage, and Unal showed COPD-related abnormalities in recent memory, construction, attention, language, and orientation, with correlated functional impairment. Also, as hypoxia increases in severity, motor skills may become impaired (Reitan & Wolfson, 1993). Although regular oxygen use can lead to improvement in scores on some tests, variability in test performance, particularly on measures of executive functioning, is common in patients with this disease.

OBSTRUCTIVE SLEEP APNEA

Obstructive sleep apnea (OSA) occurs in more than 25% of individuals over the age of 65 and is particularly prevalent in males (Beers & Berkow, 2000). Factors that contribute to OSA include excessive weight, smoking, high blood pressure, and alcohol and sedative abuse. Research regarding the cause of cognitive impairment associated with OSA is unclear, but deficits are believed to result from hypoxemia, chronic sleep deprivation, or a combination of the two. Areas of impaired performance on neuropsychological testing include executive skills, attention, memory, and psychomotor speed (Bliwise, 2002; Shochat & Pillar, 2003). Many individuals who suffer from this disorder are noncompliant with treatment, which usually involves regular use of a continuous positive airway pressure (CPAP) device at night; therefore, it is difficult to determine with certainty whether cognitive skills improve with prescribed medical and behavioral intervention (Naegele et al., 1998). Sleep deprivation is associated with pro-inflammatory cytokine excess, a condition that will be discussed in more detail in the section that follows.

INFLAMMATION

Inflammation is a complex immunologic reaction to infection, tissue injury, or immunologic stimulation. Systemically, it involves fever and synthesis of *acute phase proteins* by the liver; locally it is characterized by increased vascular permeability and blood flow, influx of neutrophils at the site of injury, and edema. The process is mediated by a number of substances, but some of the most important are cytokines, which belong to a large and complex self-regulating group of soluble low molecular-weight extra-cellular signaling proteins that modulate the immune system (L. R. Watkins, Hansen, Nguyen, Lee, & Maier, 1999; Witko-Sarsat, Rieu, Descamps-Latscha, Lesavre, & Halbwachs-Mecarelli, 1990).

Cytokines may be either pro-inflammatory or anti-inflammatory, and a self-organizing equilibrium between the two types both facilitates the immune response and constrains the system's tendency to cause severe illness secondary to runaway inflammation. The coordinated dynamic activity of the various classes of cytokines and receptors allows the appropriate development of inflammation, plus its downregulation when it is no longer necessary (Frieri, 1999; Gabay & Kushner, 1999). The major pro-inflammatory cytokines, which include interleukin-1 (IL1-α and IL1-ß), interleukin-6 (IL6), and tumor necrosis factor-alpha (TNF-α) among others, promote inflammation. They are regulated and modulated by other molecules, including anti-inflammatory cytokines such as IL4, IL10, and IL13.

Pro-inflammatory IL-6 is found in increased levels in the aging brain and seems to play a major role in aging. Its presence in the brain is associated with such conditions as anemia, frailty, and anorexia. Godbout and Johnson (2004) note that IL6 in the brain can be toxic and will likely affect both cognition and motivation. Interferon-α, along with IL6, IL1, and TNF-α, stimulates *sickness behavior*, which includes myalgias, apathy, lassitude, fever, depression, and learning and memory impairment—in short, many of the signs and symptoms of infectious illnesses (Banks, Farr, La Scola, & Morley, 2001; Dunn, Swiergiel, & de Beaurepaire, 2005; Parnet, Kelley, Bluthe, & Dantzer, 2002; Simen, Duman, Simen, & Duman, 2006; L. M. Watkins & Maier, 2000).

In addition to increased effects of pro-inflammatory cytokines, aging is accompanied by a two- to fourfold increase in plasma/serum levels of inflammatory mediators such as C-reactive protein (CRP; Godbout & Johnson, 2004; Krobbe, Pedersen, & Bruunsgaard, 2004).

C-reactive protein has been shown to be a predictor of cognitive decline. It is a sensitive acute-phase protein whose levels increase in response to inflammation, infection, and tissue damage. Several studies have found an increased short-term risk of cardiac events in patients with elevated levels of CRP and fibrinogen, and elevated levels of lipoprotein-associated phospholipase A2 are additional strong predictors of risk (Packard et al., 2000). A recent study by Aiello et al. (2006) showed that persons with higher levels of antibody to cytomegalovirus (CMV) experienced a faster rate of cognitive decline over a 4-year period than did elderly individuals with lower levels. C-reactive protein did not modify the relationship between viral antibody levels and cognitive decline.

Total plasma homocysteine (tHcy) also predicts cognitive decline (Dufouil, Alperovitch, & Ducros, 2003). Elevated tHcy levels increase the risk of arterial disease and stroke, partially explaining the relationship to cognitive dysfunction; however, there appears to be a direct neurotoxic effect as well (Clarke, Daly, & Robinson, 1991; Hankey & Eikelboom, 2005). In a recent study by Raamt, Kalmijn, Mali, Zandvoort, and van der Graff (2006), high tHcy affected all domains of cognition except executive function on formal neuropsychological assessment. Although differences in scores of younger subjects in the study were small, the negative effects of tHcy on cognition became more significant with subjects' increasing age.

DISTURBANCES IN WATER AND ELECTROLYTE BALANCE

Disorders of water and mineral metabolism occur frequently in older persons due mainly to decreased renal function and the negative effects of many commonly prescribed medications. Maintenance of normal composition of extracellular fluid (ECF) is vital for normal cellular function, and alteration in ECF causes impaired mental status, disrupted peripheral nerve conduction, and decreased muscle strength (Godwin-Austen & Bendall, 1990).

Renal Disease

The incidence of chronic renal failure increases with age, and impaired cognition often accompanies endstage renal disease (Lass, Buscombe, & Harber, 1999). Uremic encephalopathy accounts for 10% of delirium in the elderly (Lipowski, 1994); in fact, the condition is almost always present in elderly patients who suffer from acute deterioration in renal function. Fatigue, apathy, impaired attention and concentration, and subtle motor changes occur early in the course of renal failure, and with further deterioration, coma and seizures are common (Burn & Bates, 1998). Treatment of uremic encephalopathy, after which cognitive functioning occasionally improves, involves correction of the underlying renal disease and in some cases, hemodialysis. A progressive decline in cognition has been associated with chronic dialysis, however, and although a switch to aluminum-free water in dialysate and aluminum chelating agents has significantly reduced the incidence of this type of dementia, patients frequently experience an episode of delirium at the initiation of treatment (Burn & Bates, 1998).

Dehydration

Dehydration is the most common fluid disturbance in the elderly and also is a major risk factor for delirium in hospitalized or nursing home patients (Inouye, 2000; Reyes-Ortiz, 1997). Treatment involves removal of certain medications and hydration with isotonic saline until hemodynamic stability is achieved. Dehydrated patients usually become hypernatremic, but when large doses of diuretics lead to water depletion, hyponatremia can occur. Mental changes associated with both conditions include altered consciousness, confusion, and delirium. Such symptoms may be more difficult to detect and assess in the elderly because dehydration is common in patients with an underlying dementia. In hospital and nursing home settings, psychiatrists or psychologists often are asked to evaluate and manage episodes of disturbed behavior exhibited by dehydrated patients (Godwin-Austen & Bendall, 1990).

Malnutrition

Epidemiologic studies have shown that older adults typically consume less than two-thirds of the recommended daily allowance of many important nutrients (Morley, Glick, & Rubenstein, 1995). Protein-calorie malnutrition, which is correlated with morbidity and mortality, occurs in as many as 30% to 50% of elderly patients in nursing homes and hospitals (Bernard, 2004; Gariballa & Sinclair, 1998). Magnesium deficiency can occur in conjunction with marked protein-calorie malnutrition, diuretic therapy leading to excess renal loss, and the delirium tremens that results from heavy alcohol consumption or alcohol withdrawal. Pellegra, or nicotinic acid deficiency, can cause memory loss, lethargy, depression, irritability, hallucinations, and paranoia. This deficiency may be difficult to diagnose in the elderly due to the similarity and subsequent misattribution of these disturbances to a psychiatric disorder or cortical dementia (Godwin-Austen & Bendall, 1990).

VITAMIN B12 DEFICIENCY

Vitamin B12 levels tend to decrease in older persons, in part due to malabsorption, but also secondary to conditions such as pancreatic insufficiency and atrophic gastritis. Pernicious anemia, which mainly affects older persons, can result from an inability to utilize B12 when taken orally. Patients with B12 deficiency often report fatigue, weakness, and parasthesias in their hands and feet. Cognitive changes associated with B12 deficiency include deficits in abstract reasoning and complex problem solving, decreased verbal fluency, impaired visuoconstructional and perceptual skills, and problems with delayed verbal recall. Although many of the problematic neurologic signs resolve with supplementation, cognitive impairment rarely disappears completely even with treatment (M. E. Meadows, Kaplan, & Bromfield, 1994).

CHRONIC PAIN

With aging, conditions such as bone and joint disorders, back problems, and arthritis increase the likelihood of chronic pain. Assessment of pain in older adults may be challenging, however, as many patients consider it to be a normal part of getting old, and many who have cognitive impairment may not communicate effectively about their pain. Pain frequently interferes with daily functioning (Clark, Stump, Hui, & Wolinsky, 1998; Hicks et al., 2005), and although its interference may reflect limitations associated with the stiffness of osteoarthritis, both acute and chronic pain can have an adverse effect on cognitive functioning. Hart, Martelli, and Zasler (2000) reviewed a number of studies in which they found that although effects on functioning could be mediated by depression or other forms of emotional distress, pain stimuli seemed to impact neural networks that underlie information processing. Grigsby, Rosenberg, and Busenbark (1995), for example, found that the speed and capacity of information processing among chronic pain patients was equivalent to, or worse than, that of individuals with mild to moderate traumatic brain injuries.

Apkarian et al. (2004) used magnetic resonance imaging to measure the volume of a number of different brain regions in patients with chronic back pain and found reduced volumes of dorsolateral prefrontal cortex bilaterally, and also of the right thalamus. After normalization of brain volumes, the pain patients showed 5% to 11% less neocortical gray matter than did the controls, a finding which the authors note is "equivalent to the gray matter volume lost in 10 to 20 years of normal aging" (p. 10410). These results strongly suggest that chronic pain not only affects brain structure, but does so in a manner related to the duration of pain.

ADVERSE DIRECT AND INTERACTIVE EFFECTS OF MEDICATION

Older adults take more prescription and over-the-counter (OTC) medications than any other age group, and due to age-related changes in drug metabolism, absorption, distribution, and excretion, there is an increased risk of toxicity leading to dementia-like symptoms that in many cases can be reversed or arrested if properly identified and managed (Cafiero, 2004). Inappropriate medication use in older patients has been identified as a serious problem, with 21.3% of community-dwelling older Americans receiving at least 1 of 33 potentially inappropriate medications (Zhan, Sangl, & Bierman, 2001). Patients in poor health who take more medications are at significantly greater risk of problematic interactions. Also, medication compliance may be an issue even when medications are appropriately prescribed (Tangalos & Zarowitz, 2006), and some research has shown a noncompliance rate that varies from 26% to 50% in patients over the age of sixty (van Eijken, Tsang, & Wensing, 2003). Many of the side effects of medications in the elderly involve confusion or oversedation, and the presence of either of these conditions in a patient who is being assessed could indicate a potentially reversible cause for his or her cognitive impairment.

Medication use of any type should be identified and documented as part of a thorough assessment of an older person's mental capacity. In addition to the individual negative effects of many prescription medications such as those listed previously, many seemingly harmless OTC medications such as cold and allergy drugs, plus common chemicals such as those found in tobacco and frequently consumed beverages and foods, can interfere with cognition. For example, alcohol, nicotine, and the caffeine in coffee, tea, colas, and chocolate can interact with prescription medication to produce changes in cognition. If possible, information regarding usage of the latter substances, as well as a complete list of prescription and nonprescription medications, should be obtained from the patient or his or her caregivers. In cases involving patients who are taking complex or multiple medications with likely adverse effects or interactions, consultation with a physician or pharmacologist is advised. Table 3.1 provides a very basic summary of medications with known adverse effects on mental and emotional status.

Chemotherapy

There is considerable evidence that medications used in cancer treatment can have significant effects on different aspects of cognition. This phenomenon has been studied most vigorously in women with breast cancer, and although many studies have methodologic limitations, the majority involving both high-dose and standard-dose chemotherapy show an adverse effect. One of the earliest investigations, conducted by

Table 3.1   Selected Medications with Possible Side Effects

Drug Class	Generic Name	Confusion	Depression	Anxiety
Analgesics	Codeine, meperidine, propxyphene	X	X	X
Antiarrhythmics	Digoxin, disopyramide	X	X	X
Antibiotics and antivirals	Acyclovir, ciprofloxacin, metronidazole	X	X	
Antihistamines	Cetirizine, dimenhydrinate, diphenhydramine, loratadine	X		
Antihypertensives	Atenolol, metoprolol, propranolol, methyldopa	X	X	X
Anti-inflammatories	Naproxen, ibuprofen	X		
Anti-Parkinsonian medications	Amantadine, levodopa, selegiline	X	X	X
Corticosteroids	Methylprednisolone, prednisone	X	X	
Cough suppressants and decongestants	Dextromethorphan, pseudoephedrine	X		
Sleep medications	Eszopiclone, zolpidem, zeleplon	X	X	

Silberfarb, Philibert, and Levine (1980), found that women who received chemotherapy scored significantly worse on testing than those who did not, and affective disturbances did not account for the differences in cognitive functioning. Of interest, the majority of the patients were 50 years of age or older; therefore, the authors hypothesized that age was a risk factor in the development of cognitive impairment following chemotherapy treatment.

Brezden, Phillips, Abdolell, Bunston, and Tannock (2000) assessed cognitive functioning using a researcher-administered screening tool (the High Sensitivity Cognitive Screen) and a self-report measure. Women who were receiving chemotherapy at the time had significantly lower scores on a summary cognitive score and more severe impairment in memory and language than did the healthy controls. Women who had completed chemotherapy obtained scores intermediate between the current chemotherapy group and the healthy controls. Disturbances in mood did not account for changes in cognitive status. Other authors (Ahles & Saykin, 2001; Hurria et al., 2006; Schagen, Hamburger, Muller, Boogerd, & van Dam, 2001; Schagen et al., 1999, 2002; van Dam et al., 1998; Wieneke & Dienst, 1995) have discussed similar findings. A. Stewart and colleagues (A. Stewart, Bielajew, Collins, Parkinson, & Tomiak, 2006), in a meta-analysis of studies of chemotherapy and cognition, concluded that for most women with breast cancer, chemotherapy produces cognitive effects that are "subtle but consequential."

For at least some patients treated with chemotherapy, effects on cognition can persist for many years. Ahles et al. (2002) administered a battery of neuropsychological tests to breast cancer and lymphoma survivors who had completed their therapies an average of 10 years prior to testing. Persons who had undergone chemotherapy were more likely to score in the impaired range on testing than those who received local therapy, and deficits were especially evident on tests of verbal memory and psychomotor functioning. For most patients, there appears to be some degree of recovery of cognitive functioning over time, but for a subgroup of patients, cognitive deficits persist and may never return to pretreatment levels. Silverman et al. (2006) reported changes in cerebral blood flow in the areas of frontal cortex, cerebellum, and basal ganglia as long as 5 to 10 years following chemotherapy. Although a number of issues remain to be resolved regarding the long-term effects of cancer treatment, and most of the research to date has been conducted with breast cancer patients, it is essential to consider chemotherapy effects as important determinants of cognitive functioning among older adults.

MEDICAL ASSESSMENT OF ACUTE CONFUSION OR DELIRIUM

Most physicians and almost every geriatrician will complete a basic medical dementia workup when evaluating a patient who shows signs of significant cognitive decline. A thorough medical dementia workup is especially important when the patient presents as acutely confused or delirious (National Institutes of Health, 1987; Streim, 2004). Elements that are usually part of a basic medical dementia workup include:

- Medical history.
- Chart review (including identification of all current or recently administered medications), including PRNs (medications taken as needed).
- Results of physical and mental status examinations.
- Laboratory test results: complete blood count, electrolyte panel, screening metabolic panel, thyroid function, vitamin B12 and folate levels, urinalysis, test for syphilis, and electrocardiogram.
- Based on findings from the patient's history, chart review, and physical and mental status examination, procedures such as a chest x-ray, brain CT scan or MRI, lumbar puncture, test for human immunodeficiency antibodies, or electroencephalogram may be added.

CONCLUSION

Completion of a comprehensive assessment of an older person's mental or decisional capacity is time consuming and reliant on many skills. In addition to a grasp of basic principles of neuropsychology, familiarity with changes associated with the aging process, and an ability to identify and differentiate between delirium and dementia, knowledge of the effects of medical disorders and medications is crucial. An acute confusional state may be the only obvious initial clinical manifestation of a life-threatening medical illness, or it may indicate the presence of a less serious medical condition that can lead to comorbidity or potentially preventable disability in frail or very old adults. The clinical signs and symptoms of impaired cognition secondary to medical illness also may worsen existing impairment associated with one of the more common forms of dementia. This chapter summarizes selected medical conditions and medications that can adversely affect cognition in the elderly, but additional reading and study are strongly advised. Familiarity with medical tests and procedures undoubtedly is useful; however, a thorough evaluation ideally should include consultation with multiple disciplines in the medical profession. Thoughtful, thorough assessment is of vital importance when issues of mental capacity are in question, as a partial evaluation based on limited or poorly understood information could have potentially damaging consequences for an elderly person.

REFERENCES

Ahles, T. A., & Saykin, A. (2001). Cognitive effects of standard-dose chemotherapy in patients with cancer. *Cancer Investigation, 19,* 812–820.

Ahles, T. A., Saykin, A., Furstenberg, C. T., Cole, B., Mott, L. A., Skalla, K., et al. (2002). Neuropsychological impact of standard-dose systemic chemotherapy in long-term survivors of breast cancer and lymphoma. *Journal of Clinical Oncology, 20,* 485–493.

Aiello, A. E., Hann, M. N., Blythe, L. B., Moore, K., Gonzalez, J. M., & Jagust, W. (2006). The influence of latent viral infection on rate of cognitive decline over 4 years. *Journal of the American Geriatrics Society, 54,* 1046–1054.

Antonelli, I. R., Marra, C., Giordano, A., Calcagni, M. L., Cappa, A., Basso, S., et al. (2003). Cognitive impairment in chronic obstructive pulmonary disease: A neuropsychological and spect study. *Journal of Neurology, 250,* 325–332.

Apkarian, A. V., Sosa, Y., Sonty, S., Levy, R. M., Harden, R. N., Parrish, T. B., et al. (2004). Chronic back pain is associated with decreased prefrontal and thalamic gray matter density. *Journal of Neuroscience, 24,* 10410–10415.

Arbib, M. A., Érdi, P., & Szentágothai, J. (1998). *Neural organization: Structure, function, and dynamics.* Cambridge, MA: MIT Press.

Asimakopoulou, K. G., Hampson, S. E., & Morrish, N. J. (2002). Neuropsychological functioning in older people with type 2 diabetes: The effect of controlling for confounding factors. *Diabetic Medicine, 19,* 311–316.

Bagchi, N., Brown, T. R., & Parish, R. F. (1990). Thyroid dysfunction in adults over the age of 55 years: A study in an urban, U.S. community. *Archives of Internal Medicine, 140,* 785–787.

Baldini, I. M., Vita, A., Mauri, M. C., Amodei, V., Carrisi, M., & Bravin, S. (1997). Psychopathological and cognitive features in subclinical hypothyroidism. *Progress in Neuro-Psychopharmacology and Biological Psychiatry, 21,* 925–935.

Banks, W. A., Farr, S. A., La Scola, M. E., & Morley, J. E. (2001). Intravenous human interleukin-1 alpha impairs memory processing in mice: Dependence on blood-brain barrier transport into posterior division of the septum. *Journal of Pharmacology and Experimental Therapeutics, 299*, 536–541.

Barzel, U. S. (1995). Hypothyroidism. *Clinical Geriatric Medicine, 11*, 239–249.

Beers, M. H., & Berkow, R. (Eds.). (2000). *The Merck manual of geriatrics* (3rd ed.). Whitehouse Station, NJ: Merck Research Laboratories.

Bernard, M. (2004). Nutrition. In M. A. Forciea, E. P. Schwab, D. B. Raziano, & R. Lavizzo-Mourey (Eds.), *Geriatric secrets* (3rd ed., pp. 95–103). Philadelphia: Hanley & Belfus.

Blake, M. J. F. (1967). Time of day effects of performance in a range of tasks. *Psychonomic Science, 9*, 349–350.

Bliwise, D. L. (2002). Sleep apnea, APOE4, and Alzheimer's disease: 20 years and counting? *Psychosomatic Research, 53*, 539–546.

Bodnar, R. J., Commons, K., & Pfaff, D. W. (2002). *Central neural states relating sex and pain*. Baltimore: Johns Hopkins University Press.

Brezden, C. B., Phillips, K. A., Abdolell, M., Bunston, T., & Tannock, I. F. (2000). Cognitive function in breast cancer patients receiving adjuvant chemotherapy. *Journal of Clinical Oncology, 18*, 2695–2701.

Burn, D. J., & Bates, D. (1998). Neurology and the kidney. *Journal of Neurology, Neurosurgery, and Psychiatry, 65*, 810–921.

Cafiero, A. C. (2004). Geriatric pharmacotherapy. In M. A. Forciea, E. P. Schwab, D. B. Raziano, & R. Lavizzo-Mourey (Eds.), *Geriatric secrets* (3rd ed., pp. 29–35). Philadelphia: Hanley & Belfus.

Clark, D. O., Stump, T. E., Hui, S. L., & Wolinsky, F. D. (1998). Predictors of mobility and basic ADL difficulty among adults aged 70 years and older. *Journal of Aging and Health, 10*, 422–440.

Clarke, R., Daly, L., & Robinson, K. (1991). Hyperhomocysteinemia: An independent risk factor for vascular disease. *New England Journal of Medicine, 324*, 866–871.

Cugell, D. W. (1988). COPD: A brief introduction for behavioral scientists. In A. J. McSweeny & I. Grant (Eds.), *Chronic obstructive pulmonary disease: A behavioral perspective* (pp. 1–18). New York: Marcel Dekker.

Davis, J. D., Stern, R. A., & Flashman, L. A. (2003). Cognitive and neuropsychiatric aspects of subclinical hypothyroidism: Significance in the elderly. *Current Psychiatric Reports, 5*, 384–390.

Donahue, J. G., Choo, P. W., Manson, J. E., & Platt, R. (1995). The incidence of herpes zoster. *Archives of Internal Medicine, 155,* 1605–1609.

Dufouil, C., Alperovitch, A., & Ducros, V. (2003). Homocysteine, white matter hypointensities, and cognition in healthy elderly people. *Annals of Neurology, 53,* 214–221.

Dugbartey, A. T. (1998). Neurocognitive aspects of hypothyroidism. *Archives of Internal Medicine, 158,* 1413–1418.

Dunn, A. J., Swiergiel, A. H., & de Beaurepaire, R. (2005). Cytokines as mediators of depression: What can we learn from animal studies? *Neuroscience and Biobehavioral Reviews, 29,* 891–909.

Everson, S. A., Helkala, E., Kaplan, G. A., & Salonen, J. T. (2001). Atherosclerosis and cognitive functioning. In S. Waldstein & M. F. Elias (Eds.), *Neuropsychology of cardiovascular disease* (pp. 105–120). Hillsdale, NJ: Erlbaum.

Fornek, M., & Henning, K. (2004). Infection control in long-term care facilities. In M. Forciea, E. P. Schwab, D. B. Raziano, & R. Lavizzo-Mourey (Eds.), *Geriatric secrets* (3rd ed., pp. 267–274). Philadelphia: Hanley & Belfus.

Frieri, M. (1999). Corticosteroid effects on cytokines and chemokines. *Allergy and Asthma Proceedings, 20,* 147–159.

Gabay, C., & Kushner, I. (1999). Acute-phase proteins and other systematic responses to inflammation. *New England Journal of Medicine, 340,* 448–454.

Gariballa, S. E., & Sinclair, A. J. (1998). Nutrition, aging, and ill health. *British Journal of Nutrition, 80,* 7–23.

Godbout, J. P., & Johnson, R. W. (2004). Interleukin-6 in the aging brain. *Journal of Neuroimmunology, 147,* 141–144.

Godwin-Austen, R., & Bendall, J. (1990). *The neurology of the elderly.* London: Springer-Verlag.

Gray, S. L., Lai, K. V., & Larson, E. B. (1999). Drug-induced cognition disorders in the elderly: Incidence, prevention, and management. *Drug Safety, 21,* 101–122.

Grigsby, J., & Osuch, E. (2007). Neurodynamics, state, agency, and psychological functioning. In C. Piers, J. P. Muller, & J. Brent (Eds.), *Self-organizing complexity in psychological systems* (pp. 37–81). Lanham, MD: Rowman & Littlefield.

Grigsby, J., Rosenberg, N. L., & Busenbark, D. (1995). Chronic pain is associated with deficits in information processing. *Perceptual and Motor Skills, 81,* 403–410.

Guo, Z., Winblad, B., & Vitanen, M. (1997). Clinical correlates of low blood pressure in very old people: The importance of cognitive impairment. *Journal of the American Geriatric Society, 45*, 701–705.

Haan, M. N., Shemanski, L., Jagust, W. J., Manolio, T. A., & Kuuler, L. H. (1999). Predictors of cognitive change in the elderly: Does ApoE4 change the course of cognitive decline due to atherosclerosis or diabetes? *Journal of the American Medical Association, 282*, 40–46.

Hampson, E. (1990a). Estrogen-related variations in human spatial and articulatory-motor skills. *Psychoneuroendocrinology, 15*, 97–111.

Hampson, E. (1990b). Variations in sex-related cognitive abilities across the menstrual cycle. *Brain and Cognition, 14*, 26–43.

Hampson, E., & Kimura, D. (1988). Reciprocal effects of hormonal fluctuations on human motor and perceptual-spatial skills. *Behavioral Neuroscience, 102*, 456–459.

Hankey, G. J., & Eikelboom, J. W. (2005). Homocysteine and vascular disease. *Lancet, 354*, 407–413.

Hart, R. P., Martelli, M. F., & Zasler, N. D. (2000). Chronic pain and neuropsychological functioning. *Neuropsychology Review, 10*, 131–149.

Hicks, G. E., Simonsick, E. M., Harris, T. B., Newman A .B., Weiner, D. K., Nevitt, M. A., et al. (2005). Cross-sectional associations between trunk muscle composition, back pain, and physical function in the health, aging and body composition study. *Journals of Gerontology Series A: Biological Sciences and Medical Sciences, 60*, 882–887.

Ho, P. M., Arciniegas, D. B., Grigsby, J., McCarthy, M., Jr., McDonald, G. O., Moritz, T. E., et al. (2004). Predictors of cognitive decline following coronary artery bypass graft surgery. *Annals of Thoracic Surgery, 77*, 597–603.

Hofman, A., Ott, A., Breteler, M. M. B., Bots, M. L., Slooter, A. J., van Harskamp, F., et al. (1997). Atherosclerosis, apolipoprotein E, and prevalence of dementia and Alzheimer's disease in the Rotterdam Study. *Lancet, 249*, 151–154.

Hogervorst, E., Boshuisen, M., Riedel, W., Willeken, C., & Jolles, J. (1999). The effect of hormone replacement therapy on cognitive function in elderly women. *Psychoneuroendocrinology, 24*, 43–68.

Hurria, A., Rosen, C., Hudis, C., Zuckerman, E., Panageas, K. S., Lachs, M. S., et al. (2006). Cognitive function of older patients receiving adjuvant chemotherapy for breast cancer: A pilot prospective longitudinal study. *Journal of the American Geriatrics Society, 54*, 925–931.

Inouye, S. K. (2000). Prevention of delirium in hospitalized patients: Risk factors and targeted intervention strategies. *Annals of Medicine, 32*, 257–263.

Kevorkian, R. (2006). Cytokines and the care of the older adult. *Annals of Long-Term Care, 14*, 34–40.

Kimura, D. (1999). *Sex and cognition.* Cambridge, MA: MIT Press.

Krobbe, K. S., Pedersen, M., & Bruunsgaard, H. (2004). Inflammatory mediators in the elderly. *Experimental Gerontology, 39*, 687–699.

Lass, P., Buscombe, J. R., & Harber, M. (1999). Cognitive impairment in patients with renal failure is associated with multiple-infarct dementia. *Clinical Nuclear Medicine, 24*, 561–565.

Lie, J. T. (1994). Pathology of occlusive disease of the extracranial arteries. In F. B. Meyer (Ed.), *Sundt's occlusive cerebrovascular disease* (2nd ed., pp. 25–44). Philadelphia: Saunders.

Liesker, J. J., Postma, D. S., Beukema, R. J., ten Hacken, N. H., van der Molen, T., Riemersma, R. A., et al. (2004). Cognitive performance in patients with COPD. *Respiratory Medicine, 98*, 351–356.

Lipowski, Z. J. (1994). Acute confusional states (delirium) in the elderly. In M. L. Albert & J. E. Knoefel (Eds.), *Clinical neurology of aging* (2nd ed., pp. 347–362). New York: Oxford University Press.

Lishman, W. A. (1997). *Organic psychiatry* (3rd ed.). Oxford: Blackwell Press.

Martin, R. J., & Whitehouse, P. J. (1990). The clinical care of patients with dementia. In N. L. Mace (Ed.), *Dementia care: Patient, family, and community* (pp. 22–31). Baltimore: Johns Hopkins University Press.

McCall, A. L., & Figlewicz, D. P. (1997). How does diabetes mellitus produce brain dysfunction? *Diabetes Spectrum, 10*, 25–32.

Meadows, M. E., Kaplan, R. F., & Bromfield, E. B. (1994). Cognitive recovery with vitamin B12 therapy: A longitudinal neuropsychiatric assessment. *Neurology, 44*, 1764–1765.

Mennemeier, M., Garner, R. D., & Heilman, K. M. (1993). Memory, mood and measurement in hypothyroidism. *Journal of Clinical and Experimental Neuropsychology, 15*, 822–831.

Morley, J. E., Glick, A., & Rubenstein, L. Z. (1995). *Geriatric nutrition: A comprehensive review* (2nd ed.). Philadelphia: Lippincott Williams & Wilkins.

Muldoon, M. F., Waldstein, S. R., & Jennings, J. R. (1995). Neuropsychological consequences of antihypertensive medication use. *Experimental Aging Research, 21*, 353–368.

Naegele, B., Pepin, J. L., Levy, P., Bonnet, C., Pellat, J., & Feuerstein, C. (1998). Cognitive executive dysfunction in patients with obstructive sleep apnea syndrome (OSAS) after CPAP treatment. *Sleep, 21,* 392–397.

National Institutes of Health. (1987). Differential diagnosis of dementia diseases. *Journal of the American Medical Association, 258,* 3411–3416.

Newman, M., Blumenthal, J. A., & Mark, D. B. (2004). Fixing the heart: Must the brain pay the price? *Circulation, 110,* 3402–3403.

Newman, M., Croughwell, N., Blumenthal, J., White, W., Lewis, J., Smith, L., et al. (1994). Effect of aging on cerebral autoregulation during cardiopulmonary bypass: Association with postoperative cognitive dysfunction. *Circulation, 90,* 243–249.

O'Brien, D., Baurer, R., Yarandi, H., Knauf, D., Bramblett, P., & Alexander, J. (1992). Patient memory before and after cardiac operations. *Journal of Thoracic and Cardiovascular Surgery, 104,* 1116–1124.

Osterwell, D., Syndulko, K., Cohen, S. N., Pettler-Jennings, P. D., Hershman, J. M., Cummings, J. L., et al. (1992). Cognitive function in non-demented older adults with hypothyroidism. *Journal of the American Geriatrics Society, 40,* 325–335.

Oudenaarde, I., Takkenberg, J. M., van der Velden, E., Chalfont, L., Wesnes, K., & van Herverden, L. A. (2000). Neuropsychologic dysfunction after CABG: Standard cardiopulmonary bypass versus off-pump CABG. *Critical Care, 4*(Suppl. B), 6.

Ozge, C., Oage, A., & Unal, O. (2006). Cognitive and functional deterioration in patients with severe COPD. *Behavioral Neurology, 17,* 121–130.

Packard, C. J., O'Reilly, S. J., Caslake, M. J., McMahon, A. D., Ford, I., Cooney, J., et al. (2000). Lipoprotein-associated phospholipase A2 as an independent predictor of coronary heart disease. *New England Journal of Medicine, 343,* 1148–1155.

Papademetriou, V. (2005). Hypertension and cognitive function: A review of the literature. *Geriatrics, 60,* 20–24.

Parnet, P., Kelley, K. W., Bluthe, R. M., & Dantzer, R. (2002). Expression and regulation of interleukin-1 receptors in the brain: Role in cytokine-induced sickness behavior. *Journal of Neuroimmunology, 125,* 5–14.

Phillips, S. M., & Sherwin, B. B. (1992a). Effects of estrogen on memory function in surgically menopausal women. *Psychoneuroendocrinology, 17,* 485–495.

Phillips, S. M., & Sherwin, B. B. (1992b). Variations in memory function and sex steroid hormones across the menstrual cycle. *Psychoneuroendocrinology, 17*, 497–506.

Pickup, J. C., & Williams, G. (Eds.). (1997). *Textbook of diabetes* (2nd ed.). Oxford: Blackwell Science.

Raamt, F. A., Kalmijn, S., Mali, W., Zandvoort, J. E., & van der Graff, Y. (2006). Homocysteine level and cognitive function in patients with arterial disease: The second manifestations of Arterial Disease Study. *Journal of the American Geriatrics Society, 54*, 575–579.

Reitan, R. M., & Wolfson, D. (1993). *The Halstead-Reitan Neuropsychological Test Battery: Theory and clinical applications* (2nd ed.). Tuscon, AZ: Neuropsychology Press.

Reyes-Ortiz, C. A. (1997). Dehydration, delirium, and disability in elderly patients. *Journal of the American Medical Association, 278*, 287–288.

Roos, K. L. (2002). Nonviral infectious diseases of the nervous system. In J. L. Sirven & B. L. Malamut (Eds.), *Clinical neurology of the older adult* (pp. 349–362). Philadelphia: Lippincott Williams & Wilkins.

Runge, T. M., & Runge, M. S. (2004). Limiting brain and lung damage after coronary artery bypass grafting: An alternative to conventional coronary artery bypass graft. *Clinical Cardiology, 27*, 594–598.

Ryan, C. M., & Geckle, M. O. (2000). Circumscribed cognitive dysfunction in middle-aged adults with type 2 diabetes. *Diabetes Care, 23*, 1486–1493.

Schabbing, R. W., & Corboy, J. R. (2002). Viral illnesses in the nervous system of the elderly. In J. L. Sirven & B. L. Malamut (Eds.), *Clinical neurology of the older adult* (pp. 363–371). Philadelphia: Lippincott Williams & Wilkins.

Schagen, S. B., Hamburger, H. L., Muller, M. J., Boogerd, W., & van Dam, F. S. (2001). Neurophysiological evaluation of late effects of adjuvant high-dose chemotherapy on cognitive function. *Journal of Neuro-Oncology, 51*, 159–165.

Schagen, S. B., Muller, M. J., Boogerd, W., Rosenbrand, R. M., van Rhijn, D., Rodenhuis, S., et al. (2002). Late effects of adjuvant chemotherapy on cognitive function: A follow-up study in breast cancer patients. *Annals of Oncology, 13*, 1387–1397.

Schagen, S. B., van Dam, F. S., Muller, M. J., Boogerd, W., Lindeboom, J., & Bruning, P. F. (1999). Cognitive deficits after postoperative adjuvant chemotherapy for breast carcinoma. *Cancer, 85*, 640–650.

Shanker, V. (2002). Neurological complications of systemic disease: GI and Endocrine. In J. Sirven & B. Malamut (Eds.), *Clinical neurology of the older adult* (pp. 395–404). Philadelphia: Lippincott Williams & Wilkins.

Shochat, T., & Pillar, G. (2003). Sleep apnea in the older adult. *Drugs and Aging, 20*, 551–560.

Silberfarb, P. M., Philibert, D., & Levine, P. M. (1980). Psychosocial aspects of neoplastic disease: Pt. II. Affective and cognitive effects of chemotherapy in cancer patients. *American Journal of Psychiatry, 137*, 597–601.

Silverman, D. H. S., Dy, C. J., Castellon, S. A., Lai, J., Pio, B. S., Abraham, L., et al. (2007). Altered frontocortical, cerebellar, and basal ganglia activity in adjuvant-treated breast cancer survivors 5 to 10 years after chemotherapy. *Breast Cancer Research and Treatment, 103*, 303–311.

Simen, B. B., Duman, C. H., Simen, A. A., & Duman, R. S. (2006). TNF-alpha signaling in depression and anxiety: Behavioral consequences of individual receptor targeting. *Biological Psychiatry, 59*, 775–785.

Stehman, J. M., Strachan, G. I., Glenner, J. A., Glenner, G. G., & Neubauer, J. K. (1996). *Handbook of dementia care.* Baltimore: Johns Hopkins University Press.

Stewart, A., Bielajew, C., Collins, B., Parkinson, M., & Tomiak, E. (2006). A meta-analysis of the neuropsychological effects of adjuvant chemotherapy treatment in women treated for breast cancer. *Clinical Neuropsychologist, 20*, 76–89.

Stewart, R. J., & Liolitsa, D. (1999). Type 2 diabetes mellitus, cognitive impairment and dementia. *Diabetic Medicine, 16*, 93–112.

Stein, D. P., Dambrosia, J. M., & Dalakas, M. C. (1995). A double-blind placebo-controlled trial of amantadine for the treatment of fatigue in patients with the post-polio syndrome. *Annals of the New York Academy of Science, 753*, 296–302.

Streim, J. E. (2004). Confusion and amnesia. In M. Forciea, E. P. Schwab, D. B. Raziano, & R. Lavizzo-Mourey (Eds.), *Geriatric secrets* (3rd ed., pp. 41–46). Philadelphia: Hanley & Belfus.

Stuss, D. T., Perkin, I., & Guzman, D. A. (1997). Chronic obstructive pulmonary disease: Effects of hypoxia on neurological and neuropsychological measures. *Journal of Clinical and Experimental Neuropsychology, 19*, 515–524.

Swan, G. E., Carmelli, D., & LaRue, A. (1998). Systolic blood pressure tracking over 25 to 30 years and cognitive impairment in older adults. *Stroke, 22*, 2334–2340.

Tangalos, E. G., & Zarowitz, B. J. (2006). Medication management in the elderly. *Annals of Long-Term Care, 14*, 27–31.

Trojan, D. A., Colet, J. P., & Shapiro, S. (1999). A multicenter, randomized, double-blinded trial of pyridostigmine in post-polio syndrome. *Neurology, 53*, 1225–1233.

van Dam, F. S. A. M., Schagen, S. B., Muller, M. J., Boogerd, W., van de Wall, E., Droogleever Fortuyn, M. E., et al. (1998). Impairment of cognitive function in women receiving adjuvant treatment for high-risk breast cancer: High-dose versus standard-dose chemotherapy. *Journal of the National Cancer Institute, 90*, 210–218.

van Eijken, M., Tsang, S., & Wensing, M. (2003). Interventions to improve medication compliance in older patients living in the community: A systematic review of the literature. *Drugs and Aging, 20*, 229–240.

Vibha, D., Kalita, J., Agarwal, R., & Misra, U. K. (2006). Coronary artery bypass surgery: Does it lead to cognitive impairment? *Annals of Indian Academy of Neurology, 9*, 145–151.

Volpato, S., Guralnik, J. M., Fried, L. P., Remaley, A. T., Capppola, A. R., & Launer, L. J. (2002). Serum thyroxine level and cognitive decline in older women. *Neurology, 244*, 1055–1061.

Waldstein, S. R., Jennings, J. R., Ryan, C. M., Muldoon, M. F., Shapiro, A. P., Polefrone, J. M., et al. (1996). Hypertension and neuropsychological performance in men: Interactive effects of age. *Health Psychology, 15*, 102–109.

Waldstein, S. R., Siegel, E. L., Holder, L. E., Snow, J., Rothman, M. I., Zoarski, G. H., et al. (1997). Neuropsychological, neuroanatomical, and neurophysiological correlates of hypertension in older adults: Preliminary findings. *Psychosomatic Medicine, 56*, 449–456.

Walstra, G. J., Teunisse, S., van Gool, W. A., & van Crevel, H. (1997). Reversible dementia in elderly patients referred to a memory clinic. *Journal of Neurology, 244*, 17–22.

Watkins, L. M., & Maier, S. F. (2000). The pain of being sick: Implications of immune-to-brain communication for understanding pain. *Annual Review of Psychology, 51*, 29–57.

Watkins, L. R., Hansen, M. K., Nguyen, K. T., Lee, J. E., & Maier, S. F. (1999). Dynamic regulation of the proinflammatory cytokine, interleukin-1 beta: Molecular biology for the non-molecular biologists. *Life Science, 65*, 499–481.

Wieneke, M. H., & Dienst, E. R. (1995). Neuropsychological assessment of cognitive functioning following chemotherapy for breast cancer. *Psycho-Oncology, 4,* 61–66.

Witko-Sarsat, V., Rieu, P., Descamps-Latscha, B., Lesavre, P., & Halbwachs-Mecarelli, L. (2000). Neutrophils: Molecules, functions, and pathophysiological aspects. *Laboratory Investigation, 80,* 617–653.

Zhan, C., Sangl, J., & Bierman, A. (2001). Potentially inappropriate medication use in the community-dwelling elderly: Findings from the Medical Expenditure Panel Survey. *Journal of the American Medical Association, 286,* 2823–2829.

—⇒◆⇐—

Impact of Dementia on Decision-Making Abilities

Stacey Wood and Betty E. Tanius

This chapter describes the brain regions involved in decision-making processes and discusses the implications for individuals with dementia processes. The first section of the chapter discusses current understanding of decision making from neuropsychology, forensic psychology, and neuroscience. In the second section, two common types of dementia disorders are used to illustrate how decisional processes may be impacted by cognitive disorders.

IMPLICATIONS FOR ASSESSMENT

Dementia processes can influence an individual's ability to reason and make good decisions, placing them at higher risk for fraud and exploitation. Decision making is a complex cognitive process that involves multiple brain systems and thus, can be impacted by a diverse range of injuries. This chapter begins by discussing some contemporary ideas regarding decision processes and brain regions involved in decision making. We then present three cases to illustrate two common types of dementia and how dementia can influence decision making.

Current Frameworks for Understanding Decision Making

Neuroscience of decision making and the related field of neuroeconomics have emerged in the past 5 years and have added tremendously to our knowledge of brain systems involved in decision making (Zak, 2004). One of the major themes of this line of research has been examining the role that emotion may play in decision making and the integration of emotion and cognition in decision processes.

A number of dual-process models have been proposed to classify decision processes, usually separating intuitive/emotional processes from higher cognitive processes (Sanfey, Lowenstein, McClure, & Cohen, 2006). For this review, we are using Kahnemans' (2003) framework, System 1 and System 2, as a heuristic for conceptualizing decision making. System 1 is described as intuitive, automatic, fast, emotional, rule based, and holistic. For example, your ability to quickly judge height or express a consumer preference may be viewed as *System 1* types of decisions. Clinically, this system may come into play when a client expresses an intuitive judgment to trust another person. Kahneman described this system as one of instant access and several researchers have speculated that this system may be relatively secure as one ages. Further, it is possible that older adults may rely relatively more on intuitive decision making (e.g., Peters, Finucane, MacGregor, & Slovic, 2000; Peters, Hess, Västfjäll, & Auman, in press; Yates & Patalano, 1999). *System 2* is described as analytic, effortful, flexible, and slow. Decisions that require a weighing of costs and benefits or calculation are examples of System 2 types of decisions. Another example of a System 2 type of decision is choosing between two types of medical treatments or two types of insurance plans. In this case, information regarding options is retrieved and compared on different attributes. A good deal of everyday decision making requires the dynamic involvement of both systems.

Traditionally, neuropsychologists have employed the construct of executive functioning to questions regarding decision-making capacity. This construct includes a range of processes including initiation, flexibility, working memory, and persistence (MacPherson, Phillips, & Sala, 2002). Conceptually, executive functioning, with its emphasis of online processing and flexibility may be best understood as most like System 2.

Neuroscience of Decision Making

In broad terms, there is evidence of distinct neural circuits dedicated to the automatic and affective aspects of System 1 decision making versus the more deliberate, conscious System 2 decision processes. Neuroscientists have identified brain regions involved in reward, loss, and what appears to be a region involved in the integration of reward information and cognitive information including the basal ganglia and ventromedial aspect of the frontal lobes (e.g., Elliott, Newman, Longe, & Deakin, 2003; Kuhnen & Knutson, 2005). Conversely, System 2 types of decision processes have been more consistently associated with dorsolateral aspects of the frontal lobes.

The role of the ventromedial frontal (VMF) lobe in risky decision making became well known approximately 14 years ago following the work of Antonio Damásio (1994). Prior to this work, the dominant theories in decision making either minimized the role of emotion or discussed emotion as a distraction to rational decision making. In contrast, Damásio's somatic marker hypothesis places emotion as the central player in healthy decision making. Drawing on his extensive clinical and research experience with brain-injured patients, Damásio theorized that healthy decision makers are able to draw on their affective signals and integrate them into their cognitive processes. Individuals with brain injuries to the VMF region are unable to do this and thus, cannot benefit from these types of somatic cues. Clinical examples of poor decision making in VMF lobe patients included difficulties with holding a job, managing family relationships, and reading social cues (Bechara, Damasio, Tranel, & Damásio, 1997).

Bechara and colleagues (1997) developed a gambling task, now known as the Iowa Gambling Task (IGT) to conduct experimental assessments of the role the VMF lobe may play in decision making. The IGT requires participants to draw from one of four decks, simply labeled A, B, C, and D. Two of the decks have high payouts but even higher losses. The other two decks, the "good decks" have relatively lower payouts but lower losses resulting in better performance over time. Healthy individuals may begin by sampling all of the decks, sample more frequently from the bad decks, but over time tend to migrate to selecting primarily from the good decks.

Bechara et al. (1997) added measures of skin conductance response (SCRs) to the IGT to assess autonomic reactivity. They hypothesized that behavioral measures of performance would correlate with physiologic measures of SCRs and that those with strong reactivity to losses would do best on the task. Overall, their original results support this theory. Since that time, there have been hundreds of studies using this task with different clinical populations. Over time, some consistent criticisms have been made regarding the IGT including the ability of the task to localize to the VMF region, the role of explicit cognitive factors such as memory on performance, and the difficulty of replicating the anticipatory SCR findings (e.g., Busemeyer & Stout, 2002; Fellows, 2004; Maia, & McClelland, 2004). However, in general, the somatic theory has been validated in that it is generally accepted that emotion plays an important role in decision making and that the VMF region is critical for the integration of reward signals and higher cognitive processes (e.g., Khunen & Knutson, 2005; Smith, Dichaut, McCabe, & Pardo, 2002).

The VMF region is extensively connected to subcortical brain regions involved in emotion and reward (Fellows, 2004). These regions, which include midbrain dopamine nuclei, basal ganglia structures, and limbic regions, are involved in detecting the presence of reward and in signaling reward. For example, in studies using functional imaging, images of rewarding stimuli, such as primary reinforcers like food and secondary reinforcers such as money, will activate this reward pathway (Kuhnen & Knutson, 2005). This system will be activated when a participant receives a reward while playing a gambling type task. There is evidence that the system is deactivated when a participant fails to win on a particular trial. In contrast, a separate neural circuit appears to be involved in the presence of negative stimuli. For example, when participants are faced with a potential loss or experience a loss, activation of insula regions and amygdala regions are more likely (Paulus, Rogalsky, Simmons, Feinstein, & Stein, 2003). Taken together, there is considerable evidence for both a reward and a loss pathway that is dissociable from higher cognitive, cortical regions involved in decision making.

In contrast, System 2 decision processes that involve working memory and the conscious weighing of pros and cons appear to be more highly related to activations of dorsolateral prefrontal regions. Dorsolateral prefrontal regions have been consistently linked to cognitive flexibility, the ability to encode new information and to plan (e.g., MacPherson et al., 2002). In studies examining the ability to delay gratification, increased dorsolateral prefrontal activation was seen on trials where participants rationally chose to delay gratification rather than to receive an immediate but less valuable reward (McClure & Laibson, 2004). Other cortical regions that have been linked to decision making include the parietal lobe for calculation and frequency estimates and the temporal lobe for long-term memory.

Neuropsychological assessments of these types of processes fall under the category of *executive functioning* and *working memory*. Common neuropsychological tests used to assess executive functioning include the Wisconsin Card Sorting Test, the Stroop test, and Word Fluency tests (Lezak, 1995). Neuropsychologists do not have well-standardized clinical tools to assess the rapid automatic processes involved in System 1 types of decisions.

In summary, the neuroscience of decision making is complex and involves both cortical and subcortical regions. Decision making appears to involve multiple cortical processes and diverse brain regions. Thus, there can be no *capacimeter* that can tap into one localized brain region involved in decision making. That being said, there is consensus on the critical role played by frontal regions (both VMF and dorsolateral prefrontal cortex), and injury to frontal regions would likely disrupt decision processes. Although a typical assessment of capacity includes measures of executive functioning, they typically do not include an assessment of risk taking and the reward/loss pathways. Because only experimental measures are available presently, clinicians must augment their batteries with functional instruments to gain this additional information. For example, including a measure of financial capacity and a well-designed clinical interview may allow a clinician to comment on past risk-taking behavior and potential response to reward.

Moving from Neuroscience to Clinical Settings

Next, we review what is known regarding healthy aging and decision making, and then we discuss the impact that Alzheimer's disease and vascular dementia may have on decision processes, both at initial presentation and after some progression.

Precise patterns of decision-making abilities and how they change across the life span are still emerging. Work in this area has consistently emphasized that older and younger adults ultimately make the same decisions on many decision tasks, although they may use different strategies to reach their endpoint. For example, in a study of older and younger women with breast cancer, older women were found to be less likely to seek out a second opinion or additional material regarding their options but ultimately chose the same course of treatment as younger women with the same condition (Park, 1999). In a study using the IGT, older and younger adults both performed well, with younger adults capitalizing on their strong memory abilities, and older adults relying more on affective cues (which deck previously held a loss or win) when making their decisions (Wood, Busemeyer, Koling, Cox, & Davis, 2005). Taken together, these results suggest that as decision strategies and motivations change with age, brain regions relevant to decision processes may also change. Another theme that has emerged in this area is that older adults may have difficulty on tasks where there is increased complexity and cognitive demands. In a study of heath care decision making, older adults were more likely as a group to make errors in terms of consistency and comprehension. The IGT demonstrated that as cognitive demands increased, both groups made more errors. These results suggest that older adults will not perform as well as younger adults with decisions that place high demands on working memory.

In summary, this emerging literature highlights the deliberative and affective processes that underlie decision making and potential dissociations in the decision making of younger and older adults. Older adults as a group are thought to rely more on affective processes in their decision making (System 1) than on deliberative processes (System 2). In support of this concept, MacPherson and colleagues (2002) reported that older adults demonstrate age-related impairment on tasks associated with the dorsolateral prefrontal cortex (DLPFC), but not those associated with VMF lobe. Thus, as we age, we may shift to using more System 1 types of processes to adapt to age-related changes in System 2 neuroanatomy. The related, problem-solving literature suggests that everyday problem-solving abilities decline with age and that these changes are related to changes in cognitive functioning. However, these differences are lessened when the problem to be solved is social rather than cognitive, suggesting that when VMF (System 1) regions are activated, older adults perform well (e.g., Blanchard-Fields, Mienaltowski, & Baldi Seay, 2007; Thornton & Dumke, 2005).

In terms of implications for clinicians, research on older adults suggests that there may be less of a relationship between traditional neuropsychological measures and real-world decision making than that found in younger adults. In the real world, older adults appear to be using compensatory strategies, such as an increased reliance on System 1, and are more likely to seek the input of experts in their decision making (Yates & Patalano, 1999). Thus, impairments on neuropsychological measures of executive functioning may not correspond to equally severe impairments in real-world decision making. Therefore, it is important to include a functional assessment as part of any capacity evaluation so that these potential dissociations can be brought to light.

How Dementia Disrupts Decision Making

Dementia, in general, is often disruptive to decision processes, but the specific effects are dependent on the clinical population in question, brain regions impacted by the disorder, and the presentation (early versus late). The neuroscience of the decision-making field and neuroeconomics has yet to tackle questions regarding how specific dementias impact decision making. In the following section, we consider two specific dementia processes to illustrate how each may impact decision making, drawing on the fields of neurology, neuropsychology, and forensic geropsychology.

Alzheimer's Disease and Decision Making

Alzheimer's disease is initially characterized by difficulties with new learning and changes in at least one other cognitive domain, which may include language, visuoperceptual skills, and/or executive functioning. Language symptoms typically begin with anomia or marked word finding difficulties and changes in verbal fluency. If perceptual disturbances are present early, they usually include topographical disorientation and difficulty copying complex figures. There are commonly changes in personality that may include apathy/indifference, sadness, or delusions. In terms of decisional capacity, an individual at this stage will have vulnerabilities in decisions that load heavily on learning new information. Difficulties with language should not be as much of a concern in the earliest stages as long as clients have plenty of time to express themselves. Perceptual disturbances could impair calculations necessary for financial decisions. It is possible that changes in personality such as a lack of awareness of new limitations could lead to poor judgments and negatively impact decision making. Indifference may result in errors in accounting or home maintenance, while a lack of initiative may result in unpaid bills.

Alzheimer's disease primarily impacts medial temporal regions at the beginning of the disease, areas important for converting short-term memories into long-term memories (Cummings & Benson, 1992). As it progresses, other brain regions become compromised by the disease, including the parietal lobe and frontal regions. The parietal lobes are associated with language functioning, calculation, and object recognition. Changes in language processing have been associated with impairments on standard instruments used to assess ability to consent to medical treatment (Gurrera, Moye, Karel, Azar, & Armesto, 2006). Changes in basic calculation have been found to be predictive of impairments on assessments of financial decision making (Martin et al., 2003). Both VMF and dorsolateral prefrontal regions of the frontal lobe will eventually be compromised by Alzheimer's disease resulting in impairments in both executive functioning and emotional aspects of decision making. These changes disrupt cognitive aspects of decision making such as being able to keep information *online* as one weighs a decision and the ability to integrate feedback into the decision process.

At this point in the illness, decision-making incapacity may or may not be determined to be impaired depending on the decision in question. Verbal retrieval has been found to be a strong predictor of medical decision making (Moye, Karel, Gurrera, & Azar, 2006). Early dementia can pose difficulties for the recall of information such as medical or financial data that may impair decision making. Making comparisons of alternatives in either medical treatments or investment decisions would be especially challenging for an individual at this stage of early dementia. However, recent research has demonstrated that most individuals in the earliest stages of dementia would not meet the legal criteria for incapacity and should be encouraged to participate in decision making (Moye et al., in press).

Case Example: Early Alzheimer's Disease (Roughly 1 to 3 Years since Onset)

Mr. J. Smith, a 68-year-old retired physician, was referred by his primary care doctor for an evaluation of cognitive functioning secondary to concerns regarding memory loss. His family reported that he had been less attentive to work at their home that included the care of several horses, a long-standing hobby. Neuropsychological testing done at that time revealed overall high average to superior functioning with the exception of verbal recall, which was low average at the 20th percentile. Clinical recommendations made at that time included a diagnosis of mild cognitive impairment with a recommendation for follow-up examination in 18 to 24 months and a recommendation for neuroimaging. J.S. had good insight into his limitations and had hired an accountant to assist with bill paying. Because J.S. was primarily experiencing difficulties with memory recall, it was recommended that he use support (written information/organizers) when planning for the future, but recommendations for guardianship were not made.

As the disease progresses, roughly 2 to 10 years following onset, the client will demonstrate increased difficulty with memory, including more severe loss of remote memory. Language impairments will progress to a fluent aphasia with marked anomia and word finding difficulties. The client may easily become disoriented and demonstrate a poor ability to draw or construct figures to models.

Changes in executive functioning can result in poor initiation, a lack of flexibility, and poor judgment. Personality changes may become more prominent as well, with indifference becoming more marked, agitation increasing, and the presence of delusions increasing to as much as 20% of cases (Cummings, Mega, Gray, Rosemberg-Thompson, & Gornbein, 1994). Small oversights regarding home maintenance and financial matters may progress to carelessness and negligence. Decision making becomes more uniformly impaired with marked changes in the ability to initiate decisions, retrieve relevant details, and weigh options. However, there is still evidence that when presented with a simple choice regarding care, many patients with more moderate Alzheimer's disease can continue to express a choice when presented with two relatively simple options (Gurrera et al., 2006).

Case Example: Moderate to Severe Alzheimer's Disease

Mrs. G. Harris, a retired schoolteacher, was referred by her adult children for an evaluation of cognitive functioning secondary to memory and safety concerns. The adult children of the client lived in another state and were trying their best to manage her care from a distance. In clinical interview, family reported that Mrs. Harris was having difficulty keeping up with housework and expressed concern regarding her ability to shop and cook for herself. As such, the family had hired a housekeeper/cook to come in several days per week to assist with her care. However, Mrs. Harris disliked having a stranger in her home and accused the housekeeper of stealing and fired her. Mrs. Harris reported that she was living alone, completely independently with no assistance. She reported that she did not need any additional assistance and showed very limited insight into her memory difficulties. She had recently suffered a fall and had been briefly hospitalized. On neuropsychological testing, Mrs. Harris was not oriented to time and was unable to recall the current or past president. She scored at the second percentile on tasks assessing immediate and delayed verbal memory. She also demonstrated severely impaired performance on tasks assessing executive functioning and visuoperceptual construction. Her language abilities were somewhat better, although she performed below average on a task assessing word-finding abilities. Assessment of personality revealed the presence of suspiciousness and delusions regarding theft. In this case, clinical recommendations included the need for a more structured setting and assistance with decision making. A guardianship hearing was held granting her adult son guardianship over estate and person. Mrs. Harris was presented with several potential options for housing including moving to a local assisted living facility, or moving in with either her adult son or daughter. She was consistently able to express a preference to live with her son. The son planned to sell Mrs. Harris's home and move her to his home where he and his wife could care for her.

Vascular Dementia and Decision Making

Vascular dementia has a prevalence rate of about 6% in individuals over 60 and the rate increases with age (Cummings & Benson, 1992). Vascular dementias include those caused by small strategically located single strokes, dementias following a hemorrhagic event, and dementias resulting from ischemic tissue changes. The clinical characteristics of the dementia depend on the specific vessels involved. Large vessel disease impacting the carotid or cerebral arteries can result in cortical symptoms including aphasia, apraxia, and amnesia. Injury to smaller vessels may result in a more subcortical presentation that includes apathy, poor memory recall, and poor executive functioning, In general, neuropsychological profiles of vascular dementias contain features of both cortical and subcortical dementias including deficits in orientation, changes in memory recall, impairments in executive functioning, and potentially, changes in language and visuospatial abilities. Personality changes and changes to executive systems are very common (Cummings & Benson, 1992). The course of vascular dementia is variable. Some researchers have noted a stepwise course that results in periods of decline followed by plateaus. However, the disease is ultimately progressive.

Changes in executive functioning and personality emerge earlier in vascular dementia versus Alzheimer's disease and can put clients at risk for poor judgment and decision making (Looi & Sachdev, 1999). Both dorsolateral and ventromedial frontal regions can be implicated in vascular dementia resulting in poor flexibility, risk seeking, and poor response to feedback. However, given the variability of neuropsychological patterns, clients may have particular strengths and weaknesses that impact their individual decision-making abilities. Evaluations of capacity should always be domain specific rather than some, all, or none determination to capture that variability. For example, vascular dementia often results in difficulties with initiation and retrieval, so that a client may have difficulty generating options for a decision domain but can keep presented options online and express a choice.

Case Example: Vascular Dementia

Mrs. S. White was a 72-year-old woman with a long history of eccentric behavior. She was brought to the attention of adult protective services following complaints from neighbors and her senior apartment manager of odd behaviors including delusions/hallucinations and fire starting. Specifically, Mrs. White accused other residents of spreading germs and having bugs in their homes. She refused to visit a doctor's office or hospital because of concerns regarding germs. Mrs. White had adult children living in the same community, but they had been estranged for about 5 years because of her odd and somewhat inconsiderate behavior. For example, they reported that S. had come to their homes in the middle of the night requesting help with some small household task. They reported that she had also shown up at other relatives' homes (out of state) with no warning with the expectation of living with them "for awhile." Her work history included many different employers in women's apparel. They reported that she had always had a suspicious nature, but had not in times past evidenced the frank delusions and hallucinations she was currently reporting. Because of her fears regarding germs, testing was done at her residence.

On neuropsychological testing, she performed poorly on tasks of executive functioning including poor initiation, flexibility, and problem solving. She demonstrated poor insight into some of her risky behavior such as cooking on an open flame and refusal to seek medical care for what appeared to be untreated diabetes, and shoplifting at a local Wal-Mart. Magazines were piled all over her apartment and she seemed to be engaged in multiple sweepstakes-type schemes. Her memory recall was impaired, although it improved with recognition format and cuing. Language processes were intact and she could understand and produce speech. Her perceptual abilities were also intact. On clinical interview S. denied having any difficulties, despite a pending eviction. She reported seeing "bugs" all over the apartment and reiterated her concerns about seeing a physician. The neuropsychologist and family members were able to get her to the emergency room for a large bruise on her forearm, and she was admitted to an inpatient unit for further medical tests. MRI scans done at that time revealed moderate vascular dementia. Following discharge, she was moved to a more structured environment that included more supervision of medications and other safety issues.

In summary, dementia processes are ultimately disruptive to decision-making processes, but the specific impact depends on the etiology of the dementia, the stage of dementia, and the presentation of the case.

CONCLUSION

Decision making is a complex cognitive function that requires the integration of cortical and subcortical processes. Analytic, explicit decision making appears to be related to prefrontal regions including the DLPFC and its connections with other cortical regions. Intuitive, more affectively based decision making is related to a network of brain regions including ventromedial prefrontal cortex, basal ganglia regions, insular cortex, and midbrain dopamine pathways. Taken together, decision making involves both cortical and subcortical regions. Thus, there can be no capacimeter that taps into a specific decision-making region of the brain. Further, different dementia processes impair different aspects of these circuits at different points in their presentation. Each case must be examined from a cognitive, behavioral, and functional perspective to determine specific decision-making capabilities.

REFERENCES

Bechara, A., Damasio, H., Tranel, D., & Damásio, A. (1997). Deciding advantageously before knowing the advantageous strategy. *Science, 275,* 1293–1295.

Blanchard-Fields, F., Mienaltowski, A., & Baldi Seay, R. (2007). Age differences in everyday problem-solving effectiveness: Older adults select more effective strategies for interpersonal problems. *Journals of Gerontology: Series B, Psychological Sciences and Social Sciences, 62,* 61–64.

Busemeyer, J. R., & Stout, J. C. (2002). A contribution of cognitive decision models to clinical assessment: Decomposing performance on the Bechara gambling task. *Psychological Assessment, 14,* 253–262.

Cummings, J. L., & Benson, F. D. (1992). *Dementia: A clinical approach* (2nd ed.). Newton, MA: Butterworth-Heinemann.

Cummings, J. L., Mega, M. S., Gray, K., Rosemberg-Thompson, S., & Gornbein, T. (1994). The Neuropsychiatric Inventory: Comprehensive assessment of psychopathology in dementia. *Neurology, 44,* 2308–2314.

Damásio, A. (1994). *Descartes' error: Emotion, reason, and the human brain.* New York: Avon Books.

Elliott, R., Newman, J. L., Longe, O. A., & Deakin, W. J. (2003). Differential response patterns in the striatum and orbitalfrontal cortex to financial rewards in humans: A parametric functional magnetic resonance imaging study. *Journal of Neuroscience, 23*(1), 303–307.

Fellows, L. (2004). The cognitive neuroscience of human decision-making: A review and conceptual framework. *Behavioral and Cognitive Neuroscience Reviews, 3*(3), 159–172.

Gurrera, R. J., Moye, J., Karel, M. J., Azar, A. R., & Armesto, J. C. (2006). Cognitive performance predicts treatment decisional abilities in mild to moderate dementia. *Neurology, 66,* 1367–1372.

Kahneman, D. (2003). A perspective on judgment and choice: Mapping bounded rationality. *American Psychologist, 58,* 697–720.

Kuhnen, C., & Knutson, B. (2005). The neural basis of financial risk taking. *Neuron, 47,* 763–770.

Lezak, M. D. (1995). *Neuropsychological assessment* (3rd ed.). New York: Oxford University Press.

Looi, J. C. L., & Sachdev, P. S. (1999). Differentiation of vascular dementia from AD on neuropsychological tests. *Neurology, 53,* 670–675.

MacPherson, S. E., Philips, L. H., & Sala, S. D. (2002). Age, executive function, and social decision making: A dorsolateral prefrontal theory of cognitive aging. *Psychology and Aging, 17*(4), 598–609.

Maia, T. V., & McClelland, J. L. (2004). A re-examination of the evidence for the somatic marker hypothesis: What participants really know in the Iowa Gambling Task. *Proceedings of the National Academy of Sciences, 101*(45), 16075–16080.

Martin, R. C., Shannon, M. A., Darling, L., Wadley, V., Harrell, L., & Marson, D. (2003). Loss of calculation abilities in patients with mild to moderate Alzheimer's disease. *Archives of Neurology, 60*(11), 1585–1589.

McClure, S., & Laibson, D. I. (2004). Separate neural systems value immediate and delayed monetary rewards. *Science, 306,* 503–507.

Moye, J., Karel, M., Gurrera, R., & Azar, A. (2006). Neuropsychological predictors of decision-making capacity over 9 months in mild-to-moderate dementia. *Journal of General Internal Medicine, 21,* 78–83.

Moye, J., Wood, S., Edelstein, B., Armesto, J., Bower, E. H., Harrsion, J. A., et al. (in press). Clinical evidence in guardianship of older adults is inadequate: Findings from a tri-state study. *Gerontologist.*

Park, D. (1999). Aging and the controlled and automatic processing of medical information and intentions. In D. C. Park, R. Morrell, & K. Shifren (Eds.), *Processing of medical information in aging patients: Cognitive and human factors perspectives* (pp. 3–22). Mahwah, NJ: Erlbaum.

Paulus, M. P., Rogalsky, C., Simmons, A., Feinstein, J. S., & Stein, M. B. (2003). Increased activation in the right insula during risk-taking decision-making is related to harm avoidance and neuroticism. *Neuroimage, 19,* 1439–1448.

Peters, E., Finucane, M. L., MacGregor, D. G., & Slovic, P. (2000). The bearable lightness of aging: Judgment and decision processes in older adults. In P. C. Stern & L. L. Carstensen (Eds.), *The aging mind: Opportunities in cognitive research* (pp. 144–165). Washington, DC: National Academy of Sciences Press.

Peters, E., Hess, T. M., Västfjäll, D., & Auman, C. (in press). Adult age differences in dual information processes: Implications for the role of affective and deliberative processes in older adults' decision making. *Psychological Science*.

Sanfey, A., Loewenstein, G., McClure, S. M., & Cohen, J. D. (2006). Neuroeconomics: Cross currents in research on decision-making. *Trends in Cognitive Sciences, 10*(3), 108–116.

Smith, K., Dichaut, J., McCabe, K., & Pardo, J. (2002). Neuronal substrates for choice under ambiguity, risk, certainty, gains, and losses. *Management Science, 48*(6), 711–718.

Thornton, W., & Dumke, H. A. (2005). Age differences in everyday problem-solving and decision-making effectiveness: A meta-analytic review. *Psychology and Aging, 20*, 85–99.

Wood, S., Busemeyer, J., Koling, A., Cox, K., & Davis, H. (2005). Older adults as adaptive decision-makers: Evidence from the Gambling Task. *Psychology and Aging, 20*(2), 220–225.

Yates, J. F., & Patalano, A. L. (1999). Decision making and aging. In D. C. Park, R. Morrell, & K. Shifren (Eds.), *Processing of medical information in aging patients: Cognitive and human factors perspectives* (pp. 31–54). Mahwah, NJ: Erlbaum.

Zak, P. J. (2004). Neuroeconomics. *Philosophical Translations of the Royal Society of London. Series B, 359*, 1737–1748.

Social and Legal Contexts
of Capacity Decisions

5

Decision-Making Capacity: The Players

SARA HONN QUALLS

Q uestions about decision-making capacity are evident across many life domains and diverse contexts throughout the life span. Clinicians often encounter capacity questions explicitly when a legal capacity question arises or when safety concerns lead someone to a mental health professional for evaluation (Moye & Marson, 2007). Any evaluation of capacity should respect the complexity of the situation in which one person requests the review of another person's capacity. The person raising the question and the target person whose capacity is in question are only two of a potential myriad of players involved in the capacity concern.

The purpose of this chapter is to draw attention to the range of possible players involved in a capacity question and their potential roles in capacity determinations. The chapter begins by describing players in four sectors that are commonly relevant in the lives of older adults. The next section explores how those players are linked to older adults during the very time when informal and formal decision-making capacity is changing. The last section focuses on the players who may interact with mental health professionals during the process.

WHO ARE THE PLAYERS?

The lives of older adults are embedded in the same array of social structures that are relevant to younger adults, although particular players may be more or less important for older adults whose physical or mental frailty require assistance. Almost anyone in the personal or professional living environment of a person whose capacity is in question may be a relevant player because the person's fit with her environment (including the social environment) may so intensively influence her capacity (Lawton, 1982).

Family life provides a context for informal decisions about capacity across the life span, including for older adults, until risks to the social good outweigh the value of family autonomy. The informal strategies that families commonly use represent a huge policy advantage because formalizing each decision would overwhelm the legal system (Kapp, 2002). The decision to address a capacity question in a legal context does not necessarily take the decisions away from the informal care network, however. Legal rights can be transferred from a person with diminished capacity to a surrogate decision maker using tools that retain the focus on the informal support network.

Four sectors of society produce players who are often relevant to the lives of older adults and their families: legal, housing, health care, and social services.

Legal

An array of players who are often involved in legal processes related to determination of decision-making capacity is depicted in Figure 5.1. Decision-making capacity issues can engage legal processes through tools as variable as advanced directives, courtroom guardianship procedures, and adult protective services. These processes very likely involve attorneys, often including separate attorneys for various persons whose interests need to be represented (e.g., an older adult, a nursing home whose judgment is in question, a family member). Judges or magistrates make legal determinations within the court context; juries are usually not involved in decisions about capacity. Health providers are called on to provide evidence of the biological etiology of diminished capacity in formal guardianship proceedings.

People new to work with older adults may not be aware of more distal players such as financial advisors. Tax accountants, trust officers, and

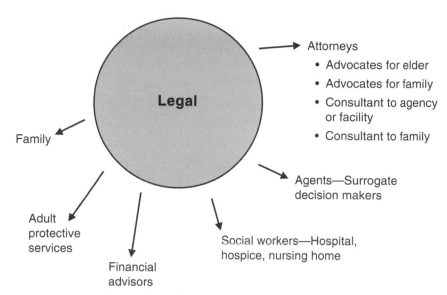

Figure 5.1   Participants in Legal Contexts

stock brokers make decisions every day about whether to trust the decision-making capacity of their clients. These players often work under service contracts that prevent them from expressing concern to anyone other than their client because of privacy concerns. This can create a difficult conflict for advisors and their clients.

Families are also players in the legal arena, as they attempt to represent their loved ones' best interests along with their own. Although only individuals have legal rights under the law, family members' rights may be infringed on by decisions about another family member. For example, the right to be cared for at home affects other family members living within that home. A guardian who chooses to place an older adult with diminished capacity into a nursing home may affect the financial inheritance of the heirs. Often, family conflicts that arise in court guardianship proceedings have their roots in long-term conflict exacerbated by proceedings that do not thoughtfully consider the stake of the players in the process.

Housing

The continuum of housing alternatives offers a very complex array of options. Community-based housing with no supportive physical characteristics or services is by far the most common residence of older adults (e.g., house or apartment). However, the array now includes options that vary based on the amount of services available and the period of time they are available (acute versus long-term), as well as the level of amenities offered. In addition, the extent to which the housing is age segregated or age integrated shapes the sets of players involved in the lives of residents.

Each housing environment brings a distinct set of players to bear on the capacity of the older adult. Figure 5.2 depicts some of the players who are commonly involved in senior housing environments such as assisted living or nursing homes. More distal players in some housing settings may also be relevant to a particular case, including health surveyors of a nursing home, ombudsmen from the Area Agency on Aging, corporate owners, or long-term care insurance company representatives. Even in an independent housing environment, the presence of other people in the household affects the picture of decision-making capacity. For example, an older adult whose capacity is being questioned may be rearing a grandchild, live with a very supportive sister or spouse, or have full responsibility for a profoundly disabled adult child.

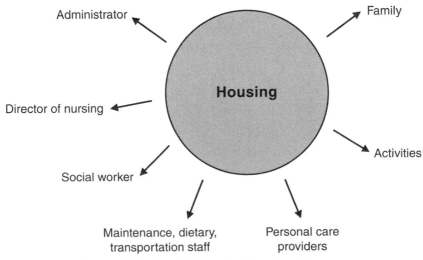

Figure 5.2   Participants in Housing Contexts

Health Care

The current health-care environment is extraordinarily complex and fragmented, so the players are not always visible to one another. Figure 5.3 depicts some of the professionals who may be providing care to an older adult as well as the array of settings that may be providing that care. The players within this domain do not necessarily know about each other. In addition, the players from other domains are highly unlikely to know who is involved and how. Electronic health-care records may help link some of these players in the near future, but for now, the burden of finding them falls to the interested party wanting the information.

Social Services

Community-based social services provide older adults with services as diverse as counseling and transportation (see Figure 5.4). The Older Americans Act funds transportation, congregate or home-delivered meals, respite

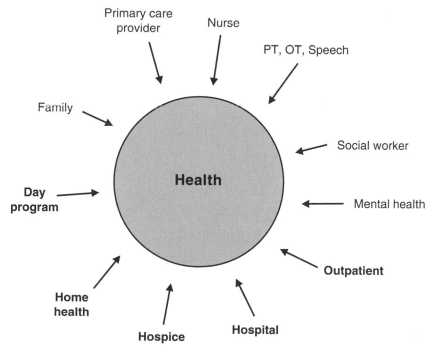

Figure 5.3   Participants in Health-Care Contexts

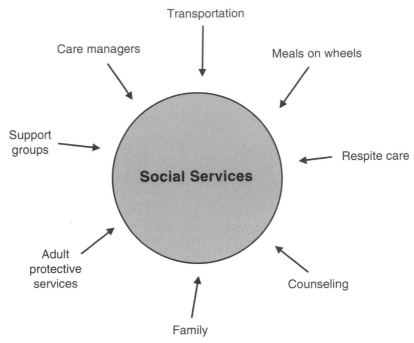

Figure 5.4   Participants in Social Services Contexts

care, and caregiver counseling and information services that are typically subcontracted by the Area Agency on Aging to local providers. Local governments provide adult protective services when an older adult is at risk and unwilling or unable to cooperate in making changes to protect their own basic safety. Long-term care insurance funds some of these services, when they are required to maintain the person in the least-restrictive setting possible. A wide array of health and human service agencies and informal networks also provide services in this category.

HOW ARE THE PLAYERS INVOLVED?

The health professional involved in capacity decisions needs an accurate view of the players involved in the process to provide evaluation data in language and format that is useful to the participants. Figure 5.5 depicts a typical sequence of events involving questions of legal capacity.

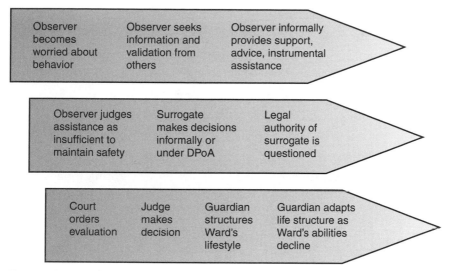

Figure 5.5   Informal and Formal Responses of Players to Changes in Decision-Making Capacity

The top row of Figure 5.5 depicts activities that may be less visible but equally important to mental health professionals involved in assessment or interventions than are the activities in the second row. Key questions in the assessment process relate to who noticed what and what they have already tried to do to address their concerns. *Any* player noted previously, along with many not mentioned specifically, could play these vital roles of problem detection, initial assessment, and early intervention. Reconstructing the history of these steps is critical because it helps identify key players, and it helps put current concerns about safety in perspective. For example, consider the scenario in which an adult child in a distant state calls Adult Protective Services to seek an intervention leading toward guardianship because she believes the home health aide who bathes her mother is incompetent to recognize potentially life-threatening signs of falls. If the mother likes the home health aide and does not want the daughter involved, a psychologist may be called in to evaluate the mother's decision-making capacity. Even more common is the reverse of this scenario in which an older adult fires the home health aide who was hired by her family to maintain her at home safely.

The context of the question shapes the assessment process signifi-cantly. In both of the previous scenarios, family members are acting on behalf of an older adult whom they deem unable to manage life safely. In the typical scenario, no legal decision has been made to appoint or ac-knowledge the legal authority of family over the older adult until the older adult protests the family's authority to override her decisions. In other words, most decision capacity questions are raised without an ap-peal for guardianship or even activation of a durable power of attorney. The family or other concerned party simply wants information about an older person's ability to be safe within a particular context. Family mem-bers provide 80% of elder care, with the vast majority presumably offered under these informal arrangements.

Scientists can tell us relatively little about this interpersonal stage in the process of evaluating and supporting decision-making capacity. In-deed, I can find no studies of family perspectives on the processes just prior to the legal step of guardianship. However, we can draw from a re-lated literature that has examined the social-cognitive responses of ob-servers to the same period of time when dementia makes functioning in daily life difficult. The studies did not examine specifically those events that led to guardianship, but did offer insight into the interpretation of those difficulties and initial help-seeking efforts.

Uncertainty about what warrants intervention is a common theme among lay observers of signs of dementia. Retrospective studies of fam-ily members of persons with dementia report that they recognized the signs of declining cognitive abilities approximately 1 year before they began seeking medical evaluations (Knopman, Donahue, & Gutter-man, 2000). Looking back on that period, families describe themselves as uncertain about whether their observation warranted involvement or not, so they hesitated to intrude on their loved one's independence (Knopman et al., 2000; Ross et al., 1997). Help seeking does not occur until safety is a point of concern, thus delaying assessments until well into midstage dementia (Nichols & Martindale-Adams, 2006). Even when seeking help, caregivers often label the problem inaccurately despite their ability to describe serious cognitive impairments (Qualls et al., 2005).

This uncertainty apparently centers on the challenge of interpreting the everyday behaviors through which cognitive decline is evidenced. Our lab has conducted a series of studies demonstrating that although lay observers have a reasonably accurate understanding of Alzheimer's disease (AD), they are not very effective at identifying signs of cognitive decline in daily activities (Williams, 2007). Detection rates rise as symptom intensity increases and are stronger when the symptoms match observers' schema for AD primarily as a memory disorder (Berryman, 2003). However, when the behavior problems are more characteristic of executive dysfunction (e.g., poor initiation, disinhibition, poorly organized behavior), laypersons may appraise the situation as problematic, but are far more confused about how to interpret those signs or what kind of help to seek than when memory symptoms dominate (Berryman, 2003; Williams, 2007).

These findings suggest that the informal processes presented in the first row of Figure 5.5 are fraught with delayed observations and inaccurate interpretations, and thus likely to generate ineffective initial efforts to solve the problem. More research is needed to help understand how families and friends respond to observations of unsafe behavior and under what conditions those informal efforts are insufficient. How a formal question of capacity is raised, by whom, and what is hanging on the outcome of any formal assessment or legal process all come in to play in an examination of those first-row processes.

The second row in Figure 5.5 depicts the actions that accrue when someone is deemed incapable. The initial processes occur relatively informally in most cases because families simply step in. Several factors shape whether the intrusive action is viewed as welcome assistance or meddling, including: who steps in and how, the impact of the target person's impairment on his or her insight into the scope of the problem, and the implications of the surrogate's actions. Even agencies or residential facilities have stepped in rather informally to assist a declining client, although recent scrutiny of legal rights more commonly generates a desire for formal assessment.

The simpler cases are those where the elder is receptive to assistance. Also relatively simple are cases where the person needing assistance has legal documents detailing surrogate preferences. Even when the question of who will become the surrogate is relatively straightforward, the process of determining whether the timing is right for transferring authority from the target older adult to their chosen proxy is not simple. Far more confusing are situations in which the elder has not specified a surrogate or there are multiple versions of legal documents completed at different points in time that name different people.

The final row in Figure 5.5 tracks the process through a legal determination made in court. Once the formal procedure is completed in the courtroom, multiple players are still involved in implementing the guardianship responsibilities. The court-appointed guardian may have been granted full or partial responsibility for all aspects of the older adult's life. The guardian's responsibilities may include oversight and choices about all or only some of the following life domains on behalf of the older adult: living arrangements, health care, personal care, legal, and financial arrangements. Any change in the person's functioning is likely to require alteration to those arrangements, so the responsibility requires regular involvement.

Mental health professionals can be involved in almost any phase of the complex sequence that unfolds; usually, in a far less linear way in real human lives than Figure 5.5 implies. Indeed, multiple players also are involved in numerous ways at various points in this process and this may be confusing to any one player. Consider this example:

 ## Case Example: Who's on First?

A nursing assistant agrees with a resident's daughter (who visits the resident regularly) that the resident should be provided with any treats she desires because her life is so limited that she is often depressed. Both of them take the resident small treats almost daily. The physical therapist working on contract with the facility has obtained the resident's agreement to a treatment plan that requires the resident to lose weight to gain mobility. The legal surrogate decision maker (the resident's daughter who lives in another state and visits monthly) insists on strength exercises for her mother and strict adherence to a weight-loss diet with hopes that her mother will regain independent mobility. Escalating conflict between the sisters becomes problematic for the facility social worker when the sisters both threaten legal action against the facility for not enforcing an appropriate standard of care. You are asked for an evaluation of the mother's capacity to make nutritional decisions and to judge whether the local daughter's visits need to be restricted because of her refusal to adhere to the food limitations.

Mental health professionals often play the role of evaluator in the process. Chapter 12 describes many other aspects of expertise (in addition to evaluation) that are needed. The diverse roles of mental health professionals require them to respect and investigate the range of players involved in care.

CONCLUSION

The potential set of players involved in capacity decisions is remarkably diverse and linked to the older person with threads that are often invisible at first glance. Assessments of decision-making capacity require thoughtful analysis of the impact of various players on the person's functioning as well as on the process of determining his or her capacity. The players are very relevant to legal standards that include assessment of the person's cognitive abilities, daily functioning abilities, values and wishes, and potential for functioning under improved environmental conditions. Professionals coming into this practice area for the first time need to become familiar with the range of players and how they can shape both the formal and informal processes of gauging decision-making capacity in another person.

REFERENCES

Berryman, K. B. (2003). *The effect of memory and executive function cue presentation on the recognition of problem existence in early dementia.* Unpublished master's thesis, University of Colorado, Colorado Springs.

Kapp, M. B. (2002). Decisional capacity in theory and practice: Legal process versus "bumbling through." *Aging and Mental Health, 6,* 413–417.

Knopman, D., Donahue, J. A., & Gutterman, E. M. (2000). Patterns of care in the early stages of Alzheimer's disease: Impediments to timely diagnosis. *Journal of the American Geriatric Society, 48,* 300–304.

Lawton, M. P. (1982). Competence, environmental press, and the adaptation of older people. In M. P. Lawton, P. G. Windley, & T. O. Byerts (Eds.), *Aging and the environment: Theoretical approaches* (pp. 33–59). New York: Springer.

Moye, J., & Marson, D. C. (2007). Assessment of decision-making capacity in older adults: An emerging area of practice and research. *Journal of Gerontology: Psychological Sciences, 62B,* P3–P11.

Nichols, L. O., & Martindale-Adams, J. (2006). The decisive moment: Caregivers' recognition of dementia. *Clinical Gerontologist, 30,* 39–52.

Qualls, S. H., Layton, H., Stephens, M., Hiroto, K., Williams, A., Altayli, B., et al. (2005, October & November). *Family caregivers of elderly seek counseling services primarily for cognitive disabilities.* Poster session presented at the annual conferences of the Coleman Institute, Boulder, CO, and the Gerontological Society of America, Orlando, FL.

Ross, G. W., Abbott, R. D., Petrovitch, H., Masaki, K. H., Murdaugh, C., Trockman, C., et al. (1997). Frequency and characteristics of silent dementia among elderly Japanese-American men. *Journal of the American Medical Association, 277,* 800–805.

Williams, A. (2007). *Impact of variations in context and format of presentation on accuracy of identification of Alzheimer's disease symptoms.* Unpublished master's thesis, University of Colorado, Colorado Springs.

CHAPTER

6

⟹◆⟸

A Primer for
Legal Proceedings

Wayna M. Marshall, Catherine Seal, and Lynn Vanatta-Perry

When a person's cognitive abilities begin to decline, legal and medical/mental health professionals should work together to determine what that person needs and to ensure that those needs are being met. Unfortunately, these professionals often speak their own unique languages and are not always adept at communicating with each other to accomplish the task. Our goal in this chapter is to clarify the legal process and terminology. We address the typical players and the process, the legal questions the court is trying to answer, jurisdiction and how it affects the process, options when no one is available to help, alternatives to court proceedings, and what happens under complex conditions of dual diagnosis or when there is a contested hearing.

THE LEGAL PLAYERS AND THE LEGAL PROCESS

In every legal proceeding, a variety of players fill prescribed roles. These players are the parties to the action. The primary parties include: the respondent, the petitioner, the petitioner's attorney, the court visitor, the *guardian ad litem*, the attorney for the respondent, the guardian, the conservator, and the judge or magistrate. It is important to recognize that the labels for the parties may vary from state to state. For example, instead of a guardian and conservator, there may be a guardian of the person and a guardian of the property. Whatever the label, the roles of the parties are essentially the same.

A respondent is the person whose cognitive abilities are in question. The respondent is entitled to be represented by an attorney. This attorney expresses the respondent's wishes to the court. The court may appoint another attorney—the guardian ad litem—to represent the best interests of the respondent. If the court determines that the respondent needs assistance in making decisions about medical care, treatment, and placement, a guardian will be appointed. If the decisions involve financial matters, a conservator will be appointed.

To bring a matter before the court, a petition must be filed explaining the facts and circumstances of the respondent and requesting that the court make certain determinations regarding the respondent. The person filing the petition is called the petitioner. The petitioner can be any person or organization interested in the welfare of the respondent, ranging from a family member to the adult protective division of the local social services department. The petition must be accompanied by a report from an independent professional addressing the cognitive abilities of the respondent.

Once a petition has been filed with the court, a court visitor is appointed to act as the court's eyes and ears and to gather background information. The court visitor has access to all of the respondent's records. In addition, the court visitor will talk with the respondent, the petitioner, the proposed guardian and/or conservator, care providers, and medical professionals.

After the court visitor files a report with the court, a hearing on the appointment of a guardian and/or conservator is set. At the hearing, the court will take testimony from the respondent, the petitioner, the guardian ad litem, and any other witnesses who may be able to provide the court with assistance in making a determination regarding the relief requested in the petition.

THE LEGAL QUESTIONS

The two primary questions that the court is trying to answer are: (1) Does the respondent meet the definition of an incapacitated or protected person? and (2) If so, who should be appointed as guardian and/or conservator?

In Colorado, for example, a distinction is made between a person who is incapacitated and a person who is in need of protection. A finding of incapacity allows the court to appoint a guardian to make medical decisions. A guardianship is, by default, limited; therefore, based on the level of the respondent's incapacity, the court determines to what extent the guardian should be involved in the decision-making process. For example, the respondent may be capable of deciding what to eat and wear but not where to live and which medications to take.

If the court finds that the respondent is unable to manage finances, the court may place the respondent under a protective arrangement and appoint a conservator. In this situation, there is no need for a finding of incapacity. Just as in the guardianship scenario, the court determines the level to which the conservator should be involved in the financial matters of the respondent. For example, the respondent may be perfectly capable of paying monthly bills but may be baffled by larger investments. In that situation, the conservator would manage the investments, probably in consultation with the respondent, while the respondent would continue to maintain some sense of independence by handling the day-to-day operating account.

Obviously, for the court to make these kinds of determinations, evidence must be presented that clearly delineates the respondent's abilities. The court will rely on anecdotal evidence, but prefers that this evidence be supported by independent professional reports in the form of neuropsychological evaluations and functional assessments. The neuropsychological evaluation explains *why* the respondent is not capable of handling all aspects of life by reporting and interpreting testing results. The functional assessment tells *how* this is manifested in everyday life. Both types of reports are invaluable for the court.

JURISDICTION

In what state and county is the guardianship or conservatorship filed? In most states, a petition for the appointment of a guardian of the person is filed in the state and county where the person resides, while a petition for the appointment of a conservator of the property can be filed in any county of any state where the person owns real estate, as well as in the state and county where the person resides. In this discussion, *guardianship* or *guardianship of the person* refers to a legal proceeding to appoint an individual as guardian to make medical decisions and personal care decisions, while the term *conservatorship* or *conservatorship of the property* is used to refer to a legal proceeding to appoint an individual as conservator to make financial decisions and to manage property.

Sometimes, a person who is traveling out of state, possibly visiting a relative or spending the winter months in a more temperate climate, has a sudden and immediate, but perfectly legitimate, need for management of their person and/or property. On some occasions however, an individual with suspect motives travels from one jurisdiction to another with a person to file a guardianship and/or conservatorship matter in a jurisdiction where there is a perceived advantage to the person seeking appointment. On rare occasions, parties in more than one state file guardianship and/or conservatorship cases at the same time, and there are significant questions as to which state actually has authority to make appointments in these *dueling petition* matters.

The National Conference of Commissioners on Uniform State Laws is drafting a proposed law for states to adopt, which would provide the courts with a process for determining which jurisdiction has priority in multijurisdiction cases. The proposed law sets up a standard for determining a "home state" for every proposed "incapacitated person" based on the person's length of residency. The solution is modeled after laws already in place that govern child custody jurisdiction and is designed to discourage transporting individuals to jurisdictions other than their usual place of residence for the purpose of filing guardianship and/or conservatorship cases. The proposed law also deals with such matters as dueling petitions that have been filed in more than one jurisdiction setting up guidelines for courts to use to determine which jurisdiction is the most appropriate.

WHAT HAPPENS WHEN THERE IS NO ONE TO HELP?

Often, the adult protective division of the social services department in a jurisdiction is the petitioner for the individual with no family. The referral to adult protective services is made by someone who has concerns that an individual may lack capacity to effectively manage his or her affairs. Other petitioners may be friends or caregivers. Sometimes, a hospital discharge planner is the party referring the matter to adult protective services, because the individual is not deemed able to participate in the discharge planning and a decision maker is needed. In many states, "interested parties" to a guardianship and/or conservatorship case is a category far broader than is typical in court proceedings. Often, the goal is to involve any individual who might have actual knowledge about or concern for the person.

Some states have an office of public guardian, who serves when there is no one else. Many states do not and the result is a frantic search for friends, caregivers, or community volunteers to serve as guardian of the person, unless the individual has sufficient resources to pay for a professional guardian. Likewise, with conservator of the property, some states have an office of public conservator, but many do not. For those individuals who have assets or income sufficient to warrant doing so, a professional may be appointed. For those individuals without such resources, friends and community volunteers are the only alternative.

ALTERNATIVES TO GUARDIANSHIP AND/OR CONSERVATORSHIP

Mechanisms other than guardianship and conservatorship are available to assist older adults whose capacity for autonomous decision making is declining. Assistance from family members may help the individual to manage affairs despite his or her deficits, relying on informal help rather than formal processes (see Qualls, Chapter 12, this volume). When necessary, restraining orders can be used to help protect an individual from physical or financial abuse. An individual can sign a *power of attorney*, delegating authority to someone he or she trusts to manage the individual's financial affairs, provided the individual has the capacity to execute the power of attorney at the time it is signed (a good tool for preplanning, but renegade agents can do great harm because there is no supervision of the agent). An individual can also sign a *medical durable power of attorney*; delegating authority to someone he or she trusts to make decisions about the individual's person (again, a good preplanning tool, but selection of an agent is critical).

In the absence of a legal document delegating authority, most states have a procedure for the family to nominate one individual to act as decision maker, known as a *proxy decision maker*. In a harmonious family facing an immediate medical crisis, this can be the procedure that allows medical providers to treat without having informed consent from the person. The limits to the authority of the medical proxy are unknown, but often long-term care facilities and others do not accept a proxy for ongoing personal care decisions.

DUAL DIAGNOSIS

Individuals with a mental illness diagnosis must meet certain standards to be involuntarily placed into a facility for treatment. In many states, a guardian cannot consent to mental health treatment against the wishes of the individual. Therefore, an individual under guardianship has to meet the same standards for involuntary placement as individuals who are not under guardianship.

In many states, the following must be proven in a mental health proceeding before commitment can take place:

- The individual must be a danger to other people.
- The individual must be a danger to him or herself.
- The individual is unable to provide for his or her basic needs, such as food, clothing, and shelter.

In contrast, the criteria for guardianship may vary from state to state. For example, in Colorado, the definition of "incapacitated person" means

an individual other than a minor, who is unable to effectively receive or evaluate information or both or make or communicate decisions to such an extent that the individual lacks the ability to satisfy essential requirements for physical health, safety or self-care, even with appropriate and reasonably available technological assistance. (Colorado Revised Statutes, Section 15-14-102(5))

One dilemma is that under guardianship, a person may be deprived of liberty by being placed in a secured unit of a skilled nursing facility, if this is the least restrictive placement for meeting the person's care needs. If the individual requires such placement or treatment for a mental illness, he or she is being denied due process rights to a mental health commitment process before such placement occurs.

A second dilemma focuses on where such individuals should be placed, if they require mental health treatment. Medicare reimbursements for psychotherapy and other mental health services are lower than for physical illnesses, except for Alzheimer's disease and dementia, for which medication management is reimbursed at the rate of physical illness. Unfortunately, while outpatient reimbursement is higher, residents of such facilities have difficulty making office visits.

WHEN THINGS GET MESSY: THE CONTESTED HEARING

A final hearing is always necessary to appoint a guardian of the person or conservator of the property. After the petition is filed (the pleading is what initiates the court case), a process of informing the respondent of the nature and scope of the proceeding, appointment of professionals, and investigation takes place. The professionals' efforts are focused on gathering evidence to inform the court, or, to prove or disprove the allegations in the petition. Frequently, a neuropsychological evaluation has been completed prior to the petition being filed and may be the basis for the petitioner's allegation that the respondent lacks capacity (in the case of a guardianship) or is impaired (in the case of a conservatorship). The court must make findings, based on evidence presented at the hearing with the respondent present (unless the respondent is excused), that the respondent is incapacitated or impaired, in whole or in part, and that a guardian and/or conservator, with limited or unlimited authority, must be appointed. The petition sets forth the facts that must be proved by the petitioner with clear and convincing evidence.

Many final hearings are uncontested. The evidence presented is stipulated to by the parties and is presented to the court without objection. The parties have agreed to the basic terms and to a plan of action to be carried out by the appointed guardian and/or conservator. Sometimes the final hearings are contested. The respondent may disagree with the appointment of a guardian or conservator, believing that one is unnecessary and that he or she is not incapacitated or impaired in any way. Family members or other interested parties may disagree about whether the respondent is incapacitated or impaired, who should be guardian or conservator, the appropriate placement and level of care being proposed for the respondent, the specific terms of the appointment, or whether the appointment should be limited or unlimited.

A court hearing is a formal setting, presided over by a judge or magistrate, at which the parties are allowed to present evidence and make statements following established legal rules of evidence and procedure. If the hearing is contested, the court may enter a case management order that directs the parties to file a disclosure statement before the final hearing date. The statement lists specific factual and legal issues to be resolved by the court; factual and expert witnesses and a description of their testimony; and exhibits and descriptions of exhibits, including reports, records, pictures, and other documents to be offered into evidence by parties. The case management order may also require a statement of efforts that have been made to resolve the case by negotiation and a statement of each party's attitude toward additional efforts to resolve the conflicts.

Opening statements may be allowed, in which case, the petitioner makes the first statement, followed by the other parties. The party filing the petition, the petitioner, has the initial burden of proof. It is the petitioner's responsibility to present evidence that supports the allegations in the petition. The petitioner calls witnesses one by one to testify under oath. Through those witnesses, documents may be offered into evidence. Once the petitioner has examined a witness, other parties may cross-examine the witness. After all parties have asked questions, the judge or magistrate may ask questions of the witness. After the petitioner offers all of his or her evidence, other parties may offer evidence, that is, witnesses to rebut the testimony of the petitioner's witnesses. The petitioner may again offer evidence to rebut the other parties' evidence. Once all parties have offered their evidence, the parties may be allowed to make closing arguments or statements. The judge or magistrate then makes his or her findings of fact and conclusions of law and enters an order.

The petitioner has the obligation to prove the allegations in the petition by clear and convincing evidence. A petitioner with the burden of proof can use evidence produced by any party to persuade the court. If the petitioner fails to meet his or her burden of proof, the court cannot grant the relief requested in the petition. A fact or proposition has been proved by "clear and convincing evidence" if, considering all the evidence, the court finds it to be highly probable and the court has no serious or substantial doubt.

The primary use of expert testimony in guardianship and conservator proceeding is in proving or disproving incapacity and impairment. The petitioner must prove that the respondent is incapacitated or impaired, based on the applicable legal standard. Experts can disagree.

Credentials of expert witnesses—education, degrees, training, experience, board certifications, specialties, and published works—are used to establish their qualifications as experts. Most of the time, the parties stipulate to an expert witness's credentials, meaning that the parties do not question that the expert witness has the credentials to testify as an expert. When the parties do not stipulate as to the credentials, the first set of questions asked of the expert in direct examination is designed to prove credentials. Other parties may then *voir dire* (ask questions immediately after direct examination, before the witness testifies) the expert witness on his or her credentials.

Once the witness is qualified as an expert, questions are asked designed to substantiate and offer into evidence the expert's opinion. Those questions relate to the witness's familiarity with the respondent, the nature and scope of examination and testing performed on the respondent by the witness and others, the records reviewed by the expert, the findings, and the conclusions or opinions based on the findings.

Most of the time, the expert has prepared a written report. Questions are typically based on the report. Cross-examination questions may be designed to point out limitations of the testing procedures, methodology, and reasonable conclusions that may be drawn from the testing.

Broadly defined, *due process of law* means compliance with fundamental rules for fair and orderly proceedings (e.g., notice, opportunity to appear and be heard, right to effective counsel). In the context of guardianship proceedings, these rules are designed in recognition of the respondent's potential loss of autonomy and decision-making authority. Personal liberty and property rights of the respondent stand to be materially changed by the court.

Thus, there are strict rules of notice in guardianship and conservatorship proceedings. The respondent must be personally served with a notice of the final hearing. The notice must state that the respondent is required to be physically present at the hearing unless excused by the court. Failure to personally serve the respondent deprives the court of jurisdiction, which precludes the court from granting the petition for permanent orders. Failure to serve other interested parties is procedural, not jurisdictional, and therefore does not prevent the court from appointing a guardian or conservator.

Some courts may require the parties who are in disagreement to participate in some form of mediation before a final hearing. If there are legal issues, the parties may agree to mediation before a professional mediator or a retired judge and may agree to be bound by the decision of the mediator. If there are family dynamic issues, the parties may agree to less formal mediation by using the services of psychology professionals. In that case, the goal may be to maintain family relationships, maximize the respondent's autonomy, or maintain and respect the respondent's privacy.

The courtroom is a place where all parties have a forum to speak and are required to listen, but it may not be the best place to do so. Often, respondents simply want symbolic recognitions that they remain in control of certain abilities or retain certain values. Allowing demented respondents to keep control of small accounts of their own funds to spend on anything they want, including donations to political parties not supported by others in their families, or to make all decisions concerning aspects of their living situations, may avoid contested hearings.

CASE EXAMPLES

The following are three common scenarios demonstrating how the issues discussed previously can translate into everyday life.

 ### Case Example: The Dueling Experts

Susan, a case manager with a local senior service provider, We Care, visits Maybelle, age 80, one of their meals-on-wheels clients. This was the periodic visit to see if Maybelle could benefit from other services provided by We Care. During the visit, Susan recognizes the smell of an unwashed body. Susan excuses herself to visit the bathroom and finds that the tub is unusable. Susan also notices alcohol bottles in several parts of the house. Maybelle downplays the challenges of maintaining hygiene without a tub and explains that her grandson, Mike, comes regularly to bring pizza and beer and that she has not cleaned it up since last week. The mess is far greater than what could have been created in a week. There is no food in the refrigerator. Susan also notices that Maybelle has significant bruising on her arms and legs. Maybelle does not know how the bruising happened, it just did. Susan is not able to convince Maybelle to accept the regular or one-time services of a housekeeper or a handyman to fix the bathtub. Mike can provide what she needs. Maybelle has not seen a doctor in years; there was no reason. However, she does agree to Susan coming to visit her the following week.

The following week, Susan visits Maybelle and finds the same conditions. Maybelle does not recall their last visit. Maybelle explains that Mike visited once that week, took her check (she was not sure what check it was) to the bank to deposit it into her account, but he has not been back since. Susan notices a significant amount of mail on Maybelle's table. The mail is unopened and a piece of mail is addressed to Mike at Maybelle's address. Maybelle again declines the services of a housekeeper and handyman. She does appreciate the food she gets from the nice man everyday, but she does not eat most of it. She will get to the mail when she feels up to it. While at Maybelle's home, a neighbor comes by to visit and to see if Maybelle needs anything. When Susan introduces herself, the neighbor seems appreciative that some one is looking after Maybelle. She states that she is worried about Maybelle but is not specific as to why. Susan gives the neighbor her contact information and both the neighbor and Susan leave.

The following day the neighbor calls Susan. She wants to be specific about her concerns. The grandson has been seen coming and going from Maybelle's home at all hours of the day and night. Sometimes, shady looking people accompany him. This has been going on for about 6 months. Maybelle has not been seen out of her home during that time. Other than the meals-on-wheels delivery, no one else has been seen visiting Maybelle during this time period.

Susan contacts the department of human services to investigate. The department determines that Maybelle's real estate taxes have not been paid this year, her gas and electricity have been turned off at least once in the past 5 months, she has no telephone, she has $5.00 in her bank account, Mike is a signatory on her bank account and he has been depositing her social security checks and withdrawing large sums of cash. Mike states that he has been using the cash to pay bills and to purchase food and medications for Maybelle. He is unable to produce any documentation regarding the use of the cash. Mike moved into the home 6 months ago to "take care of Maybelle" at her request. Mike's mother, who is Maybelle's daughter and who lives in another state, knows about the arrangement. She believed her mother needed help and her son needed a place to stay. It was a win-win situation.

Maybelle consents to a neuropsychological evaluation. The evaluation is done in the doctor's office over a period of a week and two visits. The results show significant deficits, particularly in short-term memory. A medical examination is recommended. The conclusion is that Maybelle does not have the capacity to manage her financial affairs and that she needs 24-hour supervision.

The department, through the county attorney's office, files a petition for the appointment of a conservator and guardian for Maybelle. The department recommends that We Care be appointed guardian and conservator. We Care does not believe Maybelle should remain in her home. If necessary, the home can be sold and the proceeds of the sale used to support appropriate placement. They are investigating appropriate placement. Maybelle is still resistant to seeing a medical doctor for an examination.

Mike and his mother object to the appointment of We Care. If a guardian and/or a conservator are needed, they believe they should be appointed cofiduciaries. They also object to Maybelle being placed outside her home. They decide to represent their interests without the benefit of an attorney. Maybelle wants to remain in her home. She wants Mike to live with her and to provide any assistance she needs. The court appoints an attorney to represent Maybelle and what she wants. The court also appoints a guardian ad litem to represent Maybelle's best interest.

The guardian ad litem identifies the threshold issue—whether Maybelle lacks capacity. That determination will require a medical examination to rule out a medical cause for her deficits. If there is a medical cause and treatment is available, treatment will have to be initiated and Maybelle may have to be retested by a neuropsychologist. The attorney for Maybelle insists on a new neuropsychological evaluation by a doctor of his choice. He also wants an assessment by a local care manager of Maybelle's functional capacity in her home. He believes Maybelle functions quite nicely in her home and can perform most if not all of her activities of daily living with minimal assistance. He wants the neuropsychologist to determine if Maybelle has the capacity to understand and sign a power of attorney.

The case of the dueling experts has begun.

Case Example: The Balancing Act— Autonomy versus Safety

Joe, financial advisor for over 15 years to Margaret, an 85-year-old widow, notes that she has made frequent withdrawals from her investment accounts in recent months. When asked about the purpose, she always has a legitimate purchase planned. In the last 6 months, she has renovated her kitchen, purchased a new Lexus, and replaced the windows in her home. However, Joe knows that Margaret and her late husband, George, were very frugal and realizes that this spending is out of character. Finally, with the last purchase, he learns that her pastor is helping her with all of these purchases, including arranging for all the work to be done by contractors who are members of his congregation.

Joe asks you, because he knows that you work with seniors, what he should do about Margaret's spending. While she can afford these purchases, she is not wealthy, and if her health were to decline and her living expenses to increase, there is a possibility that she could outlive her money. The final straw is when Margaret brings Joe a power of attorney form that designates her pastor as agent and revokes a former power of attorney, in which Margaret had designated her niece, Sarah, as agent. Joe asks Margaret why she signed this document, and her answer is that Sarah is too busy with her own parents and her three children, and that the pastor suggested she name him instead. She tells Joe that the pastor has offered to handle her checking account for her, and that she has agreed to this arrangement. Joe is very concerned about accepting the authority of this new agent on his client's brokerage accounts. He wants to know if he should call the niece to tell her what has happened.

You tell Joe that he could report this situation to the local department of human services adult protective services division, and let the department know that he is concerned about financial exploitation. However, Joe believes that if Margaret learns that he has done so, she will fire him, and not only will he lose her business, but he may also lose any ability to provide oversight on this situation. And, as there is no imminent threat to Margaret on the known facts, the matter may not receive much attention from the governmental agency.

Joe could contact Sarah using an official notice stating that she is no longer the agent on these accounts and that he is therefore unable to provide any further information to her. This, under most banking privacy regulations, would not be a breach as he is only informing the niece that she may no longer have access to information. If she calls him, it is most likely that he will not be able to divulge any further information than what was provided in the letter.

Joe decides not to call adult protective services and sends the letter to Sarah. He never hears from Sarah. Two months later, Margaret calls to say that she is making a donation to the pastor to aid him personally in his ministry. This donation is the largest single withdrawal she has ever made from her brokerage account. The next day, the pastor calls to say that he is coming in to sign the paperwork for Margaret on the withdrawal.

Now, despite his misgivings, Joe calls adult protective services. The intake worker asks several questions, most of which Joe cannot answer. Is Margaret really capable of handling her own financial matters? Are there any other signs that might show a decline in ability, that is, overdrawn checking accounts, real estate taxes unpaid, health insurance premiums or medical bills unpaid? Joe does not know the answer to these questions.

The case is assigned an intake worker to investigate the concerns. In most states, the party making the report may choose to be anonymous.

The caseworker has several questions. Does Margaret show any signs of inability to care for herself? A visit to the home is the first step to see if her living environment raises any concerns. When interviewed, Margaret is quite angry at the implication that she needs any help or is having any problems. The home is fairly tidy, with little clutter and the yard is well kept. The caseworker engages Margaret in conversation regarding the numerous improvements, including the modern kitchen and the new windows. She explains that her pastor has encouraged her to make these improvements. The caseworker asks about whether she has designated any agents under powers of attorney. Margaret discloses the power of attorney form she signed naming the pastor. She says the pastor told her she needed to do that, because her former agent, Sarah, would just put her in a home if she was too much trouble. She says, "he has promised to have his granddaughter move in to take care of me if I need help, so that I won't ever have to leave." When asked about whether she has made any gifts to the pastor, Margaret says she is planning to do that in her will, but that she hasn't made any gifts at this time.

The caseworker calls Sarah. Sarah visits her aunt about twice a month and takes her out shopping at the grocery store and to the beauty parlor. Sarah says that she has been concerned about the pastor's influence but has been unable to convince her aunt that the pastor may have ulterior motives. Sarah says, "If I push the issue too much, she accuses me of trying to protect my inheritance. Because I love my aunt and want to be able to spend time with her and keep an eye on her, I've just tried to stay out of it." The caseworker asks Sarah if she would serve as conservator if one were necessary. Sarah agrees to do so.

In many counties with understaffing and budget issues, if the investigation doesn't establish a clear case of exploitation, it is entirely possible that the county attorney would be unable to devote resources to the matter. Without some documentation as to Margaret's abilities or any concrete evidence of exploitation, the case may be closed at this point, with the caseworker suggesting to Sarah that she contact an attorney and pursue conservatorship on her own. The key element at this time is Margaret's abilities.

Sarah calls the caseworker to report that she has discovered that Margaret has failed to pay her real estate taxes for 2 years and the property has gone to tax sale. The county attorney is now willing to file and request that a conservator be appointed to manage Margaret's financial affairs.

There are several key issues:

- The new spending pattern, which is contradictory to Margaret's former lifestyle.
- The trusted fiduciary changes from niece to pastor, at the suggestion of the pastor.
- Gifts made to the pastor that are out of character.
- Margaret's report that the pastor has promised she won't have to leave her home.

Without the evidence of unpaid property taxes, there is no real evidence that Margaret requires assistance. Even with the evidence of unpaid taxes, which is sufficient to file for financial protection, it is likely that more evidence will be required for success in a conservatorship proceeding. The changes in spending, change of fiduciary and gifts to the pastor are choices a competent individual may make, without challenge.

Case Example: A Family Solution That Respects Autonomy

Mary is an elderly widow with two children, Jack and Jill. The children are worried that Mary may no longer be safe in her own home and that she may be forgetting important things such as paying her bills, keeping doctors' appointments, and taking medications. To anyone else, Mary would appear to be handling everything just fine since her husband's death a few years ago. The children notice that their mother is no longer keeping her home spotless. In fact, during recent visits, they notice that she has been piling all of the mail, including bills, on a table in the kitchen. They also notice that she doesn't appear to be bathing regularly and seems to be losing weight. When the children approach Mary, she denies having any problems. The children visit Mary's doctor and her local bank but are stonewalled because they don't have any authority to access her records.

Jack and Jill apparently do have their mother's best interests at heart but are at a loss what to do next. How can they help Mary while respecting her independence?

Jack and Jill make an appointment with an elder law attorney. The attorney suggests that they approach their mother gently with their concerns and assure her that they are not going to take over her life and that her wishes will remain their primary focus. Because Mary's wishes are critical to any decision that might be made, they may discuss the option of visiting with the attorney as a family so that Mary can learn what powers of attorney are, how to limit them, and what the advantages might be for her. In addition, they can discuss as a family what alternative measures might have to be taken in the future, if Mary's health or decision-making abilities decline and if she decides not to sign powers of attorney.

Additionally, they could discuss the idea of Jack and Jill meeting with Mary and her doctor to discuss nonintrusive testing, such as a neuropsychological evaluation, to determine whether there actually are any medical problems that need to be addressed. In this situation, a functional assessment would also be a useful tool to determine how Mary's day-to-day decision making is affected. Just as in the discussion with the attorney, the doctor could be the one to instigate the discussion of any testing thereby allowing Jack and Jill to be supportive rather than adversarial by stressing that this type of diagnosis is a preventive measure to ensure her safety and autonomy. Once again, the focus is on Mary, her wishes, and her needs.

Another piece of this puzzle is the protection of Mary's finances. While meeting with the attorney, Jack and Jill could discuss some options with their mother, such as signing a power of attorney to allow at least one child the authority to assist her formally. Another option might be to allow one child to monitor her accounts online without the formality of a power of attorney. If some unusual behavior is detected, Mary and her children could meet with the banker and possibly the attorney to put safeguards in place at that time. Maybe Mary could manage a small account for her monthly bills, while being assisted by her children with major investments.

The moral of the story is that no matter what medical and financial problems may exist, Mary will continue to be a person worthy of love and respect from her children and the community. Jack and Jill should consider their mother's wishes, her history, and her fears when deciding how far to intrude into her life. Certainly, it is appropriate for Jack and Jill to express and act proactively on their concerns. However, Mary should still be allowed to make some decisions that her children might not agree with while preserving her autonomy. Ultimately, a team approach with Mary as the team's captain, at least nominally, will produce results that are the most satisfying and easy to implement for all parties involved.

CONCLUSION

A fundamental legal principal guiding all professionals involved with a person with declining capacity, including a court, is the right of the person to make autonomous decisions, unless the person lacks the capacity to do so. Assistance should be provided only when and to the extent necessary given the nature and level of incapacity. As the case examples demonstrate, there is a tension between this principal and the desire to protect the person from bad decisions. The situation may be further complicated by the competing needs, desires, and limitations of other individuals and institutions in the person's life. The following Helpful Resources provide detailed information regarding common issues that arise in adult protective proceedings.

Understanding the parameters, expectations, and constraints of court proceedings and the alternatives to court proceedings is essential to formulating a plan to meet the needs of a person with declining capacity. A court proceeding may not be the optimal method of determining issues related to incapacity, but it is the final forum in which competing opinions can be aired and a decision made. This process heavily relies on psychological professionals in determining the nature and extent of older adults' decision-making capacity. Therefore, it is critical that those professionals understand the context in which their opinions will be used.

HELPFUL RESOURCES

www.alz.org
Alzheimer's Association: The Alzheimer's Association provides information about Alzheimer care, support, and research.

www.annuitytruth.org
Annuity Truth: This is a web site offered by H.E.L.P. (Healthcare and Elder Law Programs Corporation), which is a nonprofit education and counseling center, provides impartial information to older adults and their families on elder care, law, finances, consumer protection, and more.

www.ffiec.gov/nicpubweb/nicweb/SearchForm.aspx
Bank search: This database is maintained by the Federal Reserve System and is useful in searching for the successor to an institution when you uncover old passbooks and certificates of deposit with the name of a bank that is no longer in operation.

www.benefitscheckup.com
Benefits checkup: Connects thousands of people every day to private or government programs that help them pay for prescription drugs, health care, utilities, and other needs.

www.medicareadvocacy.org
Center for Medicare Advocacy: Staffed by attorneys, paralegals, nurses, and information management experts, the Center for Medicare

Advocacy represents thousands of individuals in appeals of Medicare denials.

www.cms.hhs.gov
Centers for Medicare and Medicaid Services: This is the U.S. Department of Health and Human Services web site.

www.ababooks.org
Legal Guide for Americans over 50, authored by ABA Commission on Law and Aging staff, is a complete revision and update of an earlier book in the ABA Legal Guide series. Important material from the first edition has been expanded, and new chapters on elder abuse, marriage and divorce, financial planning for incapacity, and advance planning for health-care decisions were added. The new edition also contains dozens of practical tips, warnings of pitfalls, steps to take, and helpful web sites. The book is available for purchase online or by calling the ABA Service Center at 800-285-2221.

www.medicare.gov/default.asp
Medicare: One useful link on this site is a comparison feature, allowing you to compare two or more nursing homes in a particular area: www .medicare.gov/NHCompare/Home.asp?version=alternate&browser=IE%7 C6%7CWin2000&language=English&defaultstatus=0&pagelist=Home& CookiesEnabledStatus=True.

www.medicarerights.org/Index.html
Medicare Rights Center: The largest independent source of health-care information and assistance in the United States for people with Medicare. Founded in 1989, MRC helps older adults and people with disabilities get good, affordable health care.

www.psychlaws.org/LegalResources/Index.htm
Mental health law information: Whether you are a legislator working to strengthen your state's treatment laws, an attorney representing a person with severe mental illness, or an individual searching for information on a family member's rights under the law, the information on this page can assist you in understanding the complexities of mental illness law and what must be done to strengthen existing statutes.

www.myziva.net
My Ziva: A free, objective and easy-to-use nursing home resource for prospective residents, caregivers, and health-care professionals. We help you find and compare nursing homes.

www.naela.com
National Academy of Elder Law Attorneys: A nonprofit association that assists lawyers, bar organizations, and others who work with older clients and their families. Established in 1987, the Academy provides a resource of information, education, networking, and assistance to those who deal with the many specialized issues involved with legal services to the elderly and people with special needs.

www.n4a.org
National Association of Area Agencies on Aging: Operates the Eldercare Locator, a free national service (800-677-1116, www.eldercare.gov), which links older adults and their family caregivers to aging information and resources in their own communities. This service is supported by a cooperative agreement with the Administration on Aging, U.S. Department of Health and Human Services.

www.elderabusecenter.org/default.cfm
National Center on Elder Abuse: A national resource for elder rights, law enforcement and legal professionals, public policy leaders, researchers, and the public. The Center's mission is to promote understanding, knowledge sharing, and action on elder abuse, neglect, and exploitation.

www.nccnhr.org/default.cfm
National Citizens' Coalition for Nursing Home Reform: Provides information and leadership on federal and state regulatory and legislative policy development and models and strategies to improve care and life for residents of nursing homes and other long-term care facilities.

One item available for purchase from this site that is useful for clients: *Nursing Homes: Getting Good Care There,* by Sarah Greene Burger, Virginia Fraser, Sara Hunt, and Barbara Frank. New second edition published by the National Citizens' Coalition for Nursing Home Reform.

www.unclaimed.org
National database for unclaimed property: If you think an individual may have a bank account or other asset that they have lost track of, consult this web site.

www.pdrhealth.com
PDRHealth: Provides drug information in layman's terms.

CHAPTER

7

Culture and Medical Decision Making

MICHELE J. KAREL

Cultural attitudes, beliefs, and practices—related to racial, ethnic, religious, regional, and other influences—inform all aspects of medical decision making. Culture informs beliefs about the meanings, causes,
and cures of illness; what or who can help when illness strikes; as well as
who should be involved in making decisions about medical care (e.g., the
patient, family, community, doctor, and/or other healers). Not all Americans share Western medical assumptions about illness, treatment, and
decision making. In decision making, individual autonomy or self-
determination has become a primary value over the past few decades;
thus, informed consent has become the cornerstone of American medical
ethics. The topic of this book—concern for decision-making capacity in
older adults—reflects this Western cultural value of self-determination
where older adults have the right to make their own decisions while they
are capable of doing so; and, if they become incapable, where decision
making is deferred to a surrogate decision maker to, ideally, represent the
older adult's preferences. While all cultures share concern for dignity and
respect of older adults, the ways in which health-care decisions are typically made and the values and beliefs guiding decisions vary considerably
across cultural groups.

This chapter examines cultural influences on medical decision making because those influences may have implications for the assessment of

decision-making capacity of older adults from varying cultural back-grounds. The chapter is divided into four major sections: (1) a review of the demographic context, (2) consideration of broad issues in culture and medical care, (3) cultural influences on decision making in geriatric care, and (4) implications of cultural issues for the assessment of medical decision-making capacity.

A DIVERSE AGING POPULATION

The U.S. population is increasing in diversity, and the same is true for the aging population. In 2004, 81.9% of adults age 65 and over were classified as non-Hispanic White by the U.S. Census Bureau. By 2050, projections are that only 61.3% of adults aged 65 and over will be non-Hispanic White, 17.5% of older adults will be Hispanic, 12.0% Black, 7.8% Asian, and 2.7% other races alone or in combination (Federal Interagency Forum on Aging-Related Statistics, 2006).

Within these ethnic groups, the percentages of adults over age 65 vary. In 2000, 14.4% of non-Hispanic Whites were age 65 or over, while the proportion of older adults in Hispanic, Black, and Asian groups were 4.9%, 8.1%, and 7.8% (U.S. Census Data, as cited in Spector, 2004).

A significant minority of older adults now living in the United States were born outside of the United States. According to 2000 U.S. Census data, 90.5% of older adults were born in the United States, 6.9% were foreign-born naturalized citizens, and 2.7% were foreign-born noncitizens. Further, a significant minority of older adults do not use English as their first language. According to 2000 U.S. Census data, 6.7% of adults over age 65 speak non-English at home and speak English less than "very well," while 5.9% of older adults speak non-English at home but also report speaking English "very well." The majority, 87.4%, report speaking only English at home (Gist & Hetzel, 2004). In certain U.S. communities, the proportions of older adults who were born outside the United States or who speak languages other than English are much larger. In 2000, the most common regions of birth for foreign-born individuals of any age were Central America (34%), Asia (26%), Europe (15%),

Caribbean (10%), South America (7%), and other (8%; U.S. Census Data, as cited in Spector, 2004).

Within these broad ethnic/racial groups, there are many subgroups representing various countries of origin. Each subgroup has its own traditions, values, and beliefs related to aging, illness, medical care, family caregiving, and death and dying; as well as distinct histories with regard to immigration, trauma (e.g., previous experience with war, persecution), racism, and adjustment and acculturation into American society. Among White Americans, there are many ethnic, religious, and regional subgroups with widely varying perspectives related to medical decision making. And, within all of these cultural groups, there is tremendous individual variability in terms of educational background, socioeconomic status, living arrangements, family supports, religiosity, health status, and acculturation.

CULTURAL ISSUES FOR HEALTH CARE, ETHNIC/RACIAL DISPARITIES, AND CULTURAL COMPETENCE

Culture informs all aspects of medical decision making. Beliefs about illness (what it means, what caused it); symptomatic expression of various illnesses; attribution for specific symptoms (e.g., are feelings of depression thought to represent a physical, mental, and/or spiritual problem?); what is believed to help in prevention or cure of different illnesses; and if, when, and where to go for help all influence health behaviors and decisions about medical treatments (American Geriatrics Society, 2004; Royeen & Crabtree, 2006; Spector, 2004). "Medicine itself is a cultural system with its own specific language, values, and practices that must be translated, interpreted, and negotiated with patients and their families" (Crawley, Marshall, Lo, Koenig, & the End-of-Life Care Consensus Panel, 2002, p. 676).

The Western biomedical view of health, illness, and healing is based on a mechanistic model of the human body, mind-body separation, and discounting of spirit or soul. This view differs greatly from health beliefs in other cultural traditions. For example, in many Native American traditions, health relates to harmony with the natural environment and illness is related to supernatural influences (e.g., the insertion of a foreign object into the body by an enemy, possession by a spirit, or the loss of the person's own spirit), which require intervention by a traditional healer. Similarly, many African and Asian traditions emphasize the importance of spiritual issues for health and healing, as well as the use of herbal remedies. Assessing, demonstrating respect for, and integrating cultural healing practices when appropriate into a treatment plan are all parts of good clinical care (Pachter, 1994; Xakellis et al., 2004; Yeo, 2001). Cultural issues specific to geriatric health care and decision making are reviewed later in the chapter.

Disparities in Health Care

Racial/ethnic disparities in health and quality of health care are well documented (Betancourt, Green, Carrillo, & Ananeh-Firempong, 2003; Fiscella, Franks, Gold, & Clancy, 2000; Institute of Medicine, 2002) and are important for understanding the experiences of many older adults in the health-care system. Members of minority groups have relatively high rates of many chronic diseases; are less likely to have health insurance or to access preventive, primary, and specialty health-care services; and, even when enrolled in the health-care system, are less likely to receive a range of diagnostic and medical and surgical treatment procedures. These disparities have multiple causes and are related to sociocultural barriers at multiple levels: organizational (e.g., few health-care leaders or physicians are non-White), structural (e.g., lack of interpreters, bureaucratic complexity reduces access), and clinical (e.g., provider-patient communication; Betancourt et al., 2003). Socioeconomic issues such as education, literacy, geographic access, transportation, affordable health care, and work and child-care issues are important determinants of health-care utilization and outcomes (Fiscella et al., 2000). Recent writings warn that these modifiable problems with the health-care system, rather than cultural differences in values or preferences, contribute in large part to health-care disparities (Armstrong, Hughes-Halbert, & Asch, 2006).

Cultural, communication, and relationship factors have received increased research attention as possible explanations for health-care disparities:

> These include variations in patient recognition of symptoms; thresholds for seeking care; the ability to communicate symptoms to a provider who understands their meaning; the ability to understand the prescribed management strategy; expectations of care (including preferences for or against diagnostic and therapeutic procedures); and adherence to preventive measures and medications. These factors are thought to influence patient and physician decision-making and the interactions between patients and the health care delivery system, thus contributing to health disparities. (Betancourt et al., 2003, p. 118)

Communication within the health-care encounter critically influences outcomes, like patient satisfaction, compliance with recommended treatments, and health-care decisions. A number of studies have shown that minority patients generally report lower quality interactions with their physicians; in particular, minority patients are less satisfied when seeing physicians of a different ethnic/racial background, perceiving less respect and poorer communication in those encounters. However, depending on study samples and methods, the relationship between patient-physician race concordance and various aspects of communication varies and findings are inconsistent.

For example, in a phone survey of adults in one urban area, African American patients rated visits with their physicians as less participatory and, for both Blacks and Whites, patients seeing physicians of the same race rated visits as more participatory (Cooper-Patrick et al., 1999). In a larger random phone survey of continental U.S. households, Hispanics and Asians reported lower physician relationship quality compared to Blacks and Whites. While only 10% of respondents explicitly stated a preference for a physician of their own race/ethnicity, they disproportionately reported having race-concordant regular physicians. Racial differences in satisfaction disappeared or were reversed after controlling for general physician behaviors such as showing respect and spending adequate time (Saha, Arbelaez, & Cooper, 2003). In a study that audio-taped Black and White patient visits with Black or White physicians, race-concordant visits, for both Black and White patients, were about 2 minutes longer, had slower speech, higher coder ratings of positive affect, higher patient ratings of satisfaction, and participatory decision making by their physicians (Cooper et al., 2003). However, in this study, measures of patient-centered communication did not explain differences in satisfaction between race-concordant versus discordant visits.

Issues of trust are critical in health care and are important for understanding the experiences of ethnic minorities in the health-care system and within patient-provider encounters. Accepting medical care or participating in clinical medical research requires a fair degree of trust by persons in a vulnerable position (Goold, 2002). A history of discrimination, substandard health care and, at times, frankly inhumane treatment has led to distrust of health-care systems and physicians among many African Americans and other ethnic minorities. A recent focus group study of African American patients found that trust in one's physician was related to interpersonal and technical competence of the physician, while distrust was related to expectations of racism and experimentation as well as a physician's perceived quest for profit during routine clinical care (Jacobs, Rolle, Ferrans, Whitaker, & Warnecke, 2006). Among older Japanese Americans, greater trust in one's physician was related to greater acculturation, less desire for autonomy, greater religiosity, and longer duration of the physician-patient relationship; further, Japanese physicians were trusted more than physicians of a different ethnicity (Tarn et al., 2005). For older Korean Americans, greater trust in Western medical care was related to satisfaction with health-care services, better English skills, and no experience of disrespect or discrimination in medical settings (Jang, Kim, & Chiriboga, 2005).

Cultural Competence

Cultural competence in health care, at the level of health-care delivery systems and professional clinical care, is an increasing priority for both health-care regulation and education, across professional disciplines. According to Betancourt and colleagues (2003), cultural competence in health care entails:

> understanding the importance of social and cultural influences on patients' health beliefs and behaviors; considering how these factors interact at multiple levels of the health care delivery system (e.g., at the level of structure processes of care or clinical decision-making); and, finally, devising interventions that take these issues into account to assure quality health care delivery to diverse patient populations. (p. 297)

The National Standards for Culturally and Linguistically Appropriate Services in Health Care provide guidelines for health-care organizations to ensure equal access and quality of health care for diverse populations (U.S. Department of Health and Human Services, 2001).

Many professions have developed guidelines and curricula for multicultural education: medical education in general (Betancourt, 2006; Rapp, 2006), family medicine (Culhane-Pera, Reif, Egli, Baker, & Kassekert, 1997), geriatrics (Xakellis et al., 2004), psychology (American Psychological Association [APA], 2003), psychiatry (Harris, Felder, & Clark, 2004), nursing (Sloand, Groves, & Brager, 2004), and social work (National Association of Social Workers, 2001).

In the past few years, much has been accomplished within the field of geriatrics to define core competencies for multicultural geriatric care (Xakellis et al., 2004) and to develop curricular materials (Yeo, 2001). The University of California Academic Geriatric Resource Program and the Ethnogeriatrics Committee of the American Geriatrics Society collaborated to develop a curricular framework for multicultural geriatric education that could be adapted to different academic programs. The core competencies address attitude, knowledge, and skills necessary for working effectively with diverse populations of older adults. While some issues are specific to competence for physicians, many issues are relevant for other health-care professionals (Xakellis et al., 2004).

The Collaborative on Ethnogeriatric Education has developed an outstanding online resource, the second edition of *Curriculum in*

Ethnogeriatrics (Yeo, 2001). The core curriculum modules include overview concepts; patterns of health risk; fund of knowledge; assessment; and health-care interventions, access, and utilization. Ethnic specific modules review issues for providing culturally competent health care to 12 ethnic groups: African American, American Indian/Alaska Native, Hispanic/Latino, Asian and Pacific Islander American, Asian Indian, Chinese, Filipino, Japanese, Korean, Native Hawaiian/Pacific Islander, Pakistani, and Southeast Asian. In addition, the Administration on Aging (2001) has an online resource, *Achieving Cultural Competence: A Guidebook for Providers of Services to Older Americans and Their Families,* which focuses on developing culturally competent programs.

Multiple resources regarding cultural competence development, training, and evaluation are available online. Examples include: National Center for Cultural Competence at www11.georgetown.edu /research/gucchd/nccc/, the Office of Minority Health of the U.S. Department of Health and Human Services at www.omhrc.gov, Diversity Rx at www.diversityrx.org. The web sites for the geriatric resources discussed previously are provided in the references.

GERIATRIC HEALTH CARE AND DECISION MAKING

Medical decision making in geriatric care entails everyday decisions regarding management of chronic illness, including taking medications; having diagnostic procedures or surgical interventions; arranging supportive, rehabilitative, long-term, or palliative care services in home, community, or institutional settings; and making decisions about care at the end of life. Different cultural factors are critical for all aspects of geriatric care: understandings of illness such as dementia (e.g., normal aging, brain disease, a reaction to stress or worry, craziness, possession by evil spirits); norms and expectations regarding family caregiving and the use of formal versus informal support services; views about who should make medical care decisions; and values and beliefs regarding care at the end of life (Braun, Pietsch, & Blanchette, 1999; Crawley et al., 2002;

Gallagher-Thompson et al., 2003; Haley, Han, & Henderson, 1998; Kwak & Haley, 2005; Yeo & Gallagher-Thompson, 2006).

With the exception of older adults who lack or are estranged from family connections, complex geriatric care decisions virtually always involve the family. It is normative across cultural groups for families to be involved in caregiving and medical decision making (Allen & Shuster, 2002; Haley et al., 2002; LoboPrabhu, Molinari, & Lomax, 2006). For many critical geriatric care decisions (e.g., advanced dementia or end-of-life care), the older adult is more likely to experience decisional incapacity and rely on others for decision-making support.

Truth Telling and Locus of Decision Making

There are important individual and cultural differences in preferences for diagnostic and prognostic truth telling and for the degree of active participation (by the patient versus family) in making medical care decisions (Blackhall, Murphy, Frank, Michel, & Azen, 1995; Kwak & Haley, 2005). In contrast to the modern American health-care system's emphasis on informed consent, telling patients the truth about medical diagnosis and prognosis, especially in the case of life-threatening illness, is not practiced in much of the world. In many cultures, it is believed that telling the patient the truth about a terminal illness creates undue distress, burden, and loss of hope for the patient (Kawaga-Singer & Blackhall, 2001). Even in the United States, it is only in recent decades that truth telling has become part of medical practice, and many physicians remain reluctant to share news of a dim prognosis (Christakis, 2001). Many cultural groups assume that the family, physician and/or community, and *not* the patient, are responsible for making decisions about a patient's medical care (Blackhall et al., 1995; Winzelberg, Hanson, & Tulsky, 2005).

In a study of community-residing older adults representing four ethnic groups in Los Angeles, Blackhall and colleagues (1995) found that African American and European American elders were significantly more likely than Korean American and Mexican American elders to believe that a patient with metastatic cancer should be told the truth about the cancer diagnosis (89%, 87%, 47%, and 65%, respectively). Further,

Korean American and Mexican American groups were more likely than African American or European American groups to believe that the family, and not the patient, should be told the truth about the diagnosis and prognosis. Finally, these groups differed significantly in their views on who should function as the primary decision maker in the use of life-prolonging technology. While the majority of European American (65%) and African American (60%) elders felt it should be the patient's decision, a minority of Korean American (28%) and Mexican American (41%) elders felt it should be the patient's decision; in the latter groups, elders more often stated it should be the family's decision (57% and 45% respectively).

For culturally competent clinical care, it is critical for health-care providers to understand and respect an older adult's preferences for receiving diagnostic and prognostic information (or not) and for making or delegating health-care decisions to others (Xakellis et al., 2004; Yeo, 2001). It is also important not to assume that membership in a particular ethnic or racial group implies a certain preference for truth telling or decision-making styles.

Among many individual differences, the degree of acculturation may influence an individual's perspectives on medical decision making. For example, in the case of Japanese Americans, Japanese culture values "harmonious group consensus and tacit agreement without verbal communication" (Matsumura et al., 2002, p. 536), while American culture values self-determination and open, explicit communication. Matsumura et al. (2002) compared English- versus Japanese-speaking older Japanese American adults with older Japanese adults living in Japan. Matsumura and colleagues found that while all three groups preferred group decision making; the more acculturated, English-speaking group was more likely to prefer the verbal disclosure of bad news, have a positive attitude toward advance care planning, and be willing to withdraw care at the end of life. This study also found significant variability *within* each group. Similarly, Blackhall et al. (1995) found that Mexican American elders with higher acculturation scores were more likely to believe that patients should be told the truth about their diagnosis and prognosis.

Finally, there are important cultural differences in preferred surrogate decision makers (e.g., spouse, adult child—son in particular, other relatives; Hornung et al., 1998). It is also important not to make assumptions about trusted decision makers. In some cases, friends may be trusted more than estranged family. Among gay and lesbian elders, it is critical to know if there is a trusted partner (Stein & Bonuck, 2001).

Advance Directives

The development of advance directives as legal tools to promote patient self-determination during times of decisional incapacity occurred within a Western ethical framework that values individual autonomy. Advance directives—either designation of a health-care proxy through a durable power of attorney for health care or communication of care preferences through a living will—are intended for use only when an individual is perceived to have lost the capacity to make particular health-care decisions. Thus, a finding of decisional incapacity often provides the go-ahead for a surrogate to take over medical decision making on a patient's behalf. Not surprisingly, there are significant differences among cultural groups in attitudes toward and utilization of advance directives. African American and Hispanic elders are less likely to use, and have more negative attitudes toward, advance directives (Eleazer et al., 1996; Kwak & Haley, 2005; Morrison, Zayas, Mulvihill, Baskin, & Meier, 1998; Murphy et al., 1996).

For individuals who assume that the family or doctor will make decisions on behalf of a patient (including many among the current cohort of older adults, regardless of ethnic/racial background), formal, written advance directives may be viewed as irrelevant (High, 1988; Morrison et al., 1998). Additionally, completing advance directives may not be comfortable in cultures where open discussions of illness, death, and dying are taboo; and, some ethnic elders may be reluctant to sign forms due to distrust or fear of exploitation (Kwak & Haley, 2005).

Increasingly, it is acknowledged that advance directives alone do not facilitate good advance care planning, regardless of cultural considerations (Covinsky et al., 2000; Hawkins, Ditto, Danks, & Smucker, 2005;

Singer et al., 1998). In particular, models of advance care planning and medical decision making increasingly recognize the social, rather than solely individual, nature of medical decisions, as well as limitations to the assumptions of rational choice, clear and discrete treatment preferences, and ability of surrogates to provide substituted judgment that underlie the use of advance directives (Drought & Koenig, 2002; Karlawish, Quill, Meier, & the ACP-ASIM End-of-Life Care Consensus Panel, 1999; Winzelberg et al., 2005). These emerging models of advance care planning and end-of-life care decision making are more compatible with multicultural considerations.

End-of-Life Care

Decisions about care at the end of life can be particularly agonizing for patients, families, and health-care providers. Cultural and religious perspectives on the meaning of death, what is considered a *good death*, and associated rituals for honoring the dead and grieving vary greatly and influence decisions about end-of-life care (Braun et al., 1999; Kawaga-Singer, 1994; Klessig, 1992; Koenig & Gates-Williams, 1995). It is critical for health-care providers to understand how cultural, religious, and individual/family values and beliefs underlie responses to difficult clinical situations such as whether to initiate or discontinue a life-sustaining treatment (e.g., ventilator support, tube feeding, renal dialysis). These *negotiated deaths* (Koenig & Gates-Williams, 1995) are increasingly common in the American health-care system, and research to date suggests important ethnic/racial differences in preferences for life-support interventions.

African Americans are more likely than European Americans to prefer continued use of life-sustaining interventions and less likely to have do not resuscitate (DNR) orders (Degenholtz, Thomas, & Miller, 2003; Hopp & Duffy, 2000; Kwak & Haley, 2005) for reasons including mistrust in the medical system and, frequently, Christian religious beliefs including the belief in God's power over life and death and the hope for miracles (Mouton, 2000). Research has found Hispanic Americans to be more likely than non-Hispanic Whites, but less likely than African Americans, to prefer life-support interventions (Kwak & Haley, 2005) for reasons related to religious, cultural, and educational factors (Talamantes, Gomez, & Braun, 2000). Research regarding preferences for life support remains limited for other cultural groups within the United States.

Across cultural groups, there may be distinctions between general attitudes toward life-sustaining treatments and what individuals would want for themselves (Blackhall et al., 1999). For example, in ethnographic interviews regarding attitudes toward life support, many Korean American elders expressed that, while they themselves would not want life support, they understood it was not their decision to make and the right thing for the family to do would be to prolong their lives for as long as possible (Blackhall et al., 1999).

Kawaga-Singer and Blackhall (2001) provide suggestions for addressing six important issues for end-of-life care that are influenced by culture. With all patients and families, it is important in end-of-life care to address: (1) previously experienced inequities in health care, (2) communication or language barriers, (3) religion and spirituality, (4) truth telling (how much do patients want to know?), (5) family involvement in decision making (who should be involved in making decisions?), and (6) receptivity to hospice care.

In addition to these issues, Koenig and Gates-Williams (1995) recommend evaluating all patients and families on their degree of openness in discussing diagnosis, prognosis, and death; their specific religious beliefs including beliefs about the afterlife and the possibility of miracles; how hope for recovery will be negotiated; their desire for control of events versus fatalism; their individual differences including gender, age/cohort, and power relationships within the family and in relation to the health-care team; their political and historical context, including patient and family experience with poverty, refugee status, and past discrimination or limited access to care. They also advise making use of community resources including cultural/religious leaders, translators, and family members.

These recommendations for culturally competent care at the end of life are relevant for geriatric health-care decisions across the continuum of care.

IMPLICATIONS FOR THE ASSESSMENT OF MEDICAL DECISION-MAKING CAPACITY

Cultural influences on medical decision making are relevant for all aspects of the capacity assessment process, from understanding the referral to conducting an interview using structured cognitive and decision-making capacity assessment tools and making recommendations. In this section, cultural considerations for medical decision-making capacity assessment are reviewed.

Referrals for Consent Capacity Evaluations

To date, virtually no published research exists regarding referral patterns for consent capacity evaluations and, certainly none exists for ethnic differences in such referral patterns. Consent capacity evaluations are requested when a clinical provider, team, and/or family member is concerned about a patient's ability to consent to treatment, particularly in that large gray area between a clearly capable patient (no evidence whatsoever of difficulty understanding, appreciating, reasoning) and a clearly incapable patient (comatose, severely confused; Moye, Armesto, & Karel, 2005). Further, we might speculate that a capacity evaluation is more likely to be requested when the individual patient is viewed as the appropriate, primary decision maker and, if found to lack capacity, decision-making power must be transferred to a surrogate decision maker.

In cultures in which the family, physician, and/or community are viewed as the appropriate locus for decision making, it may be less common to pursue individual consent capacity evaluations. In these cases, the concept of family decision-making capacity may be more relevant (Allen & Shuster, 2002; Winzelberg et al., 2005); that is, how can we best support families in making decisions for incapacitated older adults? However, given wide individual variability in decision-making preferences, as well as varied availability of family decision makers (some ethnic elders who might prefer family models of decision making may not have families), individual consent capacity evaluations are likely to remain relevant for older adults from diverse backgrounds.

The Evaluation Relationship/Rapport

As discussed earlier in the chapter, important clinical outcomes relate to the relationship between patients and health-care providers. Ethnic (or age, gender, primary language, educational) differences between patients and providers can be a source of discomfort or distrust for both parties. A capacity evaluation can be a particularly threatening clinical encounter because patients' basic rights to make decisions for themselves are at stake and patients are in a particularly vulnerable position (given some question about their cognitive or psychiatric functioning). Therefore, to the extent possible, it is important to create an environment in which older patients feel safe, respected, and valued.

General guidelines about multicultural assessment are important to honor (e.g., APA, 2003; Sue & Sue, 2003; Yeo, 2001). In establishing rapport with the older adult, it is helpful to be aware of culturally appropriate ways to communicate, verbally and nonverbally. In most cases, it is appropriate to greet the person with a formal term of address (Mr., Mrs.), rather than by first name. It is often helpful to begin an encounter with informal conversation before starting formal assessment. If not bedbound, invite the patient to sit where he or she feels comfortable, respecting different needs for personal space, and look for clues from the patient regarding appropriate degrees of eye contact, emotional expression, body movement (e.g., different norms regarding hand shaking), and touch.

It is very important to explain simply and clearly the purpose of the evaluation and answer any questions (and, ultimately, to document whether the patient appears able to consent to the evaluation; Moye, Karel, & Armesto, 2007). In some cases, older patients may find it uncomfortable, awkward, or frankly irrelevant to be asked questions about their medical treatment preferences, if they ultimately believe those decisions are for the doctor or family to make. In these cases, the older adult may not be particularly motivated to participate in the evaluation (Moye et al., 2005). Depending on the clinical situation and the availability of other decision makers, it can be very helpful to document if an older adult appears capable of simply stating whom they prefer to make medical decisions on their behalf, that is, to designate a health-care proxy (Mezey, Teresi, Ramsey, Mitty, & Bobrowitz, 2000). The clinical interview, which should always be conducted before administering formal cognitive or decision making assessment tools, offers an opportunity to demonstrate genuine concern and respect for the older adult's history and view of her current situation, thus helping to establish rapport.

From the perspective of the evaluator, an ongoing process of self-evaluation, of awareness of one's own values attitudes and biases, and how these may affect rapport and clinical judgment is critical (APA, 2003; Sue & Sue, 2003; Xakellis et al., 2004). In particular, evaluators must be very sensitive to situations in which they simply do not agree with a patient's health-care decision. From the evaluator's personal, family, cultural, or professional background, a patient's decision may appear quite unreasonable while, from the patient's perspective, it may be quite consistent with his or her cultural, religious, or personal values and beliefs. Certainly, the more different we are from our patients, the greater the risk for misunderstanding and biased or stereotypical judgments (APA, 2003). Even the particular professional disciplines in which we are trained influence our clinical judgments and recommendations (e.g., Kane, Bershadsky, & Bershadsky, 2006).

With specific reference to capacity judgments, some pilot data we recently collected reminds us of the potentially subjective nature of this pursuit. We found that professionals who rated stronger feelings of discomfort, frustration, or disinterest in response to a patient also judged those patients to have lower decision-making capacity (after listening to audiotaped structured decision-making capacity interviews; Moye, Karel, & Gurrera, 2006). The causal direction of these findings is not clear (e.g., perhaps individuals with decisional incapacities tend to inspire more discomfort or frustration in clinical encounters), but these results remind us that our subjective feelings about a person can affect our clinical judgments.

Language/Translation

Language differences can pose major challenges for a capacity evaluation. Such an evaluation must be conducted in the elder's primary language, ideally by an evaluator fluent in the same language. While there are increasing guidelines about the use of trained and untrained translators to facilitate communication in clinical encounters, there are no guidelines regarding the use of translators in formal clinical capacity evaluations.

Some health-care systems have professional interpreter services available with interpreters who are well trained in medical terminology, ethics, and interpreter roles (see www.diversityrx.org for information and resources). The use of untrained interpreters (e.g., a staff person who happens to speak the same language) or family members is strongly discouraged, particularly for such important and sensitive evaluations (see www.stanford.edu/group/ethnoger/, module 4). The risk of misinterpretation is high and, in the case of family members, emotional issues, confidentiality, and undue influence makes this role inappropriate in many cases. Certainly, it is entirely inappropriate for an interpreter to attempt to translate standardized cognitive, affective, or capacity evaluation tests.

Clinical Interview

The clinical interview allows the evaluator to conduct an informal mental status assessment as well as gather information about the patient's understanding of her history, current situation, concerns for the future, social supports, and values and beliefs related to current health-care decisions (Moye, 1999; Moye et al., 2007). To the extent that the patient is willing, able, and comfortable responding to questions, it is important to ask questions in the following areas: What is the patient's understanding of her current illness, the meaning that it holds (why did I get sick?), and the expected outcomes? What are her previous experiences with illness in herself or others and perhaps similar decisions faced in the past? Who are the important people in her life, and to whom does she turn for help and support? Who does she want involved in helping to make decisions regarding her medical care? What makes her life meaningful or good and what life circumstances, if any, would make life difficult to bear? What are the patient's goals at the present time (e.g., to go home, remain pain free, live as long as possible)?

Several values history or goal clarification tools designed for advance care planning purposes can help to structure such questioning (Gillick, Berkman, & Cullen, 1999; Karel, 2000; Karel, Powell, & Cantor, 2004; Pearlman, Starks, Cain, Rosengreen, & Patrick, 1998; Schwartz et al., 2003). A new capacity assessment interview, the Assessment of Capacity to Consent to Treatment Tool (ACCTT), was designed to include questions about values—valued activities and relationships, decision making preferences, and quality of life concerns—before structured questioning about medical decisions (Moye, Karel, et al., in press). These values interviews have not been studied in culturally diverse populations. However, there is some evidence that individuals with mild to moderate dementia are able to clearly and consistently express basic values related to medical decision making (Karel, Moye, Bank, & Azar, 2007).

In many cases, with the patient's consent, it is also helpful to interview family members or other significant others, as well as health-care providers, regarding the current clinical situation; the concern about the patient's decision-making capacity; their understanding of diagnosis, prognosis, and treatment options; their understanding of the patient's values, goals, and preferences; and the family's concerns about caregiving and their own emotional adjustment (e.g., Allen & Shuster, 2002).

Cognitive/Psychiatric Assessment

Often, the capacity evaluation includes formal cognitive or neuropsychological testing to ascertain the extent to which cognitive deficits in realms of attention, concentration, verbal and visual learning and memory, language, executive functioning, and verbal reasoning may be affecting decisional abilities (Department of Veterans Affairs, 1997; Moye et al., 2007). In addition, the evaluation may include formal assessment of psychiatric symptoms (e.g., depression, anxiety, psychotic symptoms) using standardized self-report or interview-based tools (Department of Veterans Affairs, 1997; Lichtenberg, 1999). In many cases, these cognitive and psychiatric assessment instruments have not been developed or validated with older adults from diverse educational, ethnic, and language backgrounds. They should be used and interpreted cautiously (Ganguli & Hendrie, 2005).

Cultural differences in the experience or expression of neurologic and psychiatric illness can be a challenge for appropriate diagnostic assessment. In the capacity evaluation, the evaluator must provide a diagnostic impression—what illness (or illnesses) is causing cognitive and/or psychiatric symptoms that underlie difficulties with medical decision-making abilities? The diagnostic impression is important in terms of implications for prognosis and treatment, that is, when and how might the condition improve over time? Evaluators must be aware of potential racial/ethnic differences in presentation of psychiatric illness. For example, late-life depression, psychosis, dementia, and behavioral symptoms of dementia may present differently across ethnic/racial groups (Cohen & Magai, 1999; Cohen, Magai, Yaffee, & Walcott-Brown, 2004; Lawrence et al., 2006; Manly & Espino, 2004; Shah, Dalvi, & Thompson, 2005; Skarupski et al., 2005).

Standardized psychological assessment tools must be used cautiously in a cross-cultural context. In a comprehensive review, Manly (2006) summarized factors that may affect neuropsychological test performance:

1. *Cultural*
   a. Language, including bilingualism, orthography (phonology, consistency), and articulatory time
   b. Acculturation, including years in the United States and level of exposure to mainstream culture
2. *Educational*
   a. Years of school
   b. Quality of education, including segregation level, teacher-student ratio, per-pupil expenditures, and length of school year
   c. Literacy level
3. *Racial socialization*
   a. Stereotype threat
   b. Perceived racism

Stereotype threat "refers to the experience of diverting attention from the task at hand to the concern that one's performance will confirm a negative stereotype about one's group" (Manly, 2006, p. 211) and may affect the self-confidence and test performance of ethnic minorities in the testing environment. In circumstances of language differences, tests cannot simply be interpreted on the spot by a bilingual translator and then assumed to reflect valid findings. It takes exhaustive research to translate and validate assessment tools across cultural groups (Manly, 2006).

Assessment of Decision-Making Abilities

A number of assessment tools have been developed to help structure the evaluation of medical decision-making capacity (Moye, Gurrera, Karel, Edelstein, & O'Connell, 2006). These tools are typically designed to help assess the four abilities required for decisional capacity—understanding, appreciation, reasoning, and choice. Cultural issues may affect the standardized assessment of each of these abilities.

Understanding refers to a patient's ability to comprehend basic diagnostic, prognostic, and treatment information, as communicated to him by a health-care provider. Understanding, then, depends in part on the adequacy of communication of information within the health-care (or assessment) encounter. At the most basic level, a patient cannot demonstrate understanding if information is provided in an unfamiliar language or at a level beyond her educational background. The research cited earlier, showing important differences in physician-patient relationships based on patient and physician race (Cooper et al., 2003; Saha et al., 2003), points to the importance of conveying information with adequate time, respect, and adjustments to account for the patient's educational and cultural background. A patient cannot provide informed consent without adequate information about the illness and risks and benefits of treatment options. Evaluators must take care to assure adequate disclosure of information before concluding that there are deficits in understanding (Moye et al., 2006).

Appreciation refers to the patient's ability to accept that they have the medical condition and trust that treatment options as described might be of benefit to them. Often, deficits in appreciation occur in the context of delusional thinking, in which a patient may understand the information presented, but deny that it relates to his own situation. In a cross-cultural context, it is possible that a patient may understand that he has a problem, but disagree with the medical conceptualization of what caused, maintains, or might treat the problem. In particular, religious/spiritual understandings of illness may appear delusional to some, but be wholly appropriate from the patient's cultural perspective.

Reasoning entails weighing the costs and benefits of various treatment alternatives in light of the anticipated consequences of different options for one's own life. The assessment of reasoning, in particular, is based on a model of decision making that emphasizes rational reasoning, that is, to be able to delineate clearly the risks and benefits of different decision options, and then compare those risks and benefits in a logical manner that yields the best decision for that person. Increasingly, however, it is recognized that humans may not approach complex decisions in such a logical manner (Dijksterhuis, Bos, Nordgren, & van Baaren, 2006) and that older adults, in particular, may use rule-based or automatic processes based on life experience and expertise (Yates & Patalano, 1999).

Older adults may state clear and valid preferences for medical care based on strongly held religious or cultural beliefs, or based on personal life experiences, but have difficulty providing a list of rational reasons for their decision (Moye, Karel, Azar, & Gurrera, 2004; Moye et al., 2005; Snyder, 1994); thus, they may score poorly on the reasoning portion of a capacity assessment tool. The extent to which decisions appear consistent with personal values, beliefs, and goals may be another important indicator of intact reasoning ability (Moye et al., 2004), and may be particularly important to consider in evaluating reasoning in racial, ethnic, or religious minorities. For example, a clear belief in the possibility of miracles, or a strong preference not to pursue any further surgical care (e.g., after surviving many difficult surgeries), may guide health-care decisions in valid ways.

The ability to express a *choice* is fairly basic but, as discussed previously, in cultures and cohorts in which the patient himself is not viewed as the appropriate decision maker, the older adult may be reluctant to express a treatment preference and prefer to defer such decisions to others.

Clinical Judgment and Recommendations

Ultimately, the evaluator makes a judgment about the patient's medical decision-making capacity as well as recommendations addressing: how to optimize the patient's participation in decision making to the extent that the patient wishes and is able to participate; whether or when further evaluation is indicated; education and support for surrogate decision makers, as appropriate; how the care team may best work with the patient and family on medical decisions, as relevant to the case. An evaluator's recommendations regarding all of these issues requires awareness and sensitivity to the cultural context—to patient and family preferences regarding decision making roles; beliefs and fears about illness, disability, caregiving, and dying; and the implications of different care decisions on the social, and caregiving, context.

CONCLUSION

Cultural context informs the assessment of decision-making capacity in older adults as it does all professional clinical activities. A variety of cultural beliefs profoundly influences decision making about medical care: beliefs regarding illness, healing, and caregiving; expectations about truth telling and locus of decision-making responsibility; and beliefs and traditions related to care at the end of life. The concern for reliable and valid assessment of an older adult's decision-making capacity comes from a cultural context that values the individual's right to self-determination in health care. While not all older adults value autonomous decision making, respect for older adults from diverse backgrounds requires that health-care providers understand whom older adults want involved in decision making and to work to ensure that their values, beliefs, and goals are represented in medical care decisions. More resources are becoming available to help clinicians develop competence in multicultural geriatric care. This chapter highlighted several themes in culture and medical decision making and provided recommendations regarding the assessment of medical consent capacity in older adults from diverse racial, ethnic, religious, or national backgrounds.

REFERENCES

Administration on Aging. (2001). *Achieving cultural competence: A guidebook for providers of services to older Americans and their families.* Retrieved December 24, 2006, from www.aoa.gov/prof/adddiv/cultural/addiv_cult.asp/.

Allen, R. S., & Shuster, J. L. (2002). The role of proxies in treatment decisions: Evaluating functional capacity to consent to end-of-life treatments within a family context. *Behavioral Sciences and the Law, 20,* 235–252.

American Geriatrics Society. (2004). *Doorway thoughts: Cross-cultural health care for older adults.* Sudbury, MA: Jones and Bartlett.

American Psychological Association. (2003). Guidelines on multicultural education, training, research, practice, and organizational change for psychologists. *American Psychologist, 58,* 377–402.

Armstrong, K., Hughes-Halbert, C., & Asch, D. A. (2006). Patient preferences can be misleading as explanations for racial disparities in health care. *Archives of Internal Medicine, 166,* 950–954.

Betancourt, J. R. (2006). Cultural competence and medical education: Many names, many perspectives, one goal. *Academic Medicine, 81,* 499–501.

Betancourt, J. R., Green, A. R., Carrillo, J. E., & Ananeh-Firempong, O. (2003). Defining cultural competence: A practical framework for addressing racial/ethnic disparities in health and health care. *Public Health Reports, 118,* 293–302.

Blackhall, L. J., Frank, G., Murhpy, S. T., Michel, V., Palmer, J. M., & Azen, S. P. (1999). Ethnicity and attitudes towards life sustaining technology. *Social Science and Medicine, 48,* 1779–1789.

Blackhall, L. J., Murphy, S. T., Frank, G., Michel, V., & Azen, S. (1995). Ethnicity and attitudes toward patient autonomy. *Journal of the American Medical Association, 274,* 820–825.

Braun, K. L., Pietsch, J. H., & Blanchette, P. L. (Eds.). (1999). *Cultural issues in end-of-life decision making.* Thousand Oaks, CA: Sage.

Christakis, N. A. (2001). *Death foretold: Prophecy and prognosis in medical care.* Chicago: University of Chicago Press.

Cohen, C. I., & Magai, C. (1999). Racial differences in neuropsychiatric symptoms among dementia outpatients. *American Journal of Geriatric Psychiatry, 7,* 57–63.

Cohen, C. I., Magai, C., Yaffee, R., & Walcott-Brown, L. (2004). Racial differences in paranoid ideation and psychoses in an older urban population. *American Journal of Psychiatry, 161,* 864–871.

Cooper, L. A., Roter, D. L., Johnson, R. L., Ford, D. E., Steinwachs, D. M., & Powe, N. R. (2003). Patient-centered communication, ratings of care, and concordance of patient and physician race. *Annals of Internal Medicine, 139,* 907–915.

Cooper-Patrick, L., Gallo, J. J., Gonzales, J. J., Vu, H. T., Powe, N. R., Nelson, C., et al. (1999). Race, gender, and partnership in the patient-physician relationship. *Journal of the American Medical Association, 282,* 583–589.

Covinsky, K. E., Fuller, J. D., Yaffe, K., Johnston, C. B., Hamel, M. B., Lynn, J., et al. (2000). Communication and decision-making in seriously ill patients: Findings of the SUPPORT project. *Journal of the American Geriatrics Society, 48,* S187–S193.

Crawley, L. M., Marshall, P. A., Lo, B., Koenig, B. A., & the End-of-Life Care Consensus Panel. (2002). Strategies for culturally effective end-of-life care. *Annals of Internal Medicine, 136,* 673–679.

Culhane-Pera, K. A., Reif, C., Egli, E., Baker, N. J., & Kassekert, R. (1997). A curriculum for multicultural education in family medicine. *Family Medicine, 29,* 719–723.

Degenholtz, H. B., Thomas, S. B., & Miller, M. J. (2003). Race and the intensive care unit: Disparities and preferences for end-of-life care. *Critical Care Medicine, 31,* S373–S378.

Department of Veterans Affairs. (1997). *Assessment of competency and capacity of the older adult: A practice guideline for psychologists.* Milwaukee, WI: National Center for Cost Containment.

Dijksterhuis, A., Bos, M. W., Nordgren, L. F., & van Baaren, R. B. (2006). On making the right choice: The deliberation-without-attention effect. *Science, 311,* 1005–1007.

Drought, T. S., & Koenig, B. A. (2002). "Choice" in end-of-life decision making: Researching fact or fiction? [Special issue III]. *Gerontologist, 42,* 114–128.

Eleazer, G. P., Hornung, C. A., Egbert, C. B., Egbert, J. R., Eng, C., Hedgepeth, J., et al. (1996). The relationship between ethnicity and advance directives in a frail older population. *Journal of the American Geriatrics Society, 44,* 938–943.

Federal Interagency Forum on Aging-Related Statistics. (2006). *Older Americans update 2006: Key indicators of well-being.* Washington, DC: U.S. Government Printing Office. Available from www.agingstats.gov.

Fiscella, K., Franks, P., Gold, M. R., & Clancy, C. M. (2000). Inequality in quality: Addressing socioeconomic, racial, and ethnic disparities in health care. *Journal of the American Medical Association, 283,* 2579–2584.

Gallagher-Thompson, D., Haley, W., Guy, D., Rupert, M., Arguelles, T., Zeiss, L. M., et al. (2003). Tailoring psychological interventions for ethnically diverse dementia caregivers. *Clinical Psychology: Science and Practice, 10,* 423–438.

Ganguli, M., & Hendrie, H. C. (2005). Screening for cognitive impairment and depression in ethnically diverse older populations. *Alzheimer's Disease and Associated Disorders, 19,* 275–278.

Gillick, M., Berkman, S., & Cullen, L. (1999). A patient-centered approach to advance medical planning in the nursing home. *Journal of the American Geriatrics Society, 47,* 227–230.

Gist, Y. J., & Hetzel, L. I. (2004). *We the people: Aging in the United States* (Census 2000 Special Reports). Washington, DC: U.S. Census Bureau. Available from www.census.gov/prod/2004pubs/censr-19.pdf.

Goold, S. D. (2002). Trust, distrust, and trustworthiness. *Journal of General Internal Medicine, 17,* 79–81.

Haley, W. E., Allen, R. S., Reynolds, S., Chen, H., Burton, A., & Gallagher-Thompson, D. (2002). Family issues in end-of-life decision making and end-of-life care. *American Behavioral Scientist, 46,* 284–298.

Haley, W. E., Han, B., & Henderson, J. N. (1998). Aging and ethnicity: Issues for clinical practice. *Journal of Clinical Psychology in Medical Settings, 5,* 393–409.

Harris, H. W., Felder, D., & Clark, M. O. (2004). A psychiatry residency curriculum on the care of African American patients. *Academic Psychiatry, 28,* 226–239.

Hawkins, N. A., Ditto, P. H., Danks, J. H., & Smucker, W. D. (2005). Micromanaging death: Process preferences, values, and goals in end-of-life medical decision making. *Gerontologist, 45,* 107–117.

High, D. M. (1988). All in the family: Extended autonomy and expectations in surrogate health care decision-making. *Gerontologist, 28,* 46–51.

Hopp, F. P., & Duffy, S. A. (2000). Racial variations in end-of-life care. *Journal of the American Geriatrics Society, 48,* 658–663.

Hornung, C. A., Eleazer, G. P., Strothers, H. S., III, Wieland, G. D., Eng, C., McCann, R., et al. (1998). Ethnicity and decision-makers in a group of frail older people. *Journal of the American Geriatrics Society, 46,* 280–286.

Institute of Medicine. (2002). *Unequal treatment: Confronting racial and ethnic disparities in health care.* Washington, DC: National Academies Press.

Jacobs, E. A., Rolle, I., Ferrans, C. E., Whitaker, E. E., & Warnecke, R. B. (2006). Understanding African Americans' views of the trustworthiness of physicians. *Journal of General Internal Medicine, 21,* 642–647.

Jang, Y., Kim, G., & Chiriboga, D. A. (2005). Health, healthcare utilization, and satisfaction with service: Barriers and facilitators for older Korean Americans. *Journal of the American Geriatrics Society, 53*, 1613–1617.

Kane, R. L., Bershadsky, B., & Bershadsky, J. (2006). Who recommends long-term care matters. *Gerontologist, 46*, 474–482.

Karel, M. J. (2000). The assessment of values in medical decision making. *Journal of Aging Studies, 14*, 403–422.

Karel, M. J., Moye, J., Bank, A., & Azar, A. R. (2007). Three methods of assessing values for advance care planning: Comparing persons with and without dementia. *Journal of Aging and Health, 19*, 123–151.

Karel, M. J., Powell, J., & Cantor, M. (2004). Using a Values Discussion Guide to facilitate communication in advance care planning. *Patient Education and Counseling, 55*, 22–31.

Karlawish, J. H. T., Quill, T., Meier, D. E., & the ACP-ASIM End-of-Life Care Consensus Panel. (1999). A consensus-based approach to providing palliative care to patients who lack decision-making capacity. *Annals of Internal Medicine, 130*, 835–840.

Kawaga-Singer, M. (1994). Diverse cultural beliefs and practices about death and dying in the elderly. In D. Wieland, D. Benton, B. J. Kramer, & G. D. Dawson (Eds.), *Cultural diversity and geriatric care: Challenges to the health professions* (pp. 101–112). New York: Haworth Press.

Kawaga-Singer, M., & Blackhall, L. J. (2001). Negotiating cross-cultural issues at the end of life. *Journal of the American Medical Association, 286*, 2993–3001.

Klessig, J. (1992). The effect of values and culture on life-support decisions. *Western Journal of Medicine, 157*, 316–322.

Koenig, B. A., & Gates-Williams, J. (1995). Understanding cultural differences in caring for dying patients. *Western Journal of Medicine, 163*, 244–249.

Kwak, J., & Haley, W. E. (2005). Current research findings on end-of-life decision making among racially or ethnically diverse groups. *Gerontologist, 45*, 634–641.

Lawrence, V., Murray, J., Banerjee, S., Turner, S., Sangha, K., Byng, R., et al. (2006). Concepts and causation of depression: A cross-cultural study of the beliefs of older adults. *Gerontologist, 46*, 23–32.

Lichtenberg, P. (Ed.). (1999). *Handbook of assessment in clinical gerontology.* New York: Wiley.

LoboPrabhu, S. M., Molinari, V. A., & Lomax, J. W. (Eds.). (2006). *Supporting the caregiver in dementia: A guide for health care professionals.* Baltimore: Johns Hopkins University Press.

Manly, J. J. (2006). Cultural issues. In D. K. Attix & K. A. Welsh-Bohmer (Eds.), *Geriatric neuropsychology: Assessment and intervention* (pp. 198–222). New York: Guilford Press.

Manly, J. J., & Espino, D. V. (2004). Cultural influences on dementia recognition and management. *Clinics in Geriatric Medicine, 20,* 93–119.

Matsumura, S., Bito, S., Liu, H., Kahn, K., Fukuhara, S., Kagawa-Singer, M., et al. (2002). Acculturation of attitudes toward end-of-life care: A cross-cultural survey of Japanese Americans and Japanese. *Journal of General Internal Medicine, 17,* 531–539.

Mezey, M., Teresi, J., Ramsey, G., Mitty, E., & Bobrowitz, T. (2000). Decision-making capacity to execute a health care proxy: Development and testing of guidelines. *Journal of the American Geriatrics Society, 48,* 179–187.

Morrison, R. S., Zayas, L. H., Mulvihill, M., Baskin, S. A., & Meier, D. E. (1998). Barriers to completion of health care proxies: An examination of ethnic differences. *Archives of Internal Medicine, 158,* 2493–2497.

Mouton, C. P. (2000). Cultural and religious issues for African Americans. In K. L. Braun, J. H. Pietsch, & P. L. Blanchette (Eds.), *Cultural issues in end-of-life decision making* (pp. 71–82). Thousand Oaks, CA: Sage.

Moye, J. (1999). Assessment of competency and decision making capacity. In P. Lichtenberg (Ed.), *Handbook of assessment in clinical gerontology* (pp. 488–528). New York: Wiley.

Moye, J., Armesto, J. C., & Karel, M. J. (2005). Evaluating capacity of older adults in rehabilitation settings: Conceptual models and clinical challenges. *Rehabilitation Psychology, 50,* 207–214.

Moye, J., Gurrera, R. J., Karel, M. J., Edelstein, B., & O'Connell, C. (2006). Empirical advances in the assessment of the capacity to consent to medical treatment: Clinical implications and research needs. *Clinical Psychology Review, 26,* 1054–1077.

Moye, J., Karel, M. J., & Armesto, J. C. (2007). Evaluating capacity to consent to treatment. In A. M. Goldstein (Ed.), *Forensic psychology: Emerging topics and expanding roles* (pp. 260–293). Hoboken, NJ: Wiley.

Moye, J., Karel, M. J., Azar, A. R., & Gurrera, R. J. (2004). Hopes and cautions for instrument-based evaluation of consent capacity: Results of a construct validity study of three instruments. *Ethics, Law, and Aging Review, 10*, 39–61.

Moye, J., Karel, M. J., Edelstein, B., Hicken, B., Armesto, J. C., & Gurrera, R. J. (in press). Assessment of capacity to consent to treatment: Challenges, the "ACCT" approach, future directions. *Clinical Gerontologist.*

Moye, J., Karel, M. J., & Gurrera, R. J. (2006). Unpublished data.

Murphy, S. T., Palmer, J. M., Azen, S., Frank, G., Michel, V., & Blackhall, L. J. (1996). Ethnicity and advance directives. *Journal of Law, Medicine, and Ethics, 24*, 108–117.

National Association of Social Workers. (2001). *NASW standards for cultural competence in social work practice.* Retrieved December 23, 2006, from www.socialworkers.org/sections/credentials/cultural_comp.asp/.

Pachter, L. M. (1994). Culture and clinical care: Folk illness beliefs and behaviors and their implications for health care delivery. *Journal of the American Medical Association, 271*, 690–694.

Pearlman, R., Starks, H., Cain, K., Rosengreen, D., & Patrick, D. (1998). *Your life, your choices: Planning for future medical decisions—How to prepare a personalized living will* (No. PB#98159437). Springfield, VA: U.S. Department of Commerce, National Technical Information Service. Retrieved January 6, 2007, from www1.va.gov/hsrd/publications/internal/ylyc.pdf.

Rapp, D. E. (2006). Integrating cultural competency into the undergraduate medical curriculum. *Medical Education, 40*, 704–710.

Royeen, M., & Crabtree, J. L. (Eds.). (2006). *Culture in rehabilitation: From competency to proficiency.* Upper Saddle River, NJ: Pearson Prentice-Hall.

Saha, S., Arbelaez, J. J., & Cooper, L. A. (2003). Patient-physician relationships and racial disparities in the quality of health care. *American Journal of Public Health, 93*, 1713–1719.

Schwartz, C., Lennes, I., Hammes, B., Lapham, C., Bottner, W., & Ma, Y. (2003). Honing an advance care planning intervention using qualitative analysis: The Living Well Interview. *Journal of Palliative Medicine, 6*, 593–603.

Shah, A., Dalvi, M., & Thompson, T. (2005). Behavioral and psychological signs and symptoms of dementia across cultures: Current status and the future. *International Journal of Geriatric Psychiatry, 20*, 1187–1195.

Singer, P. A., Martin, D. K., Lavery, J. V., Theil, E. C., Kelner, M., & Mendelssohn, D. C. (1998). Reconceptualizing advance care planning from the patient's perspective. *Archives of Internal Medicine, 158*, 879–884.

Skarupski, K. A., Mendes de Leon, C. F., Bienias, J. L., Barnes, L. L., Everson-Rose, S. A., Wilson, R. S., et al. (2005). Black-White differences in depressive symptoms among older adults over time. *Journals of Gerontology, 60*, P136–P142.

Sloand, E., Groves, S., & Brager, R. (2004, April 13). Cultural competency education in American nursing programs and the approach of one school of nursing. *International Journal of Nursing Education Scholarship, 1*(Article 6).

Snyder, A. C. (1994). Competency to refuse lifesaving treatment: Valuing the nonlogical aspects of a person's decisions. *Issues in Law and Medicine, 10*, 299–320.

Spector, R. E. (2004). *Cultural diversity in health and illness.* Upper Saddle River, NJ: Pearson Prentice-Hall.

Stein, G. L., & Bonuck, K. A. (2001). Attitudes on end-of-life care and advance care planning in the lesbian and gay community. *Journal of Palliative Medicine, 4*, 173–190.

Sue, D. W., & Sue, D. (2003). *Counseling the culturally diverse: Theory and practice* (4th ed.). Hoboken, NJ: Wiley.

Talamantes, M. A., Gomez, C., & Braun, K. L. (2000). Advance directives and end-of-life care: The Hispanic perspective. In K. L. Braun, J. H. Pietsch, & P. L. Blanchette (Eds.), *Cultural issues in end-of-life decision making* (pp. 83–100). Thousand Oaks, CA: Sage.

Tarn, D. M., Meredith, L. S., Kagawa-Singer, M., Matsumara, S., Bito, S., Oye, R. K., et al. (2005). Trust in one's physician: The role of ethnic match, autonomy, acculturation, and religiosity among Japanese and Japanese Americans. *Annals of Family Medicine, 3*, 339–347.

U.S. Department of Health and Human Services, Office of Minority Health. (2001). *National standards for culturally and linguistically appropriate services in health care.* Washington, DC: Author.

Winzelberg, G. S., Hanson, L. C., & Tulsky, J. A. (2005). Beyond autonomy: Diversifying end-of-life decision-making approaches to serve patients and families. *Journal of the American Geriatrics Society, 53*, 1046–1050.

Xakellis, G., Brangman, S. A., Hinton, W. L., Jones, V. Y., Masterman, D., Pan, C. X., et al. (2004). Curricular framework: Core competencies in multicultural geriatric care. *Journal of the American Geriatrics Society, 52*, 137–142.

Yates, J. F., & Patalano, A. L. (1999). Decision making and aging. In D. C. Park, R. W. Morrell, & K. Shifren (Eds.), *Processing of medical information in aging patients: Cognition and human factors perspective* (pp. 31–54). Mahwah, NJ: Erlbaum.

Yeo, G. (Ed.). (2001). *Curriculum in ethnogeriatrics* (2nd ed.). Stanford, CA: Collaborative on Ethnogeriatric Education. Retrieved December 24, 2006, from www.stanford.edu/group/ethnoger/.

Yeo, G., & Gallagher-Thompson, D. (Eds.). (2006). *Ethnicity and the dementias* (2nd ed.). New York: Routledge.

Clinical Evaluation
and Intervention

8

Clinical Frameworks for Capacity Assessment

Jennifer Moye

In this chapter, I describe a framework for performing clinical assessment of civil capacities of older adults. Thus, the various criminal capacities often discussed as part of forensic capacity or competency assessment are not of issue here. Instead, the clinical framework presented here is meant to apply broadly to the assessment of decision-making capacity for everyday life that commonly arises in medical settings for geropsychologists, rehabilitation psychologists, and neuropsychologists, such as capacity to manage finances, to live independently (sometimes as capacity to be "discharged home"), to provide medical consent, to drive, and other specific everyday functions.

THE RELATIONSHIP BETWEEN CAPACITY ASSESSMENT AND GENERAL PSYCHOLOGICAL ASSESSMENT

Much of capacity assessment builds on the principles and techniques of good geriatric assessment. Many of these principles are reviewed elsewhere in this book, and they include the informed and artful use of

The framework described in this chapter has been informed by my collaboration with colleagues in the VA and the American Bar Association and American Psychological Association Assessment of Capacity of Older Adults working group.

structured assessment instruments and clinical interviews that are tailored to the educational, cultural, psychological, social, and sensory characteristics of the individual being assessed. A careful consideration of the individual's acute medical status as well as the psychosocial history is foundational to solid geriatric assessment.

However, capacity assessment differs from a general psychological assessment in some important ways. Six of these factors are reviewed in this chapter. The first two factors involve the examiners and knowledge about terms and services and the utilization of a conceptual framework developed for capacity assessment. The remaining four factors relate to differences in the four phases of assessment process: prescreening, informed consent, evaluation, and postevaluation.

Knowledge of Relevant Legal Terms and Social Services

The clinical and legal meaning of *capacity* as it is being used with the individual under consideration—and the possible outcomes if the person is found to have diminished capacity—are critical to understand prior to undertaking a capacity assessment. Capacity has a broad theoretical meaning, but also specific and local meanings—as it is being applied to the specific situation (e.g., capacity to write a will versus capacity to drive) and the legal and social interventions that may assist in any specific application.

Capacity

The term *capacity* is used in both legal and clinical settings. Understanding the concept behind capacity can be challenging because the term may be misused in clinical settings. In legal settings, capacity may refer to a lawyer's determination of a client's ability to conduct legal transactions (e.g., capacity to change a will) or to a judge's determination of a person's legal abilities to make decisions or perform certain functions (e.g., capacity under guardianship). In clinical settings, capacity refers to a clinician's opinion of a person's abilities to make decisions or perform certain functions. While a clinical opinion is not a legal finding, it often serves as important evidence in legal proceedings. There are exceptions to this rule, most importantly with treatment consent capacity. Often a clinician's opinion about consent capacity is sufficient to activate the authority of a substitute decision maker—a next of kin or a health-care proxy.

The term capacity is now preferred to competency in both clinical and legal settings. The term capacity avoids the "all-or-none" baggage of the word competency (Sabatino, 1996). Decision-making capacity is task specific, not global. A person may have the capacity to make financial decisions but not medical decisions. In addition, capacity can fluctuate over time. Capacities that were diminished due to acute illness, such as postsurgical confusion, may be re-gained (McAvay et al., 2006). This point is sometimes lost in clinical settings (Ganzini, Volicer, Nelson, & Derse, 2003) when a team member proclaims "but the patient was deemed incompetent by Dr. X." For this reason it is important to be clear with team members, "for what issue was the person thought to have diminished capacity?" and "at what time and in what circumstance?" Capacity is also situational and contextual. A person's degree of capacity relates to the risk of the decision, the social environment, and resources that support or diminish the individual's functioning (Grisso, 2003).

When evaluating capacity for a specific task, such as medical consent capacity, there are important referents for the examiner. These include relevant statutory or case law that fleshes out the concept within the jurisdiction. Sometimes these can be so broad or in some states so archaic (e.g., in Massachusetts "mental weakness" is a legal standard for conservatorship) that they are not helpful. Other times the statutory or case law may be quite specific—such as requiring a listing and consideration of medications in guardianship evaluations. In addition, for some specific capacities there is an emerging empirical base and associated functional assessment tools (Moye & Marson, 2007). These are discussed in more detail in later chapters that deal with specific capacities. The goal of this chapter is to provide a general clinical framework relevant to most capacities.

Legally Authorized Substitute Decision Makers

Some common types of substitute decision makers are guardians, conservators, health-care proxies, durable powers of attorney, trustees, and representative payees. Most states also have laws in which next of kin are recognized as legally authorized medical decision makers (assuming incapacity of the patient). Evaluators should be familiar with the types of substitute decision makers that are relevant to the case, related statutes, and whether the goal of the evaluation is to support substitute decision making by such an individual.

Social Services

When performing capacity assessments of older adults, it is also important to be knowledgeable about the vast array of social services that can support an individual's functioning in the community (see Qualls, Chapter 12, this volume). These include services such as adult protective services, elder services, shared bank accounts, bill paying services, adult foster care, care management, home health services, homemaker and chore services, adult day health care, meals on wheels, transportation services, respite care, emergency lifeline systems, and other services. Usually the local Area Agency on Aging is a repository of information about available services, but it may also take some creative investigation of local communities to learn about the extent of resources available to help vulnerable elders.

Conceptual Framework

A basic conceptual framework for assessing capacity anchors the assessment process. One conceptual framework proposed by the American Bar Association (ABA) and the American Psychological Association (APA) Assessment of Capacity in Older Adults Project working group is entitled "Six Pillars of Capacity Assessment" (ABA & APA, 2006). It links closely to statutory frameworks for guardianship and the general conceptual framework for capacity assessment developed by Grisso (2003). The six pillars or domains of assessment suggested by the ABA-APA group are: medical condition, cognitive functioning, everyday functioning, values, risk of harm, and means to enhance capacity.

Medical Condition Producing Functional Disability

Documentation of the medical diagnoses is a key element in capacity determination as it is the causative factor explaining any functional disability. Grisso refers to the condition producing the disability as the "causal factor" in his model of capacity assessment (Grisso, 2003). A wide range of neurological and psychiatric conditions may impact capacity with aging—for example, Alzheimer's disease or other forms of dementia, stroke, Parkinson's disease, traumatic brain injury, Schizophrenia, Bipolar Disorder and more (Dymek, 2001; Kim, Karlawish, & Caine, 2002; see Kaye & Grigsby, Chapter 3, this volume). Some conditions may be temporary and reversible—such as delirium or depression. The identification of the causes of any cognitive or behavioral impairment leads to an understanding of the likely course, prognosis, and treatments that may help.

Cognition

Many disorders that impact capacity do so because they have a direct effect on cognitive functioning, such as dementia (see Foster, Cornwel, Kisley, & Davis, Chapter 2, this volume; Gurrera, Moye, Karel, Azar, & Armesto, 2006; Marson, Chatterjee, Ingram, & Harrell, 1996; Wood & Tanius, Chapter 4, this volume). Similarly, although psychiatric and emotional disturbance is not necessarily a cause of capacity impairment, the extent to which severe psychiatric and emotional disturbance impair cognitive abilities is also critical for understanding capacity (Grisso & Appelbaum, 1995). Some capacities, such as treatment or research consent are essentially cognitive or decisional in nature. Other capacities, such as driving or financial management, while involving a behavioral component, also rely heavily on underlying cognitive functioning (Moye & Marson, 2007). In terms of guardianship, cognitive functioning is a component of statutory standards for capacity in many states (Sabatino & Basinger, 2000). The Uniform Guardianship and Protective Proceedings Act (UGPPA; National Conference of Commissioners on Uniform State Laws, 1997) is a model statute for guardianship and also includes the cognitive functioning element in defining an incapacitated person as an individual who "is unable to receive and evaluate information or make or communicate decisions."

Everyday Functioning

Another essential in capacity assessment is what the ABA-APA group termed "everyday functioning." Functional assessment is a common component of gerontological assessment and has been appreciated by clinicians (Scogin & Perry, 1987) who categorize functioning into activities of daily living (ADLs; e.g., grooming, toileting, eating, transferring, dressing) and instrumental activities of daily living (IADLs; e.g., abilities to manage finances, health, and functioning in the home and community). The major difference between capacity assessment and general psychological assessment is this focus on functioning and the inclusion of some method to assess everyday functioning. Specific functional domains identified by the ABA-APA working group as especially relevant to capacity issues in guardianship proceedings are described in Chapter 10 of this volume as detailed in Table 10.3 on page 218. According to Table 10.3, it may be helpful to consider several broad domains of functional assessment—care of self, financial capacities, medical, home and community life, and other civil or legal issues; and within these broad domains, to identify, as much as possible, the specific issue or decision that is in need of assessment.

Individual Values, Preferences, and Patterns

A person's life experiences, race, ethnicity, culture, and religion impact his or her values and preferences (Blackhall, Murphy, Frank, Michel, & Azen, 1995; Hornung et al., 1998), and these lay the foundation for decisions (see also Karel, Chapter 7, this volume). A person may still be able to express important values underlying decisions, even with dementia, when cognitive functioning may be compromised (Karel, Moye, Bank, & Azar, 2007). Further, choices that are linked with lifetime values are rational for an individual even if outside the norm. The extent to which an individual's decisions are consistent with values is an indicator of capacity (American Bar Association, 2003). In addition, knowledge of an individual's values helps to inform the plan of care for the patient.

Risk of Harm and Level of Supervision Needed

Many capacity evaluations are, at heart, a risk assessment (Ruchinskas, 2005). Thus, the evaluation of the person and his or her medical conditions, cognitive and functional abilities, personal values and preferences, all of which impact their day to day functioning, must be analyzed in reference to the risk of the situation at hand. Does the specific treatment or research decision involve a high degree of risk? Is the home situation isolated, unsafe, or proximal to risks? An analysis of risk is not merely a consideration of the condition and its effects, but also takes into account the environmental supports and demands (Grisso, 2003). Strong social and environmental supports may decrease the risk while the lack of supports may increase it. The level of intervention or supervision recommended as a result of the capacity assessment must match the risk of harm to the individual and the corresponding level of supervision required to mitigate such risk and must include a full exploration of the least restrictive alternatives (Sabatino & Basinger, 2000; see Qualls, Chapter 12, this volume).

Means to Enhance Capacity

An essential component of a capacity assessment is a consideration of what can be done to maximize the person's functioning as described in Chapter 12 of this volume. These include practical accommodations (such as vision aids, medication reminders) and medical, psychosocial, or educational interventions (such as physical or occupational therapy, counseling, medications, or training). If improvement of capacity is possible with treatment for underlying conditions, clinical recommendations may guide the judge in deciding when to re-hear the case. Further, clinical recommendations for intervention may directly inform the individual's plan of care.

Preevaluation Screening

The need for preevaluation screening may vary by the setting. In our nursing home setting, we often find it important to clarify the purpose of the evaluation and to gather background information. When speaking with referring clinicians or treatment teams, it is helpful to ask them which specific capacities, tasks, or decisions they are concerned about. Concerns could include medical decision making, financial decision making, independent living, whether the patient can be discharged, whether the patient can drive, and so on. Once the specific capacity issue is isolated, more information on that issue is needed. For example, if the patient is refusing a medical procedure, understanding the medical procedure in detail is critical to understanding why the patient may be refusing. Is transfer to another facility involved? Is sedation involved or permitted? How will postprocedure care be delivered? Who will do the procedure? Who will be with the patient before and after the procedure? How was this information conveyed to the patient? Some capacity evaluations are obviated simply through taking more time with the patient to explain and plan for the procedure and postcare.

Such questioning may reveal that the issue at hand is not best framed—and would not be best resolved—as a capacity assessment. For example, at times, capacity questions are raised when patients and their providers or families are at odds, when what is really needed is psychological mediation to resolve a challenging or painful decision. Other times, it is important to explore whether having a substitute decision maker would help. For example, a team may raise the question about whether a patient who is refusing daily care is "competent" to refuse such care. Even if a capacity evaluation finds the patient to have diminished decisional abilities, the team still has to figure out how to provide care to the patient. At other times, a substitute mechanism may already be available (e.g., a durable power of attorney for finances or a representative payee) and a requested capacity assessment may not be needed.

In addition to gathering information about the procedure at hand and the contextual issues giving rise to a capacity evaluation request, knowing the patient's specific history relative to the situation is critical. Has the patient had trouble making decisions in the past? Has the patient had trouble with finances in the past (suffered losses, been cheated or exploited)? Has the patient had trouble living at home in the past (care of home, safety)? Who are the patient's family members, how much are they involved? If finances are an issue, what can be learned about the nature and extent of the assets? If capacity to live at home is an issue, what can be learned specifically about the home situation? Gathering a history in this way is somewhat different than processes used for a general psychological assessment—the evaluator must be deeply curious about understanding the specific environmental, contextual, and situational factors. This allows the evaluator to tailor the assessment and increases the possibility that the evaluator may uncover some novel solutions to aid the elder in maximizing capacity. Finally, the evaluator needs to judge the urgency of the request to determine when a decision on consent capacity needs to be rendered.

Informed Consent

Assuming the patient is communicative, the evaluator must attempt to obtain informed consent for the evaluation of capacity. The main goal is to inform the patient about what you are doing and why, including carefully describing the potential risks in cooperating with a capacity evaluation. The evaluator should explain why she or he has been called to evaluate capacity, what is involved (interviews, tests), the purpose of the evaluation, the potential risks (the patient may lose the right to make autonomous decisions; the patient may have a guardian appointed), and the potential benefits (information gained may help in planning for the patient's treatment or to maximize independence). The patient's reaction to each of these elements should be described in the evaluation report. Three outcomes are possible: the patient consents, the patient will not consent (refuses), or the patient cannot consent or refuse (lacks the capacity to consent to the evaluation). In the latter situation, some patients assent to the evaluation but show questionable comprehension of the risks and benefits. These same decisional deficits may be affecting the patient's capacity to consent to treatment. Describing the patient's assent detailing any areas of questionable ability to consent to the evaluation (in the absence of outright refusal; Department of Veterans Affairs, 1997) is a typical procedure, if capacity to consent to the evaluation is in question. For patients who are unable to fully consent to the evaluation, but who assent, the evaluator may usually proceed with the evaluation provided he or she has attempted to obtain informed consent and has fully disclosed the risks of the evaluation. A referral where there is questionable capacity to consent to an evaluation does not, in itself, obviate the need to disclose the risks of the evaluation or the need to attempt to obtain consent.

Evaluation

The capacity evaluation itself is quite similar to a general psychological assessment. A clinical interview with the patient is used to gain his or her perspective on psychiatric, medical, family, and social history, and perceptions on the issue at hand—values and goals (Department of Veterans Affairs, 1997). As a matter of course, a general mental status examination is completed as part of the clinical interview. Interviewing family or staff members to gain their perspectives on the patient's functioning—bearing in mind that in some cases some individuals have a conflict of interest (i.e., an exploitive family member may be motivated to make the patient appear worse than he or she is to gain control of assets)—is critical as well.

Cognitive testing to establish the "cognitive functioning" component of capacity is the next step. In nursing home settings, residents often have compromised medical status that complicates or deters administration of an extensive neuropsychological battery. However, in outpatient settings or court setting, more extensive evaluation often is possible. When only limited testing is possible, select cognitive tests that are most relevant to the diagnosis (e.g., memory tests when the individual has dementia) and to the capacity at hand (e.g., executive functioning tests to look at decisional flexibility).

As previously noted, functional evaluation is probably the most important way that capacity evaluation differs from a general psychological assessment. Here the examiner adds observation, inquiry, and direct performance-based evaluation specific to the capacity in question (ABA & APA, 2005). These are discussed in more detail in Chapters 10 and 11 of this volume.

Postevaluation

The next step is to determine the conclusions of the assessment, both general findings and capacity-related findings, and share them in clear, understandable language with the patient, medical team, relevant family members, and any referring parties. In many settings, the results of a capacity assessment can provide a clinical diagnosis and treatment recommendations, but should also clearly and directly answer the question of capacity, outline appropriate legal interventions and, whenever possible, address less restrictive alternatives. Here, the clinician must balance the information about the diagnosis, cognitive and psychiatric symptoms, and decisional functioning in view of interactive and contextual factors, such as the person's values, goals, preferences, history, and the situational risks. No cookbook exists for combining these factors; capacity conclusions are a professional clinical judgment. However, when the evaluator has carefully collected information regarding all the components, including standardized testing of cognition and behavior, the key elements to make such a judgment are at hand.

In some cases, the evaluator's job is to describe his or her capacity findings and then to leave the determination of legal capacity and appropriate actions to a judge. In other cases, the evaluator offers recommendations for disposition. For example, the clinician may conclude that a substitute decision maker is needed and recommend that a previously appointed health-care proxy be activated, or, if unavailable, that the hospital implement its policy of obtaining consent from the next of kin. Other times, the evaluator recommends that a medical decision await treatment of an underlying psychiatric or neurocognitive condition, when time allows, prior to pursuing medical treatment. The evaluation may also uncover decisional aids or cultural, language, or religious concerns that should be addressed as consent is obtained.

CONCLUSION

In conclusion, a capacity assessment builds on many of the same principles and techniques of comprehensive psychological assessment. However, it differs in some key ways. First, assessment of decision-making capacity requires knowledge of the concepts of capacity and related legal and social interventions. Second, a conceptual framework guides the capacity assessment process in sometimes murky waters. Third, capacity assessment requires special attention during the prescreening phase to ensure the appropriateness of the capacity assessment and to gather background information specific to the capacity situation and context. Fourth, capacity assessment requires an especially careful informed consent process including a warning about the risks of participating in the capacity assessment. Fifth, capacity assessment involves many of the usual aspects of psychological assessment, but adds functional evaluation. Sixth, in the postevaluation phase, capacity assessment leads evaluators to state direct opinions about whether the person has or does not have capacity for the specific task(s) in question, as well as recommendations for appropriate legal and social interventions.

REFERENCES

American Bar Association. (2003). *Model rules of professional conduction.* Washington, DC: American Bar Association.

American Bar Association & American Psychological Association Assessment of Capacity in Older Adults Project Working Group. (2005). *Assessment of older adults with diminished capacity: A handbook for lawyers.* Washington, DC: Author.

American Bar Association & American Psychological Association Assessment of Capacity in Older Adults Project Working Group. (2006). *Judicial determination of capacity of older adults in guardianship proceedings: A handbook for judges.* Washington, DC: Author.

Blackhall, L. J., Murphy, S. T., Frank, G., Michel, V., & Azen, S. (1995). Ethnicity and attitudes toward patient autonomy. *Journal of the American Medical Association, 274,* 820–825.

Department of Veterans Affairs. (1997). *Clinical assessment for competency determination: A practice guideline for psychologists.* Milwaukee, WI: Department of Veterans Affairs National Center for Cost Containment.

Dymek, M. P., Atchison, P., Harrell, L., & Marson, D. C. (2001). Competency to consent to medical treatment in cognitively impaired patients with Parkinson's disease. *Neurology, 56,* 17–24.

Ganzini, L., Volicer, L., Nelson, W., & Derse, A. (2003). Pitfalls in the assessment of decision-making capacity. *Psychosomatics, 44,* 237–243.

Grisso, T. (2003). *Evaluating competences* (2nd ed.). New York: Plenum Press.

Grisso, T., & Appelbaum, P. S. (1995). The Macarthur Treatment Competency Study III: Abilities of patients to consent to psychiatric and medical treatment. *Law and Human Behavior, 19,* 149–174.

Gurrera, R. J., Moye, J., Karel, M. J., Azar, A. R., & Armesto, J. C. (2006). Cognitive performance predicts treatment decisional abilities in mild to moderate dementia. *Neurology, 66,* 1367–1372.

Hornung, C. A., Eleazer, G. P., Strothers, H. S., Wieland, G. D., Eng, C., McCann, R., et al. (1998). Ethnicity and decision-makers in a group of frail older people. *Journal of the American Geriatrics Society, 46,* 280–286.

Karel, M. J., Moye, J., Bank, A., & Azar, A. R. (2007). Three methods of assessing values for advance care planning: Comparing persons with and without dementia. *Journal of Aging and Health, 19,* 123–151.

Kim, S. Y. H., Karlawish, J. H. T., & Caine, E. D. (2002). Current state of research on decision-making competence of cognitively impaired elderly persons. *American Journal of Geriatric Psychiatry, 10,* 151–165.

Marson, D. C., Chatterjee, A., Ingram, K. K., & Harrell, L. E. (1996). Toward a neurologic model of competency: Cognitive predictors of capacity to consent in Alzheimer's disease using three different legal standards. *Neurology, 46,* 666–672.

McAvay, G. J., Van Ness, P. H., Bogardus, S. T., Zhang, Y., Leslie, D. L., Leo-Summers, L. S., et al. (2006). Older adults discharged from the hospital with delirium: 1-year outcomes. *Journal of the American Geriatrics Society, 54,* 1245–1250.

Moye, J., & Marson, D. C. (2007). Assessment of decision making capacity in older adults: An emerging area of research and practice. *Journal of Gerontology, 62,* P3–P11.

National Conference of Commissioners on Uniform State Laws. (1997). *Uniform Guardianship and Protective Proceedings Act.* Retrieved December 29, 2006, from www.law.upenn.edu/bll/ulc/fnact99/1990s/ugppa97.htm.

Ruchinskas, R. A. (2005). Risk assessment as an integral aspect of capacity evaluations. *Rehabilitation Psychology, 50,* 197–200.

Sabatino, C. P. (1996). Competency: Refining our legal fictions. In M. Smyer, K. W. Schaie, & M. B. Kapp (Eds.), *Older adults decision making and the law* (pp. 1–28). New York: Springer.

Sabatino, C. P., & Basinger, S. L. (2000). Competency: Reforming our legal fictions. *Journal of Mental Health and Aging, 6,* 119–143.

Scogin, F., & Perry, J. (1987). Guardianship proceedings with older adults: The role of functional assessment and gerontologists. *Law and Psychology Review, 10,* 123–128.

9

The Role of Neuropsychological Assessment in Capacity Evaluations

STACEY WOOD

A thorough neuropsychological evaluation can play a critical role as part of a capacity evaluation. Neuropsychologists can provide domain specific information and diagnostic information that can be helpful to judges in consideration of limited as well as full guardianships. The language of neuropsychology is not part of the legal lexicon, which puts the onus on psychologists to understand how to translate these findings to be maximally useful to attorneys and judges. This chapter describes how neuropsychological constructs relate to legal constructs, a typical forensic neuropsychological evaluation, special issues that arise with neuropsychological evaluations of capacity, and some limitations for use of neuropsychological data. The goal of this chapter is to describe the role of neuropsychological reports in a forensic setting rather than as a guide for test selection and administration.

✍ Case Example: Aphasia

The client, a 72-year-old gentleman, suffered a left middle cerebral artery stroke resulting in language impairment 1 year ago. Apparently

6 months after the stroke, the client changed his will and advanced directives to favor his partner of 4 years versus his two adult children. The adult children are arguing that the client did not have the capacity to make those changes and that the new will and directives are not valid. According to available medical records, the client was very active and engaged with a sizable estate prior to his injury. Previous documentation noted his preference for his adult children to be named as guardians, if the need should arise. Additionally, there is a history of tension between the two adult children and his live-in partner. Since the stroke, that tension has worsened because the client's adult children and the partner differ in their opinions regarding the best treatment for the client. Currently, the domestic partner is acting as guardian.

The author was called in to assist with the case by the attorney for the adult children. A neuropsychological perspective could be useful in this type of case for a number of reasons. First, a neuropsychologist should have knowledge of different types of language disturbances and should be able to perform a detailed assessment of current language functioning. Because the neuropsychologist is being asked to make a retrospective determination of capacity, it is critical to have knowledge of the course of aphasia. Finally, the assessment should be able to identify potentially important dissociations, for example, the client may not be able to speak well but can comprehend language.

The evaluation revealed that the client primarily had expressive aphasia with some comprehension of written and spoken material. The client could understand 3 to 4 word phrases. It was not possible for him to understand written documents with phrases longer than 3 to 4 words. Because this type of aphasia is stable at 6 months, current presentation is a good indicator of the client's functioning for the past year. Further, a record review from rehabilitation being done at 6 months post injury noted a similar pattern of strengths and weaknesses. Using photographs and simple queries, we were able to assess current preferences. The client consistently expressed his desire for his adult children to be awarded guardianship. The judge determined that the client did not have testamentary capacity 6 months post injury and that he was also unable to make complex medical and financial decisions. Thus, the client's earlier will became activated.

In this type of case, one might question the ethics of the attorney who drafted the new will and directives. However, the mistake is understandable. The client had excellent social skills and was able to use gestures and his limited speech to communicate. Further, the new attorney did not have any prior history with the client on which to base his judgment. In summary, without training and experience with aphasic patients, it could be difficult to draw definitive conclusions regarding a client's decisional abilities during a routine office visit with an attorney. Thus, when a question of a language disorder arises, an attorney should seek consultation with a professional with experience and training in cognitive impairment in the elderly.

HOW NEUROPSYCHOLOGICAL CONSTRUCTS RELATE TO LEGAL CONSTRUCTS

While legal definitions of capacity vary widely from state to state, a model law—the Uniform Guardianship and Protective Proceedings Act (UGPPA)—was developed by the National Conference of Commissioners on Uniform State Laws (NCCUSL) in 1997. The UGPPA emphasizes that a person may need help in some area but not others, by defining an incapacitated person as one who is "unable to receive and evaluate information or make or communicate decisions to such an extent that the individual lacks the ability to meet essential requirements for physical health, safety or self-care, even with appropriate technological assistance" (§5-102). This definition incorporates a number of standards or tests for incapacity: a cognitive component, a functional component, and a necessity or risk component (Moye, Mlinac, Wood, Wood, & Edelstein, 2006; Sabatino & Basinger, 2000). The UGPPA also seeks to increase due process protections in many ways, including encouraging a comprehensive examination of the alleged incapacitated individual by "a physician, psychologist, or other individual appointed by the court who is qualified to evaluate the respondent's alleged impairment" (§5-306). Neuropsychological assessments are most useful in addressing the cognitive aspects of the code. But we should note, the standard does not have a pure cognitive requirement, but rather, requires that the cognitive component have some type of functional impairment that can not be eliminated with assistive technologies.

A number of papers have examined how neuropsychological constructs predict performance on treatment-capacity specific instruments such as the capacity to consent for treatment (Gurrera, Moye, Karel, Azar, & Arnesto, 2006; Marson, Ingram, Cody, & Harrell, 1995; Moye, Karel, Azar, & Gurrera, 2004). From a legal perspective, the ability to make treatment decisions requires understanding (comprehension of relevant information), appreciation (the ability to integrate relevant information with one's current situation), reasoning (the ability to rationally weigh pros and cons in light of potential consequences) and expressing a choice (the ability to communicate the decision; Moye et al., 2004). Neuropsychological performance has been found to be a significant predictor of all four measures in mild to moderate community-dwelling dementia patients of diverse etiologies (Gurrera et al., 2006).

However, it should be noted that the amount of variance in capacity assessment accounted for by neuropsychological measures varies widely. Neuropsychological performances accounted for 78% of the variance in measures that predicted understanding, including those that assessed verbal retrieval, problem solving, and general knowledge and motivation, with verbal retrieval as the strongest predictor. Neuropsychological performance accounted for 39.4% of the variance for appreciation, which drew on all of the neuropsychological domains. Reasoning was significantly predicted by neuropsychological performance (24.6% of the variance) and drew most strongly on verbal retrieval with smaller but significant relationships to general knowledge, motivation, and problem solving. Expressing a choice demonstrated the smallest relationship to neuropsychological performance (10.2% of the variance) and was not significantly correlated with specific neuropsychological domains. Expressing a choice has consistently demonstrated a smaller relationship with neuropsychological assessment tools, which implies that even moderately demented individuals who are unable to meet the core standards of understanding, appreciation, or reasoning regarding their medical decisions, may very well be able to express a choice regarding other types of decisions (Gurrera et al., 2006).

In summary, the relationship between neuropsychological measures and legal constructs used to define decisional capacity is complex and dependent on the standard of interest and the population being examined. Unfortunately, there is no such thing as a capacimeter—a gold standard tool—that can be used in all cases. However, because consistent relationships have been demonstrated between verbal retrieval, executive functioning, general knowledge, working memory, calculation abilities, and these legal constructs; a battery that includes these types of measures will be most helpful in the majority of cases (Martin et al., 2003; Moye et al., 2004). Neuropsychological tools need to be augmented with more functional tools to more completely capture the legal constructs underlying capacity.

NEUROPSYCHOLOGY IN CAPACITY ASSESSMENTS

Given that there are, at best, moderate relationships between specific neuropsychological constructs and legal standards thought to underlie decision making, you might ask what other contributions neuropsychological approaches can offer in these types of cases. Neuropsychological data can be put forth as part of the clinical evidence to specifically address a number of issues to help the court, including patterns of cognitive strengths and weaknesses, diagnostic information, consideration of assistive technologies, and prognosis.

One of the primary goals of a neuropsychological evaluation is to describe at a behavioral level a pattern of strengths and weaknesses. For example, a client may have impairment in verbal learning but have intact executive functioning and reasoning. This type of information can allow the courts to craft more specific and limited orders where appropriate. In this example, the client may need assistance with decisions that rely on memory (i.e., calling to mind past financial decisions) but be able to participate in end-of life decision making that is based on a value system.

Diagnostic information should also be obtained from a neuropsychological evaluation. The diagnosis allows for an examination of the course and prognosis of the disorder. Dementia, delirium, and depression all cause cognitive impairment that may impair decision making. However, in court it would be useful for the judge to know that there is the possibility of change that might warrant a temporary guardianship. Or conversely, when the client has a progressive disorder, the evaluation may result in a report that recommends at present a limited guardianship with the possibility of a reevaluation in a year. Diagnostic information allows for the client and his or her family to plan for the future. For example, a person in the earliest stages of dementia may be able to make many decisions but will not be able to do so in the future. Finally, if a potentially reversible cause (delirium) is identified and it is possible that the client may fully recover, then a temporary guardianship is what is most appropriate.

By the end of the evaluation, the neuropsychologist will have determined a pattern of strengths and weaknesses and diagnostic information that allows recommendations to be tailored to specific types of decision making. For example, the report may note that while memory for verbal material is impaired, memory for visual information and planning are intact.

This type of specificity can result in recommendations by a neuropsychologist that are tailored to the referral question. For example, a client may have a pattern of strengths and weaknesses that allows him to make a decision to marry (a much lower capacity standard) but one that suggests that he does not meet the standard for testamentary capacity (a higher standard). In Colorado, for example, the probate code specifically asks if there are compensations that can be made to maximize decisional abilities. The neuropsychologist's report can be used to identify potential areas that would benefit from compensation, like hearing aids or increased social support, which could lead a judge to order a more limited guardianship once those aids are in place.

A TYPICAL FORENSIC NEUROPSYCHOLOGICAL EVALUATION

In the past, physicians performed most capacity evaluations, and this practice continues to be true to some extent depending on how states define admissible evidence (Moye, 1999; Moye et al., 2006; Moye, Karel, et al., 2006). However, states with more progressive codes regularly admit and seek evidence from psychologists and neuropsychologists, in part, because of a growing appreciation of standardized assessments and also because of increased appreciation of nonphysicians' contributions (Moye, 1999).

A neuropsychologist's evaluation of capacity involves a similar overall approach to clinical cases with some important modifications. First and foremost, capacity is a legal determination made in the courtroom, and a neuropsychologist's conclusions are not binding on the court (Camp, Clayton, Epstein, & Horton, 2001; Grisso, 1994). A neuropsychologist is, thus, asked to provide clinical evidence that can be introduced to assist with the forensic issue at hand. Following a clinical model developed by Moye (1999; Moye, Chapter 8, this volume), a neuropsychological assessment of capacity includes a more extensive preassessment phase, client and collateral interviews, a typical neuropsychological battery that includes measures of verbal retrieval, language, executive functioning and reasoning, and a functional assessment.

As part of the preassessment, the neuropsychologist's first step is to determine the specific capacities in question because they may have different legal standards, which could influence recommendations. For example, an assessment of testamentary capacity is typically defined as something similar to the following California language: To determine whether or not a client has the ability to understand the nature of the testamentary act, understand and recollect the nature and situation of his or her property, and remember and understand his or her relationship to heirs (Camp et al., 2001). In contrast, the ability to consent to medical treatment requires the assessment of understanding, appreciation, reasoning, and expressing a choice. Ideally, the neuropsychologist knows the case law or statutory definitions for the specific type of capacity being assessed for the relevant jurisdiction. Next, during the pre-assessment phase, the clinician should determine if a less restrictive option might be appropriate, such as the use of a health-care proxy. In some cases, family systems issues may be driving the process toward guardianship, and mediation may be the best option. In summary, it is worthwhile to take additional time to do a preassessment of the case to understand the question being asked by the court and to evaluate less restrictive alternatives.

Next, in addition to client interviews, a forensic neuropsychological evaluation encompasses a number of collateral interviews that may include family members, caseworkers, attorneys, and law enforcement personnel depending on the referral question. These interviews provide a history of cognitive and functional abilities and assist in ascertaining the course of the alleged cognitive impairment. Forensic evaluations often require extensive record reviews including legal records, medical records, and psychological records depending on the case. Because of the additional research involved, forensic neuropsychological evaluations are often more time consuming than nonforensic clinical assessments.

SPECIAL ISSUES IN NEUROPSYCHOLOGY EVALUATIONS OF CAPACITY

There are certain types of capacity issues where a neuropsychological approach can be especially helpful. One set of issues involves cognitive impairment that is rather subtle to causal investigation. These *silent impairments* may be missed in an office visit with an attorney or physician and include pathology related to frontal lobe functioning, perceptual disorders, and to some degree, aphasia.

Research on capacity judgments conducted by experts has found that, as a group, physicians tend to overweigh memory disturbances and underweigh executive functioning impairments when making judgments regarding capacity (Marson, Earnst, Jamil, Bartolucci, & Harrell, 2000). However, the ability to plan, initiate, generate and weigh options, and respond flexibly to feedback is critical for good decision making. Neuropsychological assessment performed across domains with an emphasis on executive functioning can be very helpful in getting a clear picture of a client's true strengths and potential weaknesses. What can be particularly challenging with clients who have a focal frontal injury is that they may be able to articulate a reasonable plan but not be able to execute it. Then, during an interview situation, the client is able to express a reasonable plan and might be deemed competent. In every situation, it is important to look at discrepancies from the client's personal life between a his or her stated plan and real-world behavior.

For example, I was working with a client who complained of having difficulty paying her bills on time and feeling stress related to this difficulty. On interview, she presented as bright, warm, and articulate. She was able to talk at length about current events and state the importance of organizing bills and paying them on time. She was truly puzzled as to how her life had become so disorganized. Neuropsychological testing revealed a focal impairment with executive functioning, but otherwise she was high functioning. Neuroimaging revealed a small, bifrontal vascular injury. A functional assessment including a home visit revealed an extremely disorganized home with papers and clothing stacked everywhere. The apartment had reached a level of untidiness that in combination with consistently late rent payments resulted in an eviction. Yet, the client did not know where to start to clean up her current situation and find a new place to live. In this case, the silent frontal impairment resulted in poor decision making. Fortunately, the client's daughter was willing to step in and assist her mother with planning. She hired a housekeeper and a moving company and was able to avoid the necessity of a conservator.

Disorders of visuospatial perception, such as visual neglect or an inability to accurately copy a simple figure, may impair a client's ability to balance a checkbook, do simple calculations, or drive a car but are not necessarily apparent during an interview. In this situation, a conservator may be necessary to protect funds, and a driving evaluation may be warranted, but the client may still retain his or her ability to express wishes and make reasonable decisions.

As noted in the case example at the beginning of the chapter, individuals with aphasia can range from having near perfect comprehension to significantly impaired comprehension that can only be determined through a painstaking assessment of speech. Dissociations in terms of a client's ability to read or write may also exist. In my clinical experience, I have found that lay individuals tend to overestimate how much a person with a receptive aphasia can understand and underestimate how much a person with expressive aphasia can understand.

In summary, some cognitive disorders that can impact decision-making abilities may be difficult to detect based on a casual office interview. When working with older adults in such a setting, there are a number of warning signs that should trigger a consideration of a more formal cognitive functioning assessment. These include changes in communication style, difficulties with comprehension, problems with basic calculation at odds with clients' educational history, and lack of mental flexibility (American Bar Association Commission on Law and Aging and American Psychological Association, 2005).

A second category of special issues consists of retrospective determinations. In general, caution is warranted when asked to make a determination regarding client's decisions made in the past. Under certain circumstances, a neuropsychological approach can be useful in successfully and ethically completing such an assessment. Circumstances that improve the validity of a retrospective assessment include documentation of cognitive functioning at the time of the decision in question and a current in-person interview and assessment that allows a diagnosis to be made. Medical records from the time of the legal decision in question may contain evidence relevant to cognitive functioning. The current evaluation and diagnosis can help shed light on course and etiology. For example, if a client has a diagnosis of moderate Alzheimer's disease, it may be possible to make a definitive statement regarding their memory in the past year. However, if the client suffers from a more dynamic process like delirium, such a statement would be difficult to make. Finally, some disorders such as trauma can improve with time (at least for the first 6 months to a year) so that you could accurately predict that the client's posttraumatic cognitive abilities were likely more impaired than current performance.

SELECTING A CLINICIAN AND EVALUATING A REPORT

The optimal clinician combines clinical practice standards with an understanding of the law and cognitive disorders of the elderly. In some settings, this may be a psychologist with a title of neuropsychologist or it may be a clinical geropsychologist with extensive assessment experience. Regardless of the title of the clinician, a complete clinical report includes information regarding diagnosis, cognitive functioning, and behavioral functioning. Competent reports should take this information one step further and integrate them with the specifics of the case in question including the context of the person's life and the relevant legal standards. It is not appropriate to submit a report that is simply a summary of test scores without an integration of functional abilities and relevant legal issues (American Bar Association Commission on Law and Aging and American Psychological Association, 2005).

LIMITATIONS FOR THE USE OF NEUROPSYCHOLOGICAL DATA

As helpful as a neuropsychological approach may be in terms of determining capacity, there are some limitations and caveats to consider. To begin, clinicians trained in different approaches may use different terms to convey information regarding performance. For example, one neuropsychologist may use the term *impairment* to indicate a performance below expectation, whereas another professional might use the term only when performance is below the second percentile (Spreen & Strauss, 1998). To facilitate the interpretation of this data, it is best to examine the percentile scores themselves to make apples to apples comparisons between reports. The difference between decline and impairment offers a related clarification. A high-functioning person may experience a decline and still be scoring above the 50th percentile. Above average scores would not be considered impaired when comparing an individual's performance to age-matched peers, yet the individual may be experiencing significant change in functional abilities. For the assessment of capacity, the difference between a decline from baseline and impairment is a critical piece of evidence. The uniform probate code does not ask if the individual is performing at their optimal level, but rather that they meet basic requirements to receive and evaluate information, and to make and communicate their choices. It may be that a client has shown significant decline from a clinical perspective, but remains able to meet the legal standards for capacity. In these cases, it is important to note changes and perhaps suggest a reevaluation in the case of a progressive disorder.

The utility of neuropsychological assessment results may be limited based on the timing of the evaluation. For example, if the client is experiencing a medical crisis or is medically unstable in any way, the conclusions of the evaluation should be time limited. It may be necessary to conduct an evaluation during the throes of a medical emergency, but the report should clearly note that performance may likely change when the client is stable and explicitly recommend reevaluation at a specified time in the future.

Conclusions based solely on the paper and pencil neuropsychological tests are also limited. As reviewed earlier in this chapter, neuropsychological tests do not map directly on to legal constructs. Further, the assessment of capacity has both a cognitive piece and a functional piece (see Chapters 10 and 11 this volume). It is quite possible that two individuals with similar neuropsychological profiles may be given different determinations in a capacity hearing depending on their level of support at home and ability to compensate for their deficits. A functional assessment is a critical component when making these determinations. A forensic report should integrate the clinical data with the functional data and the case particulars.

Finally, conclusions made on the basis of screening tools such as the Folstein Mini Mental State Examination (MMSE) should be regarded as preliminary evidence. A recent review of guardianship outcomes in Colorado found that in approximately 20% of cases, screening tools served as the primary clinical evidence in civil capacity hearings (Moye, Mlinac, et al., 2006). However, the MMSE loads heavily on memory items but has little utility in capturing changes in executive functioning (Spreen & Strauss, 1998). Screening tools may be useful in getting a sense of a client's overall level of functioning but cannot provide the diagnostic or functional piece of evidence that should accompany all capacity evaluations.

CONCLUSION

Neuropsychological data, that includes a functional assessment and integration with an understanding of the legal standards relevant to the case and the context of the client's life, can play a key role as part of the clinical evidence produced in capacity hearings. Neuropsychologists can provide domain specific information regarding patterns of cognitive and behavioral strengths and weaknesses, diagnosis, and prognosis that can help the court to craft limited orders when appropriate.

REFERENCES

American Bar Association Commission on Law and Aging and American Psychological Association. (2005). *Assessment of older adults with diminished capacity: A handbook for lawyers.* Washington, DC: Author.

Camp, P., Clayton, V., Epstein, B., & Horton, N. F. (2001). Capacity and undue influence: Assessing, challenging, and defending. *Cal CEB Action Guide,* 1–82.

Grisso, T. (1994). Clinical assessment for legal competence of older adults. In M. Storandt & G. R. Vanderbos (Eds.), *Neuropsychological assessment of dementia and depression in older adults: A clinician's guide* (pp. 119–139). Washington, DC: American Psychological Association.

Gurrera, R. J., Moye, J., Karel, M. J., Azar, A. R., & Armesto, J. C. (2006). Cognitive performance predicts treatment decisional abilities in mild to moderate dementia. *Neurology, 66,* 1367–1372.

Marson, D. C., Earnst, K. S., Jamil, F., Bartolucci, A., & Harrell, L. E. (2000). Physician assessment of patient competence. *Journal of the American Geriatrics Society, 48*, 911–918.

Marson, D. C., Ingram, K. K., Cody, H. A., & Harrell, L. E. (1995). Assessing the competency of patients with Alzheimer's disease under different legal standards: A prototype instrument. *Archives of Neurology, 52*, 949–954.

Martin, R. C., Annis, S. M., Darling, L., Wadley, V., Harrell, L., & Marson, D. (2003). Loss of calculation abilities in patients with mild to moderate Alzheimer's disease. *Archives of Neurology, 60*(11), 1585–1589.

Moye, J. (1999). Assessment of competency and decision making capacity. In P. A. Lichtenberg (Ed.), *Handbook of assessment in clinical gerontology* (pp. 488–528). New York: Wiley.

Moye, J., Karel, M., Azar, A., & Gurrera, R. (2004). Capacity to consent to treatment: Empirical comparison of three instruments in older adults with and without dementia. *Gerontologist, 44*(2), 166–175.

Moye, J., Karel, M., Azar, A., & Gurrera, R. (2006). Neuropsychological predictors of decision-making capacity over 9 months in mild-to-moderate dementia. *Journal of General Internal Medicine, 21*, 78–83.

Moye, J., Mlinac, M., Wood, E., Wood, S., & Edelstein, B. (2006). Challenges in guardianship of older adults: Results of a tri-state study. *Journal of the National College of Probate Judges, 3*(2).

National Conference of Commissioners on Uniform State Laws. (1997). *Uniform Guardianship and Protective Proceedings Act.* Available from www.law .upenn.edu/bll/ulc/fnact99/1990s/ugppa97.htm.

Sabatino, C., & Basinger, S. (2000). Competency: Reforming our legal fictions. *Journal of Mental Health and Aging, 6*, 119–144.

Spreen, O., & Strauss, E. (1998). *A compendium of neuropsychological tests: Administration, norms, and commentary* (2nd ed.). New York: Oxford University Press.

CHAPTER

10

Assessment of Medical Consent Capacity and Independent Living

JENNIFER MOYE AND MICHELLE BRAUN

In this chapter, we discuss functional assessment within two domains: medical consent capacity and independent living. A third common area of functional assessment in capacity evaluation concerns financial capacities, which is discussed in Chapter 11 of this volume.

Building on the model for general clinical assessment presented in Chapter 8, this chapter focuses on the third component in the assessment process, which is the functional assessment. We also discuss some aspects of values assessment that are relevant to these functional domains. Medical consent capacity and independent living are two quite different domains of assessment. Medical consent capacity is very narrow—in practice it often involves evaluating the adequacy of the decisional process concerning a specific medical decision. It is largely a cognitive task. In contrast, independent living is a broad domain. As described by T. Grisso (1986), "the abilities are so broad that they seem to encompass almost all of the functions and skills that we employ in our adaptations to everyday life." Because these are such disparate capacity areas, we approach each in turn. For each area we address the legal basis, substitute judgment mechanisms, psychological aspects, and then discuss some specific tools and approaches for assessment.

KEY CONCEPTS

We use the term *capacity* to refer to a dichotomous (yes/no) judgment by a clinician as to whether an individual can do the task in question—make an autonomous treatment decision or live independently. In most health-care settings, questions of capacity rarely proceed to adjudication. In the medical consent area, adjudication occurs when treatment requiring judicial authorization within the jurisdiction is involved or the case is otherwise being litigated (e.g., family conflict). In the independent living area, most concerns regarding diminished capacity are managed through multiple social service, family, and medical interventions. When these are not working, not available, or other issues of risk or conflict arise, guardianship may be pursued. In this chapter, we refer to judicial determinations of capacity as *competency*.

Clinicians involved in capacity assessments should be familiar with the relevant laws in their states, including guardianship, power of attorney, and surrogate consent statutes. These are catalogued on the American Bar Association Commission on Law and Aging Web site under "legislative updates" at www.abanet.org/aging/legislativeupdates/home.shtml. Clinicians will also find useful legal educational tools regarding law and aging at this Web site.

MEDICAL CONSENT CAPACITY

Capacity from a Legal Perspective

Legal standards for medical consent capacity may include state-specific statutes on surrogate health-care decision making and/or case law standards for determining medical consent capacity. Less restrictive alternatives to guardianship, such as advance directives, durable power of attorney, and local medical center policies, such as the role of the ethics' committee or medical center director in situations of patient incapacity, are important considerations.

Incapacity as Defined in Surrogate Health-Care Decision-Making Statutes

Statutes in every state provide for surrogate health-care decision making for those individuals lacking the capacity to provide informed consent for treatment. Forty-seven states and the District of Columbia have living will laws allowing a person to make a written statement spelling out instructions about treatment or withholding or withdrawing treatment in the event of a terminal or end-stage condition or permanent unconsciousness. All 50 states and the District of Columbia have health-care power of attorney statutes (also referred to as medical power of attorney or health-care proxy) allowing an individual to appoint an agent to make health-care decisions in the event of incapacity. Some state statutes, as well as the Uniform Health-Care Decisions Act (National Conference of Commissioners on Uniform State Laws, 1993), have combined living wills and health-care powers of attorney into a comprehensive advance directive act. In addition, over 35 states and the District of Columbia have enacted statutes specifically authorizing default surrogate consent, generally by a hierarchy of family members. The Uniform Health-Care Decisions Act also provides for default surrogates (Karp & Wood, 2003).

In all of these statutes, surrogate health-care decision-making authority is triggered by a patient's lack of capacity to give informed consent for treatment. The Uniform Health-Care Decisions Act defines capacity as "the ability to understand significant benefits, risks, and alternatives to proposed health care and to make and communicate a health-care decision" (§1(3)). Various state definitions of incapacity under health-care power of attorney statutes or living will statutes provide definitions of incapacity similar to the Uniform Health-Care Decisions Act. For example, in Kentucky, capacity is defined as the ability to make and communicate a health-care decision. In Massachusetts, capacity is defined as the ability to understand and appreciate the nature and consequences of health-care decisions, including the benefits and risks of, and alternatives to, any proposed health care, to reach an informed decision. In Nebraska, an incapacitated person is defined as having an inability to understand and appreciate the nature and consequences of health-care decisions, including the benefits of, risks of, and alternatives to, any proposed health care, or the inability to communicate an informed health-care decision in any manner. Florida more succinctly defines a patient with incapacity for informed consent for health care as one who is physically or mentally unable to communicate a willful and knowing health-care decision. Other states refer to the capacity standard delineated in the adult guardianship law for the state. State-by-state citations for living will and health-care power of attorney statutes can be found on the American Bar Association (ABA) web site (www.abanet.org/aging/).

Case Law Standards for Capacity to Consent

Four standards for incapacity can be found in case law, used either individually or conjointly as a so-called "compound standard" (Appelbaum & Grisso, 1988; Drane, 1985; Roth, Meisel, & Lidz, 1977; Tepper & Elwork, 1984).

Expressing a Choice

Uncommunicative patients who cannot convey a treatment choice are seen to lack capacity. However, simply evidencing a choice does not, by itself, indicate capacity. While some degree of vacillation or ambivalence is normal, patients must be able to convey a relatively consistent treatment *choice*.

Understanding

The ability to comprehend diagnostic and treatment-related information has been recognized in many states as fundamental to capacity. *Understanding* includes the ability to remember and comprehend newly presented words, concepts, and phrases, and to demonstrate comprehension by paraphrasing diagnostic and treatment information.

Appreciation

An *appreciation* standard of capacity is the ability to relate treatment information to your own situation especially the nature of your diagnosis and the possibility that treatment would be beneficial (Grisso & Applebaum, 1998a). Thus, understanding emphasizes comprehension, while appreciation focuses on evaluation of understood information in terms of personal relevance and beliefs. Disavowal of the diagnosis or potential treatment benefit may signify a deficit in reality testing (e.g., delusional disorder) or neurologic dysfunction (e.g., anosognosia).

Reasoning

Many states have cited the ability to state rational explanations, or to process information in a logically or rationally consistent manner, as a key element of capacity. *Reasoning* has been defined as the ability to evaluate treatment alternatives by integrating, analyzing, and processing information to compare it in light of potential consequences and their likely impact on everyday life.

Substitute Judgment Mechanisms and Less Restrictive Alternatives to Guardianship

Several options are available when individuals lack the capacity to make medical decisions. First, if there is a previously appointed health-care proxy or other legally authorized decision maker in the state (such as a durable power of attorney for health care), the proxy's authority generally springs into effect on a clinical finding of incapacity. If there is no previously appointed health-care proxy, most state statutes or hospital policies allow for decisions by next of kin, and stipulate the order in which such kin may be approached (e.g., spouse, parent, child, sibling). In some cases, where there is no previously appointed health-care proxy or next of kin, hospital policies allow the treatment decision to be made by the hospital ethics committee or the hospital medical director, presuming it is not legally contraindicated. In conflictual situations or cases of extraordinary medical intervention, a guardian may be sought.

Limitations on Proxy Authority

Most states limit the authority of guardians and health-care proxies/durable powers of attorney to consent to treatment. Common limitations include the authority to make decisions concerning commitment for mental health treatment, abortion, sterilization, psychotropic medication, amputation, and electroconvulsive therapy (ECT; Richardson,

2003). Typically, these treatments require review by courts or ethics committees.

Psychological Perspective of the Task

In medical consent capacity the functional task is largely cognitive. The decisional abilities to be assessed closely map to the four case law standards previously presented—expressing a choice, understanding, appreciation, and reasoning. In applying these standards, clinicians must consider the situation and the decision at hand, and more important, how diagnostic and treatment information is relayed to the patient.

Situation Specificity

The assessment of consent capacity is situation specific. That is, an individual's capacity may vary depending on the difficulty and complexity of a medical decision. An individual with neurocognitive compromise may have diminished capacity to consent to a complex medical intervention but may retain the capacity to consent to a relatively simple medical treatment. As such, consent capacity must be evaluated for each specific informed consent situation. However, in practice, particularly in activation of proxy authority, families and clinicians may find it useful to know whether an individual has the capacity to make a current treatment decision and subsequent decisions of similar complexity. Similarly, in writing guardianship orders, especially if crafting a limited order, a judge may want information relative to an individual's capacities within key decisional domains, so that the judge can articulate those decisions for which the patient retains decisional autonomy and authority.

Decisional Complexity

The question about exactly how much information must be disclosed to the patient and how much information the patient must comprehend for adequate capacity remains unresolved. Clinicians are obligated to present information in such a way as to maximize understanding in light of an individual's level of education, language ability, and medical sophistication. Normative studies of consent comprehension provide some guidance (Park, Morrel, & Shifren, 1999), and interestingly, reveal that healthy, unimpaired adults remember and comprehend far less information than may be assumed. Further, it remains unclear to what extent understanding forms the basis for subsequent appreciation and reasoning. If an individual cannot attend to, encode, and comprehend basic information about a treatment, to what extent can he or she be expected to appreciate its significance or reason about related risks and benefits? Alternatively, one study suggests that understanding, appreciation, and reasoning do not form a hierarchical model (Grisso & Appelbaum, 1995), and from a case law perspective, these decisional abilities can be considered separately—that is, a person may lack capacity due to a failure in any one of the decisional abilities.

Disclosing Treatment Information

Clinicians are obligated to disclose information about the nature of the procedure, risks, benefits, and treatment alternatives. However, little is written about how information disclosure may impact the latter assessment of consent capacity. Disclosure formats that are more structured, organized, uniform, and brief serve to improve understanding of diagnostic and treatment information, as do simplified and illustrated guides (Dunn & Jeste, 2001). Not surprisingly, informed consent performance was improved when consent forms were left available for subsequent reference (Taub, Baker, Kline, & Sturr, 1987). These findings are supported by cognitive aging research that finds that environmental aids (e.g., cues for the retrieval of relevant information) reduce demands on cognitive resources serving working memory. In contrast, tasks that require effortful processing without such supports are more likely to reveal age-related impaired performance (Craik, 1994; Craik & Byrd, 1982; Craik & Jennings, 1992).

Furthermore, health-care decisions are influenced by the manner in which risks are framed. McNeil and colleagues (McNeil, Pauker, Sox, & Tversky, 1982) showed that participants who learned that 10% of patients die from surgery and 0% die from radiation were less likely to choose surgery compared to those who were presented with information that 100% of patients immediately survive radiation and 90% immediately survive surgery. Thus, participants are most likely to choose the more positively framed outcome, despite identical outcome probabilities.

This effect has been demonstrated in a wide range of populations (Kuhberger, 1998), including older adults asked to make medical decisions regarding life-threatening (Mazur & Merz, 1993) and less threatening outcomes (McKee, 2001).

Empirical Work

Capacity to consent to treatment in older populations is the most extensively researched of any of the civil capacities, although the overall number of studies is still small. Within these studies, findings are limited by small samples, minimal replication, and in many cases, an absence of control groups.

Together, the studies have found agreement between impairment as measured on standardized capacity measures and neuropsychological measures (Dymek, Atchison, Harrell, & Marson, 2001; Gurrera, Moye, Karel, Azar, & Armesto, 2006; Marson, Chatterjee, Ingram, & Harrell, 1996); although there are too few studies to state with confidence the exact relationships between legal standards for consent capacity and specific underlying cognitive abilities. Understanding is often strongly associated with verbal retrieval. Perhaps prevailing methods of assessing understanding should go beyond reliance on verbal retrieval and provide cues and supports to maximize comprehension and minimize memory demands (Dunn & Jeste, 2001). Appreciation and reasoning appear to rely on both memory and executive functions.

There is limited agreement between evaluations by multiple clinicians, multiple measures, or between a clinician and a measure, especially for the standards of appreciation and reasoning (Bean, Nishisato, Rector, & Glancy, 1996; Carney, Neugroschl, Morrison, Marin, & Siu, 2001; Etchells et al., 1999; Fitten, Lusky, & Hamann, 1990; Gurrera, Karel, Azar, & Moye, 2007; Marson, McInturff, Hawkins, Bartolucci, & Harrell, 1997; Moye, Karel, Azar, & Gurrera, 2004b). Together, these studies find general agreement on the legal standards important for consent capacity, but not uniform agreement on how to assess them.

These studies also find that patients who are hospitalized or in nursing homes tend to demonstrate high rates (44% to 69%) of capacity impairment (Barton, Mallik, Orr, & Janofsky, 1996; Carney et al., 2001; Dellasega, Frank, Smyer, 1996; Fitten & Waite, 1990; Frank, Smyer,

Grisso, & Applebaum, 1999; Pruchno, Smyer, Rose, Hartman-Stein, & Laribee-Henderson, 1995; Royall, Cordes, & Polk, 1997; Staats & Edelstein, 1995; Tymchuk, Ouslander, & Fitten, 1988), although the studies do not detail why or comment on the longitudinal outcome or practical implications of such findings. Some patients with dementia, but not all—especially in early stages—are impaired on consent abilities (Kim, Caine, Currier, Leibovici, & Ryan, 2001; Marson, Ingram, Cody, & Harrell, 1995; Moye, Karel, Azar, & Gurrera, 2004a; Schmand, Gouwenberg, Smit, & Jonker, 1999; Stanley, Stanley, Guido, & Garvin, 1988; Wong, Clare, Holland, Watson, & Gunn, 2000). Loss of capacity over time in dementia is attributable to declining reasoning, and was predicted by earlier problems with naming, verbal memory, and mental flexibility (Moye, Karel, Gurrera, & Azar, 2006). However, there are no studies of older patients with chronic mental illness and already fragile decisional abilities that may deteriorate further in late life. Measurement strategies developed to assess abilities in one patient group may not work as well in other patient groups.

Although newer instruments are available to assess consent capacity, normative data are not yet available (although information on mean performance in control samples is available for many measures), and test-retest reliability is rarely studied. Finally, information on race and ethnicity is provided in only two studies; little is known about the potential relationship of these characteristics to test performance.

Functional Assessment Tools

Most instruments designed to assess consent capacity offer a hypothetical vignette—the patient is asked to demonstrate understanding, appreciation, and reasoning about a hypothetical condition and his or her hypothetical treatment choices. In contrast, some instruments are designed as semi-structured interviews that allow tailoring to the specific consent situation at hand.

Vignette-Based Instruments

Capacity to Consent to Treatment Instrument

The Capacity to Consent to Treatment Instrument (CCTI; Marson et al., 1995) is based on two clinical vignettes, a neoplasm condition and a cardiac condition. Vignettes are presented orally and in writing; participants are then presented questions to assess their decisional abilities in terms of understanding, appreciation, reasoning, and expression of choice. Responses are subjected to detailed scoring criteria.

Competency Interview Schedule

The Competency Interview Schedule (CIS; Bean et al., 1996) is a 15-item interview designed to assess consent capacity for ECT. Patients referred for ECT receive information about their diagnosis and treatment alternatives by the treating clinician, and the CIS assesses decisional abilities based on responses to the 15 items.

Decision Assessment Measure

Working in England, Wong and colleagues (2000) developed a measure that references incapacity criteria in England and Wales (retention, understanding, reasoning, and communicating a choice). A standardized blood-drawing vignette is used.

Hopemont Capacity Assessment Interview

The Hopemont Capacity Assessment Interview (HCAI; Edelstein, 1999) is a medical decision-making component consisting of two clinical vignettes—treatment of an eye infection and administration of cardiopulmonary resuscitation (there are also two vignettes to assess financial capacity). The patient is introduced to general concepts of choice, risk, and benefit, followed by the two scenarios. After discussing the scenarios, patients are asked to recount factual information, explain risks and benefits, state a decision, and explain how the decision was reached.

Thinking Rationally about Treatment

The Thinking Rationally about Treatment (TRAT; Grisso & Appelbaum, 1993) assesses eight functions relevant to decision making and problem solving: information seeking (asking for additional information), consequential thinking (consideration of treatment consequences), comparative thinking (simultaneous processing of information about two treatments), complex thinking (referencing all treatment alternatives), consequence generation (ability to generate real-life consequences of the risks and discomforts described in the treatment alternatives), consequence weighting (consistent rating of activity preferences), transitive thinking (rating relative quantitative relationships), and probabilistic thinking (rating and understanding probabilities of occurrence). These functions are assessed with a hypothetical vignette and follow-up questions. The last three functions are assessed through standardized tests unrelated to the specific vignette.

Understanding Treatment Disclosures

The Understanding Treatment Disclosures (UTD; Grisso & Appelbaum, 1992) has three versions with three different vignettes: schizophrenia, depression, and ischemic heart disease. Information about the disorder and its treatments is presented in either an uninterrupted or elemental (a paragraph at a time) disclosure format. Understanding is assessed through ratings on paraphrased recall and recognition. Of note, the TRAT and UTD are precursor instruments for the MacArthur Competence Assessment Tool—Treatment, described later.

Additional Vignette Assessment Methods

A few studies are based on standardized vignettes and questions that presumably could be replicated by other investigators but do not use specifically named instruments. Research by Schmand et al. (1999) uses a vignette based on work by Sachs, Stocking, and Stern (1994) that describes physical therapy or surgery for a hip fracture. Nine questions approximate an assessment of the four decisional abilities. There is also a standardized vignette for consent to a medication research trial.

Fitten and colleagues (1990) and Fitten and Waite (1990) employ three standardized vignettes: treatment for insomnia, a procedure for diagnosis of pleural effusion, and resuscitation in the context of chronic illness. Follow-up questions address the patient's understanding of the condition, the nature and purpose of the proposed treatments and their risks and benefits, and the quality of the patient's reasoning process.

Structured or Semi-Structured Interviews

Aid to Capacity Evaluation

The Aid to Capacity Evaluation (ACE; Etchells et al., 1999) is a semi-structured assessment interview that addresses seven facets of capacity for an actual medical decision, including the ability to understand: (a) the medical problem; (b) the treatment; (c) the alternatives to treatment; (d) the option of refusing treatment; (e) the ability to perceive consequences of accepting and refusing; (f) treatment; and (g) the ability to make a decision not substantially based on hallucinations, delusions, or depression. These reflect legal standards in Ontario, Canada, but also correspond to U.S. legal standards. Questions in areas a through d assess the decisional ability of understanding. Questions in areas e and f appear to tap reasoning. Area g assesses diminished appreciation based on patently false beliefs (e.g., "Do you think we are trying to harm you?").

Capacity Assessment Tool

The Capacity Assessment Tool (CAT; Carney et al., 2001) proposes to evaluate capacity based on six abilities: (1) communication, (2) understanding choices, (3) comprehension of risks and benefits, (4) insight, (5) decision/choice process, and (6) judgment. A structured interview format is used to assess capacity to choose between two options in an actual treatment situation.

MacArthur Competence Assessment Tool—Treatment

The MacArthur Competence Assessment Tool—Treatment (Mac-CAT-T; Grisso & Appelbaum, 1998b) utilizes a semi-structured interview to guide the clinician through an assessment of understanding, appreciation, reasoning, and expressing a choice. Appreciation is assessed in two sections: whether there is "any reason to doubt" the diagnosis, and whether the treatment "might be of benefit to you." Reasoning is assessed through questions about how patients compare treatment choices and consequences and apply treatment choices to everyday situations.

Perceptions of Disorder

The Perceptions of Disorder (POD; Appelbaum & Grisso, 1992) is one instrument developed along with the TRAT and UTD, which are precursors to the MacCAT-T. The first part, "Non-Acknowledgment of Disorder," presents facts of the patient's actual disorder and then asks patients to rate agreement with those facts as applying to themselves. The second part, "Non-Acknowledgment of Treatment Potential," elicits opinions about whether treatment in general, and medication in particular, might be of some benefit. Low ratings are given when disbelief is based on grossly distorted or delusional premises.

Issues in Values Assessment

As indicated in Chapter 8, consideration of an individual's values, preferences, and perspectives is equally important as an assessment of his or her decision-making abilities. This is because information on values provides key contextual information for the treatment decision and may reveal important information about what is guiding a treatment decision that is not elicited in a more technical consideration of cognitive processing. Some questions regarding values for medical decisions appear in Table 10.1.

INDEPENDENT LIVING CAPACITY

Capacity from a Legal Perspective

The most relevant legal standards for the capacity to live independently relate to incapacity under guardianship. Guardianship is a relationship created by state law in which a court gives one person, the guardian, the duty and power to make personal and/or property decisions for an individual that the court determines to be incapacitated. Guardians are often empowered to make medical decisions on behalf of adults who lack capacity to consent. The Uniform Guardianship and Protective Proceedings Act (National Conference of Commissioners on Uniform State Laws, 1997) defines an incapacitated individual as someone who is unable to receive and evaluate information or make or communicate decisions to the

Table 10.1   Questions for Medical Consent Values Assessment

First, think about what is most important to you in your life. What makes life meaningful or good for you now?

Now, think about what is important to you in relation to your health. What, if any, religious or personal beliefs do you have about sickness, health-care decision making, or dying?

Have you or other people you know faced difficult medical treatment decisions during times of serious illness?

How did you feel about those situations and any choices that were made?

Some people feel a time might come when their life would no longer be worth living. Can you imagine any circumstances in which life would be so unbearable for you that you would **not** want medical treatments used to keep you alive?

If your spokesperson ever had to make a medical decision on your behalf, are there certain people you would want your spokesperson to talk to for advice or support (family members, friends, health-care providers, clergy, other)?

Is there anyone you specifically would **not** want involved in helping to make health-care decisions on your behalf?

How closely would you want your spokesperson to follow your instructions about care decisions, versus do what they think is best for you at the time decisions are made?

Should financial or other family concerns enter into decisions about your medical care? Please explain.

Are there other things you would like your spokesperson to know about you, if he or she were ever in a position to make medical treatment decisions on your behalf?

Source: "Using a Values Discussion Guide to Facilitate Communication in Advance Care Planning," by M. J. Karel, J. Powell, and M. Cantor, 2004, *Patient Education and Counseling, 55,* pp. 22–31.

extent that the individual lacks the ability to meet essential requirements for physical health, safety, or self-care, even with appropriate technological assistance. The 1997 Act adds an emphasis on decision making and de-emphasizes a diagnostic standard. Three states (Colorado, Minnesota, Hawaii) have statutes based on the 1997 Act, while others are based on an earlier 1982 version; still other states have incapacity standards that are particular to statutory evolution within their state.

A useful analysis of incapacity standards in state guardianship law finds that states may include one or more of the following tests or elements to define incapacity: (a) a disease or disorder, (b) cognitive or decisional impairment, (c) functional disabilities (i.e., "inability to care for self"), and (d) exceeds an essential needs threshold such that there is an unacceptable risk to the person or society (Anderer, 1990; Sabatino & Basinger, 2000). These elements are similar to a proposed general model of incapacity articulated by Grisso (2003) described in the conceptual considerations section later in the chapter. State-by-state comparison of incapacity standards for guardianship can be found on the ABA web site (www.abanet.org/aging /legislativeupdates/home.shtml).

Substitute Judgment Mechanisms and Less Restrictive Alternatives to Guardianship

When an older person has diminished capacities to live independently, a myriad of interventions may be used to support the person to remain at home. Guardianship is necessary when a substitute decision maker is required—for example, to provide legally authorized management of finances. In other cases, where there may be a high degree of risk and the individual wants to remain at home, and a guardian is useful as a substitute decision maker empowered to make decisions and arrange services to help the elder remain at home.

This chapter focuses on the assessment of capacity to live independently in those cases where a guardianship is appropriately being pursued. It is worth noting, however, that all less restrictive alternatives should be examined before pursuing guardianship. Table 10.2 presents a useful summary of less restrictive alternatives to guardianship compiled by Joan O'Sullivan, University of Maryland School of Law. Some of the alternatives provide functional assistance, while others are legal tools that provide decisional assistance. Legal tools vary by state and available social services vary by locale.

Table 10.2   Less Restrictive Alternatives to Guardianship

If the Person Needs Medical Treatment, But Is Not Able to Consent

Health-care advance directive
Any written statement a competent individual has made concerning future health-care decisions. The two typical forms of advance directive are the *living will* and the *health-care power of attorney*.

Surrogate decision making by an authorized legal representative, a relative, or a close friend
In many states, the next of kin are authorized to make some or all medical treatment decisions in the absence of a health-care advance directive or appointed guardian.

If the Problem Involves Litigation against or by the Disabled Person

Appointment of guardian ad litem
The court in which litigation is proceeding has authority to appoint a guardian ad litem solely for the purpose of representing the best interests of the individual in the litigation.

If the Problem Involves a Family Dispute

Mediation
Referring a case to mediation before a hearing offers a personal, confidential, and less intimidating setting than the courtroom, as well as an opportunity for exploring underlying issues privately.

If the Person Needs Help with Financial Issues

Bill paying services
Also called *money management services*, these assist persons with diminished capacity through check depositing, check writing, checkbook balancing, bill paying, insurance claim preparation and filing, tax and public benefit preparation, and counseling.

Utility company third party notification
Most utility companies permit customers to designate a third party to be notified by the utility company if bills are not paid on time.

Table 10.2   *(Continued)*

Shared bank accounts (with family member)
The use of joint bank accounts is a common strategy for providing assistance with financial management needs. However, if the joint ownership arrangement reaches most of the individual's income or assets, it also poses risk in its potential for theft, self-dealing, unintended survivorship, and exposure to the joint owner's creditors. A more secure arrangement is a multiple-party account with the family member or friend designated as agent for purposes of access to the account.

Durable power of attorney for finances
This legal tool enables a principal to give legal authority, as broadly or as narrowly as desired, to an agent or attorney to act on behalf of the principal, commencing either on incapacity or commencing immediately and continuing in the event of incapacity. Its creation requires sufficient capacity to understand and establish such an arrangement.

Trusts
Trusts can be established to serve many purposes, but an important one is the lifetime management of property of one who is or who may become incapacitated. They are especially useful where there is a substantial amount of property at stake and professional management is desired. Special or supplemental needs trusts and pooled income trusts are recognized under federal Medicaid and Social Security laws as permissible vehicles for managing the funds of persons with disability who depend on government programs for their care needs.

Representative payee
A person or organization authorized to receive and manage public benefits on behalf of an individual. Social Security, Supplemental Security Income (SSI), veterans' benefits, civil service and railroad pensions, and some state programs provide for appointment of a *rep payee*. Each program has its own statutory authorization and rules for eligibility, implementation, and monitoring.

Adult protective services
The term *protective services* encompasses a broad range of services. It includes various social services voluntarily received by seniors in need of support (e.g., homemaker or chore services, nutrition programs). It also includes interventions for persons who may be abused, neglected, or exploited, and which may lead to some form of guardianship.

(continued)

Table 10.2   *(Continued)*

If the Person Is Living in an Unsafe Environment

Senior shared housing programs
In shared housing programs, several people live together in a *group home* or apartment with shared common areas. *Congregate housing* refers to complexes with separate apartments (including kitchen), some housekeeping services, and some shared meals. Many congregate care facilities are subsidized under federal housing programs. Personal care and health oversight are usually not part of the facility's services, but they may be provided through other community social services.

Adult foster care
Adult foster care is a social service that places an older person, who is in need of a modest amount of daily assistance, into a family home. The program is similar to foster care programs for children. The cost varies and may be covered in part by the state social services program.

Community residential care
These are small supportive housing facilities that provide a room, meals, help with activities of daily living, and protective supervision to individuals who cannot live independently, but who do not need institutional care.

Assisted living
Assisted living facilities provide an apartment, meals, help with activities of daily living, and supervision to individuals who cannot live independently, but who do not need institutional care.

Nursing home
Nursing homes provide skilled nursing care and services for residents who require medical or nursing care; or rehabilitation services for injured, disabled, or sick persons.

Continuing care retirement communities
Also called life-care communities, CCRCs usually require the payment of a large entry fee, plus monthly fees thereafter. The facility may be a single building or a campus with separate independent living, assisted living, and nursing care. Residents move from one housing choice to another as their needs change. While usually very expensive, many guarantee lifetime care with long-term contracts that detail the housing and care obligations, as well as costs.

Table 10.2 *(Continued)*

If the Person Needs Help with Activities of Daily Living or Supervision

Care management
This is provided by a social worker or health-care professional, who evaluates, plans, locates, coordinates, and monitors services for an older person and the family.

Home health services
If the person needs medical care or professional therapy on a part-time or intermittent basis, a *visiting nurse* or *home health aide* from a *home health agency* may meet that need. Some services may be covered by Medicare or Medicaid, private insurance, or state programs.

Home care services
Homemaker or *chore services* can provide help with housework, laundry, ironing, and cooking. *Personal care attendants or personal assistants* may assist an impaired person in performing *activities of daily living*, (i.e., eating, dressing, bathing, toileting, and transferring), or with other activities instrumental to daily functioning.

Adult day care services
These are community-based group programs designed to meet the needs of functionally and/or cognitively impaired adults through an individual plan of care. Health, social, and other related support services are provided in a structured, protective setting, usually during normal business hours. Some programs may offer services in the evenings and on weekends.

Respite care programs
Respite refers to short-term, temporary care provided to people with disabilities so that their families can take a break from the daily routine of caregiving. Services may involve overnight care for some period of time.

Meals on wheels
Volunteers deliver nutritious lunchtime meals to the homes of people who can no longer prepare balanced meals for themselves. The volunteers also provide daily social contact with elders to ensure that everything is okay.

Transportation services
Because many elders cannot afford a special transit service, and are too frail to ride the bus, senior transportation services volunteers drive clients to and from medical, dental, or other necessary appointments, and remain with them throughout the visit.

(continued)

Table 10.2   *(Continued)*

Food and prescription drug deliveries
Either volunteer-based or commercially-based delivery services for food or prescription drugs, may assist those who are unable to leave their home regularly.

Medication reminder systems
This may include a weekly pill organizer box, or another pill distribution system, or telephone reminder calls.

Telephone reassurance programs
These services use volunteer to provide a daily telephone call to older persons living alone.

Emergency call system (lifeline)
Usually includes equipment added to the telephone line, plus a wireless signal button worn by the older adult. Trained responders provide emergency assistance in the event of a medical emergency in the home, such as a fall.

Home visitors and pets on wheels
Elder service agencies and other volunteer agencies may match elders with home visitors, including visiting pets, which provide social interaction and a form of monitoring.

Daily checks on the person by mail carriers
Many mail carriers, if notified that an elder at risk is living at an address, will monitor the home to insure that mail has been picked up daily, and if not, notify a designated individual.

Source: Judicial Determination of Capacity of Older Adults in Guardianship Proceedings: A Handbook for Judges, by the American Bar Association and the American Psychological Association Assessment of Capacity in Older Adults Project Working Group, 2006, Washington, DC: Author. Reprinted with permission of the American Bar Association and the American Psychological Association.

Psychological Perspective of the Task

Everyday functions have been divided into two categories: activities of daily living (ADLs) and instrumental activities of daily living (IADLs). Psychology professionals generally agree that dressing, eating, toileting, transferring or moving from one sitting position to another, walking or mobility, and bathing are all components of ADLs. There is less agreement on the main categories of IADLs and how to divide them. Several broad categories of IADLs are health-care management, financial management, and functioning in the home and community. Within these categories are many other discrete abilities described in Table 10.3.

Table 10.3 Components of Everyday Functioning Relevant for Independent Living and Adult Guardianship

Domain	Description
Care of self	Maintain adequate hygiene, bathing, dressing, toileting, dental
	Prepare meals and eat for adequate nutrition
	Identify abuse or neglect and protect self from harm
Financial	Protect and spend small amounts of cash
	Manage and use checks
	Give gifts and donations
	Make or modify will
	Buy or sell real property
	Deposit, withdraw, dispose, invest monetary assets
	Establish and use credit
	Pay, settle, prosecute, or contest any claim
	Enter into a contract, commitment, or lease arrangement
	Continue or participate in the operation of a business
	Employ persons to advise or assist him/her
	Resist exploitation, coercion, undue influence
Medical	Give/withhold medical consent
	Admit self to health facility
	Choose and direct caregivers
	Make or change an advance directive
	Manage medications
	Contact help if ill or in medical emergency
Home and community life	Choose/establish abode
	Maintain reasonably safe and clean shelter
	Be left alone without danger
	Drive or use public transportation
	Make and communicate choices about roommates
	Initiate and follow a schedule of daily and leisure activities
	Travel
	Establish and maintain personal relationships with friends, relatives, coworkers
	Determine degree of participation in religious activities
	Use telephone
	Use mail
	Avoid environmental dangers and obtain emergency help
Civil or legal	Retain legal counsel
	Vote
	Make decisions about legal documents

Source: Judicial Determination of Capacity of Older Adults in Guardianship Proceedings: A Handbook for Judges, by the American Bar Association and the American Psychological Association Assessment of Capacity in Older Adults Project Working Group, 2006, Washington, DC: Author. Reprinted with permission of the American Bar Association and the American Psychological Association.

Functional Assessment Tools

Everyday functioning can be assessed through formal means, informal means, or a combination of both. Informal methods include observing the individual or gathering information from the individual, family, and staff. Formal assessments include: (a) guardianship instruments, (b) ADL/IADL rating scales, and (c) occupational therapy (OT) instruments. Because occupational therapists often directly observe and rate ADL/IADL performance with specialized questionnaires and clinical methods, coverage of these issues is beyond the scope of this chapter. The remainder of this section provides a summary of guardianship instruments and ADL/IADL rating scales. Guardianship instruments are tools that assess independent living in the context of legal capacity. They are referred to as *tools* rather than *tests* because it is not possible to have an exact test of capacity. Capacity is a professional, clinical, and, ultimately, legal judgment. In contrast to guardianship instruments, ADL/IADL rating scales—which have been available for more than 30 years—usually categorize several aspects of daily functioning, and are often used by nurses, social workers, psychologists, and other health-care professionals. Some ADL/IADL tools are used specifically to evaluate patients with cognitive problems or dementia (because this population may have particular difficulty with daily functioning), though instruments primarily designed to track the progression of dementia (versus providing a detailed index of current everyday functioning) are beyond the scope of this chapter.

Guardianship Instruments

Decision-Making Instrument for Guardianship

The Decision-Making Instrument for Guardianship (DIG; Anderer, 1997) evaluates decisional ability in situations that may be the subject of guardianship proceedings. The instrument consists of eight simple vignettes dedicated to hygiene, nutrition, health care, residence, property acquisition, routine money management in property acquisition, major expenses in property acquisition, and property disposition. Detailed scoring criteria are used to assess different aspects of problem solving. The DIG is carefully standardized, and standard instructions, vignettes, questions, and prompts are provided with attention to differentiating between problems in reading comprehension, memory, and problem solving.

Independent Living Scales

The Independent Living Scales (ILS; Loeb, 1996) is an individually administered instrument for adults over 65 that assesses ability to care for oneself and/or property. The early version of the ILS, the Community Competence Scale (CCS), was constructed based on legal concepts with the goal of enhancing expert testimony in guardianship cases. The ILS consists of 70 items in five subscales: memory/orientation, managing money, managing home and transportation, health and safety, and social adjustment. An overall score reflects global independent functioning. The ILS manual has extensive information on norms, reliability, and validity.

ADL/IADL Scales for Older Patients (Not Specific to Dementia)

Adult Functional Adaptive Behavior Scale

The Adult Functional Adaptive Behavior Scale (AFABS; Pierce, 1996) assesses ADLs/IADLs and personal responsibility in older adults and matches clients to placement setting. It is relatively easy and brief (approximately 15 minutes) and includes 14 items: six items rate ADLs, two measure IADLs, and six tap cognitive and social functioning. Adaptive functioning is assessed through informant interview and examiner observations.

Assessing Capacity in Everyday Decision Making

Assessing Capacity in Everyday Decision Making (ACED; Lai & Karlawish, in press) is a semi-structured interview that evaluates a client's ability to make everyday decisions relating to a known functional problem (e.g., difficulty with checkbook management). Domains include: (a) understanding the problem, (b) appreciating the problem, (c) understanding the solutions, (d) understanding the benefits and harms, and (e) appreciating the benefits and harms. Initial choice, comparative reasoning, consequential reasoning, and expressing a choice are also assessed. Prompts are provided, and the use of an information sheet to accommodate short-term memory problems can be used.

Multidimensional Functional Assessment Questionnaire

The Multidimensional Functional Assessment Questionnaire (MFAQ; Center for the Study of Aging and Human Development, 1978) was developed to provide a reliable and valid method for characterizing older adults and supersedes the nearly identical Community Survey Questionnaire (CSQ, a predecessor that was also developed by the Duke Center). The MFAQ has been called "OARS," in reference to the program that developed the instrument throughout the 1970s. The MFAQ was already in use by over 50 service centers when it was published in 1978. Part A provides information in five areas of functioning, including instrumental and physical ADLs. Part B assesses utilization of services (e.g., assistance from community programs) and perceived need for services.

The Observed Tasks of Daily Living—Revised

The Observed Tasks of Daily Living—Revised (OTDL-R; Diehl et al., 2005) is a performance-based test of everyday problem solving, including nine tasks assessing medication use, telephone use, and financial management, and has been tested in diverse populations. The OTDL-R correlates with age, education, self-rated health, everyday problem solving, and measures of basic cognitive functioning.

ADL/IADL Scales for Patients with Dementia or Mild Cognitive Impairment

Cleveland Scale for Activities of Daily Living

The Cleveland Scale for Activities of Daily Living (CSADL; Patterson & Mack, 1998) is a scale that provides a detailed measure of ADLs and IADLs in individuals with dementia through informant-report using 47 items to assess 15 domains (bathing, toileting, personal hygiene, dressing, eating, mobility, medications, shopping, travel, hobbies, housework, telephone skills, money management, communication skills, social behavior, and other problems). Activities within each domain are broken into component behaviors. Factor analytic results reveal basic and instrumental ADL factors. Interrater reliability (.80 to .99) and internal consistency (.96 to .97) are high, and validity testing shows reliable differences between healthy elderly, physically impaired elderly, and elderly with three different levels of dementia severity (Patterson & Mack, 2001).

Direct Assessment of Functional Status

The Direct Assessment of Functional Status (DAFS; Loewenstein et al., 1989) is a 30 to 35 minute measure designed to stage functional impairment through direct assessment of seven skills (time orientation, communication, transportation, financial skills, shopping skills, eating skills, and dressing and grooming skills) in individuals with dementia. It requires that the patient attempt to actually perform each item (e.g., is given a telephone and asked to dial the operator) and contains a composite functional score and an optional driving subscale.

Functional Cognitive Assessment Scale

The Functional Cognitive Assessment Scale (FUCAS; Kounti, Tsolaki, & Kiosseoglou, 2006) is a 13-item scale that directly assesses six different daily activities requiring executive functioning (telephone communication, shopping, orientation in place, taking medication, personal hygiene, clothing). Seven parameters of executive functioning are assessed (awareness of the problem, working memory, planning of the solution, distribution of time, sequence of steps, accuracy of steps, and goal maintenance). Internal reliability is favorable (.89 to .92), and discriminant analysis shows that FUCAS scores can differentiate between mild cognitive impairment and moderate-severe dementia.

Issues in Values Assessment

As described for medical consent, a consideration of an individual's values is a critical component of a capacity assessment in providing important information about the personal and interpersonal context of independent living decisions. Some questions regarding values for living in the community appear in Table 10.4.

Table 10.4 Questions for Independent Living Values Assessment

Where are you living now? How long have you been there?

Does anyone live there with you? If not, do you have any fears or concerns about living alone?

Does anyone visit on a regular basis?

What family and/or friends live in your community who are important to you?

What is most important to you about where you live? What makes it home?

What kind of personal activities do you enjoy doing at home?

Are there community activities in which you enjoy participating?

What do you like about your house/apartment?

What do you not like about your house/apartment? What does not work well for you and why?

Do you feel that you can manage the house/apartment on your own? Have you noticed any changes in your abilities to manage?

Are there areas of your life that you feel you may need some assistance managing? For instance, do you have any trouble with housekeeping, yard work, preparing meals, shopping, driving, using the telephone, the mail, your health, taking medications, managing your money, or paying bills on your own?

Is there someone helping you with any of these things?

If you needed help, who would you like to help you?

Have you had any safety concerns at home? For instance, have you ever accidentally left the stove or oven on, fallen and been unable to get up by yourself, left your doors unlocked, or invited a stranger into your home?

Where would you like to live in the future?

Have you ever considered moving to a place where there would be more help for you, such as senior housing, assisted living, or a nursing home? How do you feel about that? What fears or concerns do you have?

If you were to move to senior housing, assisted living, or a nursing home, what would make it okay for you? Is there anything important that you would want to take or do in a different living situation?

Source: Judicial Determination of Capacity of Older Adults in Guardianship Proceedings: A Handbook for Judges, by the American Bar Association and the American Psychological Association Assessment of Capacity in Older Adults Project Working Group, 2006, Washington, DC: Author. Reprinted with permission of the American Bar Association and the American Psychological Association.

CONCLUSION

Medical consent capacity and independent living capacity are two very different domains of everyday functioning. Questions about these two domains may arise for older adults with neurological or psychiatric conditions. Approaches that consider the relevant legal standards and focus on the specific functional issues and related values may be useful in assessing these domains. Many instruments are available that can be used to supplement a general psychological and cognitive assessment to focus the assessment on the specific functional skills relevant to the capacity in question. Continuing research will be useful to establish the benefits and limits of these instruments.

REFERENCES

American Bar Association & American Psychological Association Assessment of Capacity in Older Adults Project Working Group. (2006). *Judicial determination of capacity of older adults in guardianship proceedings: A handbook for judges.* Washington, DC: Author.

Anderer, S. J. (1990). *Determining competency in guardianship proceedings.* Washington, DC: American Bar Association.

Anderer, S. J. (1997). *Development of an instrument to evaluate the capacity of elderly persons to make personal care and financial decisions.* Unpublished doctoral dissertation, Allegheny University of the Health Sciences, Long Beach, CA.

Appelbaum, P. S., & Grisso, T. (1988). Assessing patients' capacities to consent to treatment. *New England Journal of Medicine, 319,* 1635–1638.

Appelbaum, P. S., & Grisso, T. (1992). *Manual for perceptions of disorder.* Worcester: University of Massachusetts Medical School.

Barton, C. D., Mallik, H. S., Orr, W. B., & Janofsky, J. S. (1996). Clinicians' judgment of capacity of nursing home patients to give informed consent. *Psychiatric Services, 47*(9), 956–960.

Bean, G., Nishisato, S., Rector, N. A., & Glancy, G. (1996). The assessment of competence to make a treatment decision: An empirical approach. *Canadian Journal of Psychiatry, 41,* 85–92.

Carney, M. T., Neugroschl, J., Morrison, R. S., Marin, D., & Siu, A. L. (2001). The development and piloting of a capacity assessment tool. *Journal of Clinical Ethics, 12*(1), 17–23.

Center for the Study of Aging and Human Development. (1978). *Multidimensional functional assessment: The OARS methodology.* Durham, NC: Duke University.

Craik, F. I. M. (1994). Memory changes in normal aging. *Current Directions in Psychological Science, 3,* 155–158.

Craik, F. I. M., & Byrd, M. (1982). Aging and cognitive deficits: The role of attentional resources. In F. I. M. Craik & S. Trehub (Eds.), *Aging and cognitive processes* (pp. 191–211). New York: Plenum Press.

Craik, F. I. M., & Jennings, J. M. (1992). Human memory. In F. I. M. Craik & T. A. Salthouse (Eds.), *The handbook of aging and cognition* (pp. 51–110). Hillsdale, NJ: Erlbaum.

Dellasega, C., Frank, L., & Smyer, M. (1996). Medical decision-making capacity in elderly hospitalized patients. *Journal of Ethics, Law and Aging, 2*(2), 65–74.

Diehl, M., Marsiske, M., Horgas, A., Rosenberg, A., Saczynski, J., & Willis, S. L. (2005). The revised observed tasks of daily living: A performance-based assessment of everyday problem solving. *Journal of Applied Gerontology, 24,* 211–230.

Drane, J. F. (1985). The many faces of competency. *Hastings Center Report, 15*(2), 17–21.

Dunn, L. B., & Jeste, D. V. (2001). Enhancing informed consent for research and treatment. *Neuropsychopharmacology, 24,* 595–607.

Dymek, M. P., Atchison, P., Harrell, L., & Marson, D. C. (2001). Competency to consent to medical treatment in cognitively impaired patients with Parkinson's disease. *Neurology, 56,* 17–24.

Edelstein, B. (1999). *Hopemont Capacity Assessment Interview manual and scoring guide.* Morgantown: West Virginia University.

Etchells, E., Darzins, P., Silberfeld, M., Singer, P. A., McKenny, J., Naglie, G., et al. (1999). Assessment of patient's capacity to consent to treatment. *Journal of General Internal Medicine, 14,* 27–34.

Fitten, L. J., Lusky, R., & Hamann, C. (1990). Assessing treatment decision-making capacity in elderly nursing home residents. *Journal of the American Geriatrics Society, 38,* 1097–1104.

Fitten, L. J., & Waite, M. S. (1990). Impact of medical hospitalization on treatment decision-making capacity in the elderly. *Archives of Internal Medicine, 150,* 1717–1721.

Frank, L., Smyer, M., Grisso, T., & Applebaum, P. (1999). Measurement of advance directive and medical treatment decision-making capacity of older adults. *Journal of Mental Health and Aging, 5*(3), 257–274.

Grisso, T. (1986). *Evaluating competencies.* New York: Plenum Press.

Grisso, T. (2003). *Evaluating competences* (2nd ed.). New York: Plenum Press.

Grisso, T., & Appelbaum, P. S. (1992). *Manual for understanding treatment disclosures.* Worcester: University of Massachusetts Medical School.

Grisso, T., & Appelbaum, P. S. (1993). *Manual for thinking rationally about treatment.* Worcester: University of Massachusetts Medical School.

Grisso, T., & Appelbaum, P. S. (1995). Comparison of standards for assessing patient's capacities to make treatment decisions. *American Journal of Psychiatry, 152,* 1033–1037.

Grisso, T., & Appelbaum, P. S. (1998a). *Assessing competence to consent to treatment.* New York: Oxford University Press.

Grisso, T., & Appelbaum, P. S. (1998b). *MacArthur Competency Assessment Tool for Treatment* (MacCAT-T). Sarasota, FL: Professional Resource Press.

Gurrera, R. J., Karel, M. J., Azar, A. R., & Moye, J. (2007). Agreement between instruments for rating treatment decisional capacity. *American Journal of Geriatric Psychiatry, 15,* 168–173.

Gurrera, R. J., Moye, J., Karel, M. J., Azar, A. R., & Armesto, J. C. (2006). Cognitive performance predicts treatment decisional abilities in mild to moderate dementia. *Neurology, 66,* 1367–1372.

Karel, M. J., Powell, J., & Cantor, M. (2004). Using a values discussion guide to facilitate communication in advance care planning. *Patient Education and Counseling, 55,* 22–31.

Karp, N., & Wood, E. (2003). *Incapacitated and alone: Health care decision-making for the unbefriended elderly.* Washington, DC: American Bar Association.

Kim, S. Y. H., Caine, E. D., Currier, G. W., Leibovici, A., & Ryan, J. M. (2001). Assessing the competence of persons with Alzheimer's disease in providing informed consent for participation in research. *American Journal of Psychiatry, 158,* 712–717.

Kounti, F., Tsolaki, M., & Kiosseoglou, G. (2006). Functional Cognitive Assessment Scale (FUCAS): A new scale to assess executive cognitive function in daily life activities in patients with dementia and mild cognitive impairment. *Human Psychopharmacology: Clinical and Experimental, 21,* 305–311.

Kuhberger, A. (1998). The influence of framing on risky decisions: A meta-analysis. *Organizational Behavior and Human Decision Processes, 75,* 23–55.

Lai, J., & Karlawish, J. (in press). Assessing the capacity to make everyday decisions: A guide for clinicians and an agenda for future research. *American Journal of Geriatric Psychiatry.*

Loeb, P. (1996). *Independent Living Scales.* San Antonio, TX: Psychological Corporation.

Loewenstein, D. A., Amigo, E., Duara, R., Guterman, A., Hurwitz, D., Berkowitz, N., et al. (1989). A new scale for the assessment of functional status in Alzheimer's disease and related disorders. *Journal of Gerontology: Psychological Sciences, 44B,* 114–121.

Marson, D. C., Chatterjee, A., Ingram, K. K., & Harrell, L. E. (1996). Toward a neurologic model of competency: Cognitive predictors of capacity to consent in Alzheimer's disease using three different legal standards. *Neurology, 46,* 666–672.

Marson, D. C., Ingram, K. K., Cody, H. A., & Harrell, L. E. (1995). Assessing the competency of patients with Alzheimer's disease under different legal standards. *Archives of Neurology, 52,* 949–954.

Marson, D. C., McInturff, B., Hawkins, L., Bartolucci, A., & Harrell, L. E. (1997). Consistency of physician judgments of capacity to consent in mild Alzheimer's disease. *American Geriatrics Society, 45,* 453–457.

Mazur, D. J., & Merz, J. F. (1993). How the manner of presentation of data influences older patients in determining their treatment preferences. *Journal of the American Geriatric Society, 41,* 223–228.

McKee, D. R. (2001). *The effects of framing on younger and older adults' medical decision making.* Unpublished doctoral dissertation, West Virginia University, Morgantown.

McNeil, B. J., Pauker, S. G., Sox, H. C., & Tversky, A. (1982). On the elicitation of preferences for alternative therapies. *New England Journal of Medicine, 305,* 1259–1262.

Moye, J., Karel, M. J., Azar, A. R., & Gurrera, R. J. (2004a). Capacity to consent in dementia: Empirical comparison of three instruments. *Gerontologist, 44,* 166–175.

Moye, J., Karel, M. J., Azar, A. R., & Gurrera, R. J. (2004b). Hopes and cautions for instrument-based evaluations of consent capacity: Results of a construct validity study of three instruments. *Ethics, Law, and Aging Review, 10,* 39–61.

Moye, J., Karel, M. J., Gurrera, R. J., & Azar, A. R. (2006). Neuropsychological predictors of decision-making capacity over nine months in mild to moderate dementia. *Journal of General Internal Medicine, 21,* 78–83.

National Conference of Commissioners on Uniform State Laws. (1993). *Uniform Health Care Decisions Act.* Available from www.law.upenn.edu/bll/ulc/fnact99/1990s/uhcda93.pdf.

National Conference of Commissioners on Uniform State Laws. (1997). *Uniform Guardianship and Protective Proceedings Act.* Available from www.law.upenn.edu/bll/ulc/fnact99/1990s/ugppa97.htm.

Park, D. C., Morrel, R. W., & Shifren, K. (1999). *Processing of medical information in aging patients cognitive and human factors perspectives.* Hillsdale, NJ: Erlbaum.

Patterson, M. B., & Mack, J. L. (1998). *The Cleveland Scale for Activities of Daily Living (CSADL): Manual.* Cleveland, OH: University Alzheimer Center.

Patterson, M. B., & Mack, J. L. (2001). The Cleveland Scale for Activities of Daily Living (CSADL): Its reliability and validity. *Journal of Clinical Geropsychology, 7,* 15–28.

Pierce, P. F. (1996). When the patient chooses: Describing unaided decisions in health care. *Human Factors, 38,* 278–287.

Pruchno, R. A., Smyer, M. A., Rose, M. S., Hartman-Stein, P. E., & Laribee-Henderson, D. L. (1995). Competence of long-term care residents to participate in decisions about their medical care: A brief, objective assessment. *Gerontologist, 35*(5), 622–629.

Richardson, S. (2003). Health care decision-making: A guardian's authority. *Bifocal, 24*(4), 1–10.

Roth, L. H., Meisel, C. A., & Lidz, C. A. (1977). Tests of competency to consent to treatment. *Canadian Journal of Psychiatry, 134,* 279–284.

Royall, D. R., Cordes, J., & Polk, M. (1997). Executive control and the comprehension of medical information by elderly retirees. *Experimental Aging Research, 23,* 301–313.

Sabatino, C. P., & Basinger, S. L. (2000). Competency: Reforming our legal fictions. *Journal of Mental Health and Aging, 6*(2), 119–143.

Sachs, G. A., Stocking, C. B., & Stern, R. (1994). Ethical aspects of dementia research: Informed consent and proxy consent. *Clinical Research, 42,* 403–412.

Schmand, B., Gouwenberg, B., Smit, J. H., & Jonker, C. (1999). Assessment of mental competency in community-dwelling elderly. *Alzheimer Disease and Associated Disorders, 13*(2), 80–87.

Staats, N., & Edelstein, B. (1995, November). *Cognitive changes associated with the declining competency of older adults.* Paper presented at the annual meeting of the Gerontological Society of America, Los Angeles.

Stanley, B., Stanley, M., Guido, J., & Garvin, L. (1988). The functional competency of elderly at risk. *Gerontologist, 28*(Suppl.), 53–58.

Taub, H. A., Baker, M. T., Kline, G. E., & Sturr, J. F. (1987). Comprehension of informed consent by young-old and old-old volunteers. *Experimental Aging Research, 13,* 173–178.

Tepper, A., & Elwork, A. (1984). Competency to consent to treatment as a psycho legal construct. *Law and Human Behavior, 8,* 205–223.

Tymchuk, A. J., Ouslander, J. G., & Fitten, J. (1988). Medical decision-making among elderly people in long term care. *Gerontologist, 28,* 59–63.

Wong, J. G., Clare, I. C. H., Holland, A. J., Watson, P. C., & Gunn, M. (2000). The capacity of people with a "mental disability" to make a health care decision. *Psychological Medicine, 30,* 295–306.

CHAPTER

11

━━━◈◆◈━━━

Assessment of Financial Capacity in Older Adults with Dementia

KATINA R. HEBERT AND DANIEL C. MARSON

Financial capacity, or the capacity to manage one's financial affairs, is an advanced instrumental activity of daily living (IADL) critical to independent functioning of older adults in our society (Marson et al., 2000). It is comprised of a broad range of conceptual, pragmatic, and judgment abilities, ranging from basic skills of identifying and counting coins and currency to more complicated tasks such as preparing taxes and making investment decisions. Unlike gender-based activities like cooking, laundry, or car repair, and specific hobbies like playing bridge or tennis, all independently functioning older adults have developed a set of financial skills during their lifetimes. Financial experience does vary across individuals as a function of socioeconomic status, occupational attainment, and overall financial experience (Marson, 2001; Marson & Briggs, 2001; Marson et al., 2000). In some households, many or most financial tasks may be delegated to one spouse. Nonetheless, core financial skills (e.g., such as identifying and counting coins and currency and

This research was supported in part by an Alzheimer's Disease Center Core grant (NIH, NIA 1 P30 AG10163; Harrell, PI) and an Alzheimer's Disease Research Center grant (NIH, NIA 1P50 AG16582; Harrell, PI) from the National Institute on Aging, and a grant from the National Institute of Mental Health (NIH, NIMH 1 R01 MH55427).

conducting cash transactions) are common to all independently functioning older adults (Marson et al., 2000). More specialized financial skills (e.g., checkbook management and bank statement management) have been used by many individuals during their lifetimes; and they still possess them, even if another member of the household is currently responsible for them. Financial capacity is generic to most if not all community-dwelling older adults. Thus, this construct is particularly useful for examining the relationship between cognitive and functional decline in normal aging and dementia.

Cognition informs the development and exercise of simple and, in particular, higher order functional abilities like financial capacity (Marson & Hebert, 2006). Therefore, progressive neurodegenerative dementias such as Alzheimer's disease (AD) pose a major risk factor for financial decline (Angel & Frisco, 2001; Demers, Oremus, Perrault, Champoux, & Wolfson, 2000) and incapacity in older adults (Marson & Briggs, 2001; Marson et al., 2000). Impairments in financial skills and judgment are often the first functional changes demonstrated by patients with early dementia (Willis, 1996). At initial evaluation, family complaints of financial decline in patients with early AD often accompany concerns of significant memory loss (Marson, 2001). Patients with early AD may neglect to pay bills, repetitively pay bills, have problems balancing the checkbook, or exercise poor financial judgment falling prey to telephone and mail fraud scams (Overman & Stoudemire, 1988). Empirical research has provided evidence of select impairment of financial performance in preclinical stages of AD (Griffith et al., 2003; Okonkwo, Wadley, Griffith, Ball, & Marson, 2006) as well as progressive declines across an increasing number of financial activities and abilities in mild to moderate AD (Marson, 2001; Marson et al., 2000). Therefore, financial capacity is similar to other higher order functional capacities such as medical decision making and driving, which have also been found to decline as a consequence of AD (Drachman & Swearer, 1993; Hunt et al., 1997; Marson, Ingram, Cody, & Harrell, 1995).

The power of individuals to control their own finances represents a fundamental element of autonomy in our society, such that its loss may result in psychological and social consequences for AD patients and their families (Marson, 2001). Loss of decisional autonomy has been linked to declines in mental well-being, personal control, the ability to cope with changes and stressors, and physical health (Moye, 2003). Families may feel burdened, ill equipped, or unable to take on the responsibility of managing their loved ones' finances. As with driving privileges (Hebert, Martin-Cook, Svetlik, & Weiner, 2002), dementia patients may actively resist relinquishing financial control resulting in family distress and conflict. In the absence of appropriate clinical assessment, families are often left wondering how they can best accommodate for financial difficulties and when it may be necessary to revoke the financial privileges of a spouse or parent with AD.

Significant economic and legal consequences may also occur as a result of declining financial capacity. Failure to pay bills or difficulty handling basic financial tasks may lead to bounced checks, disconnection of services, property repossession, and poor credit ratings. Impaired financial judgment may result in loss of assets intended for long-term care or inclusion in an estate will (Marson, 2001). From a legal perspective, diminished or impaired mental capacity is associated with increased vulnerability to financial fraud and exploitation (Nerenberg, 1996). Older adults are disproportionately targeted for scams and other types of consumer fraud ("Woman Out," 1996). Furthermore, older adults with diminished capacity are more susceptible to undue influence (otherwise referred to as improper persuasion or coercion) by family members and third parties (Spar & Garb, 1992). Individuals with preclinical or mild AD, who are cognitively impaired but seemingly "normal," may be at greatest risk for poor financial decisions and exploitation (Marson, 2001). In some cases, financial incapacity may result in loss of decisional autonomy and the appointment of a guardian and conservator by the court for the protection of the person and his or her estate (Moye, 2003). Loss of financial capacity may also have legal implications that extend beyond the individual's death. For instance, an individual's last will and testament may be contested and ruled invalid and void by the probate court, if evidence is presented that the testator (or person making the will) lacked sufficient knowledge of the nature and extent of his or her assets at the time the will was executed (Marson & Hebert, 2005; Marson, Huthwaite, & Hebert, 2004).

Despite its importance to current mental health and legal practice, financial capacity has been surprisingly neglected in the medical-legal literature (Grisso, 2003; Lieff, Maindonald, & Shulman, 1984; McKay, 1989; Toffoli & Herrmann, 1993). Lack of detailed conceptual models and standardized instruments for assessing financial capacity may have contributed to the dearth of clinical research in this area. Prior gerontological research has addressed the ability of older adults to manage their finances, and numerous measures of everyday living skills incorporate financial items (Ashley, Persel, & Clark, 2001; Leckey & Beatty, 2002; Loewenstein et al., 1989; Mahurin, DeBettignies, & Pirozzolo, 1991; Willis et al., 1998). However, these measures cover a diverse range of functional abilities and are not specific to financial capacity. Only recently have detailed conceptual models and standardized assessment instruments been developed and systematic empirical studies of financial capacity been conducted (Cramer, Tuokko, Mateer, & Hultsch, 2004; Griffith et al., 2003; Marson, 2001; Marson et al., 2000; Okonkwo et al., 2006; Van Wielingen, Tuokko, Cramer, Mateer, & Hultsch, 2004).

The primary purpose of this chapter is to provide clinicians with a basic understanding of financial capacity and its assessment. First, we present a clinically based conceptual model of financial capacity that operates according to three levels, including specific financial abilities, broad domains of financial activity, and overall financial capacity (Marson, 2001). Next, we describe four general approaches to the assessment of financial capacity: clinical interview format, observational rating scales (self and informant report), and performance-based measures, as well as neuropsychological assessment as a secondary approach. Last, we review recent psychometric studies of financial capacity in normal aging and patients with AD and mild cognitive impairment (MCI).

CONCEPTUAL MODEL OF FINANCIAL CAPACITY

Financial capacity is not a unitary construct. Rather it represents a broad continuum of activities and specific skills (Marson & Hebert, 2005). Accordingly, Marson and colleagues propose a model of financial capacity that operates at three levels: (1) specific financial tasks and abilities, (2) broader domains (or categories) of financial activity, and (3) overall financial capacity. Each domain of financial activity and its constituent financial tasks were reviewed and approved by a panel of physicians, gerontologists, an attorney, and a judge with considerable knowledge of the financial capacity construct and found to be relevant for independent functioning within the community (Marson & Briggs, 2001; Marson et al., 2000). This model has been the basis for instrument development and ongoing studies of financial capacity in AD and other clinical populations (Griffith et al., 2003; Marson & Briggs, 2001; Marson et al., 2006; Okonkwo et al., 2006).

Nine domains of financial activity have been identified, including basic monetary skills, financial conceptual knowledge, cash transactions, checkbook management, bank statement management, financial judgment, bill payment, knowledge of personal assets and estate arrangements, and investment decision making (Griffith et al., 2003; Marson et al., 2000). Domains were selected based on their relevance to psychologists who treat and evaluate persons at risk for financial incapacity (i.e., older adults and persons with dementia) as well as their relevance to legal criteria for financial competency (Marson, 2001; Marson et al., 2000).

Each domain of financial activity is further broken down into constituent tasks or abilities that emphasize understanding and pragmatic application of skills relevant to a specific domain (Marson, 2001; Marson et al., 2000). For instance, the domain of financial conceptual knowledge involves understanding concepts such as loans and savings, and using this information to select advantageous interest rates. Similarly, bill payment involves not only understanding what a bill is and why it should be paid, but also accurately reviewing a bill and preparing it for mailing. Therefore, tasks represent abilities that constitute broader, clinically relevant domains of financial activity (Marson & Hebert, 2005). Each task may be categorized as simple or complex based on the level of cognitive resources it appears to require (Marson, 2001; Marson et al., 2000). Domain-level financial activities and task-level financial abilities are presented in Table 11.1.

Table 11.1   Revised Financial Conceptual Model: 18 Tasks, 9 Domains, and 2 Global Measures of Overall Capacity

Domain/ Task Level	Task Description	Task Difficulty
Domain 1 Basic Monetary Skills		
Task 1a Naming coins/currency	Identify specific coins and currency	Simple
Task 1b Coin/currency relationships	Indicate relative monetary values of coins/currency	Simple
Task 1c Counting coins/currency	Accurately count groups of coins and currency	Simple
Domain 2 Financial Conceptual Knowledge		
Task 2a Define financial concepts	Define a variety of simple financial concepts	Complex
Task 2b Apply financial concepts	Practical application/computation using concepts	Complex
Domain 3 Cash Transactions		
Task 3a 1-item grocery purchase	Enter into simulated 1-item transaction; verify change	Simple
Task 3b 3-item grocery purchase	Enter into simulated 3-item transaction; verify change	Complex
Task 3c Change/vending machine	Obtain change for vending machine use; verify change	Complex
Task 3d Tipping	Understand tipping convention; calculate/identify tips	Complex
Domain 4 Checkbook Management		
Task 4a Understand checkbook	Identify and explain parts of check and check register	Simple
Task 4b Use checkbook/register	Enter into simulated transaction; pay by check	Complex
Domain 5 Bank Statement Management		
Task 5a Understand bank statement	Identify and explain parts of a bank statement	Complex
Task 5b Use bank statement	Identify specific transactions on bank statement	Complex

Table 11.1 (Continued)

Domain/ Task Level	Task Description	Task Difficulty
Domain 6 Financial Judgment		
Task 6a Detect mail fraud risk	Detect and explain risks in mail fraud solicitation	Simple
Task 6c Detect telephone fraud risk	Detect and explain risks in tele-phone fraud solicitation	Simple
Domain 7 Bill Payment		
Task 7a Understand bills	Explain meaning and purpose of bills	Simple
Task 7b Prioritize bills	Identify overdue utility bill	Simple
Task 7c Prepare bills for mailing	Prepare simulated bills, checks, envelopes for mailing	Complex
Domain 8 Knowledge of Assets/ Estate	Indicate/verify asset ownership, estate arrangements	Simple
Domain 9 Investment Decision Making	Understand options; determine returns; make decision	Complex
Global 1 Sum of Domains 1–7	Overall functioning across tasks and domains	Complex
Global 2 Sum of Domains 1–8	Overall functioning across tasks and domains	Complex

Source: "Impaired Financial Abilities in Mild Cognitive Impairment: A Direct Assessment Approach," by H. R. Griffith et al. 2003, *Neurology*, 60(3), p. 450. Copyright 2003, American Academy of Neurology. Reprinted with permission.

Last, clinicians are often called on to make overall judgments of an individual's financial capacity, particularly in the context of guardianship and conservatorship hearings where decisional competency must be determined (Marson, 2001; Moye, 2003). Such global judgments require integration of information concerning an individual's task- and domain-level financial performance, his or her judgment skills, and informant report of financial abilities. Competency is ultimately a categorical judgment or classification made by a clinician or legal professional (Marson & Hebert,

2005). Therefore, overall financial capacity reflects both a clinical and legal construct (Marson, 2001).

According to Griffith and colleagues (2003), the current conceptual model of financial capacity has three levels: (1) specific financial abilities or tasks, each of which is relevant to a particular domain of financial activity; (2) general domains of financial activity, which are clinically relevant to the independent functioning of community-dwelling older adults; and (3) overall financial capacity, which reflects a global measure of capacity based on the summation of domain- and task-level performance.

METHODS OF ASSESSING FINANCIAL CAPACITY

Using the previously described conceptual model as a framework, three common approaches used by clinicians in reaching a determination regarding an older adult's financial capacity are discussed next including (1) clinician interview, (2) self- and informant-report (or observational) measures, and (3) performance-based (or psychometric) measures. Neuropsychological testing is also useful for identifying cognitive deficits that may potentially interfere with an older adult's ability to perform financial tasks.

Clinical Interview

The clinical interview is the most commonly used method for assessing financial capacity. However, few if any guidelines for conducting clinical interviews of financial capacity have been proposed (Marson, 2001). As such, clinicians vary considerably in how they assess capacity as well as their subsequent capacity determinations (Marson, McInturff, Hawkins, Bartolucci, & Harrell, 1997). A thorough clinical interview of financial capacity should address broad domains of financial activity (i.e., checkbook management) as well as the specific financial tasks that support these activities (i.e., writing a check and recording in a checkbook register; Cramer et al., 2004; Van Wielingen et al., 2004).

The conceptual model described previously provides a framework on which to base a clinical interview of financial capacity. Emphasis should be placed on those financial activities necessary for independent living within the community, such as conducting cash transactions, writing a check, and paying bills. Clinicians should inquire about the number and type of financial activities that are impaired as well as the amount of help needed by patients to complete financial activities. Individuals who require only verbal prompting to initiate or complete paying bills are qualitatively different in terms of financial capacity than individuals who require actual hands on assistance and supervision in paying bills or who are completely dependent on others to perform this task (Marson, 2001).

Psychologists should also consider an individual's level of previous experience with a task as well as his or her past opportunities to perform a task, prior to rendering a determination regarding financial capacity (Marson, 2001). For instance, it would be inappropriate to assume that a person who demonstrates difficulty making investment decisions is declining in financial capacity if he or she has never performed this task or if his or her investment portfolio has been managed by a spouse or financial advisor (Marson, 2001). As such, psychologists should differentially weigh financial performance and place greater emphasis on those activities and abilities required for independent living within the community. Recognizing the need for a semi-structured interview approach assessing financial capacity, Marson and colleagues (2006) developed the Semi-Structured Clinical Interview for Financial Capacity.

The Semi-Structured Clinical Interview for Financial Capacity

The Semi-Structured Clinical Interview for Financial Capacity (SCIFC) is a clinician administered, semi-structured assessment interview of financial capacity (Marson et al., 2006). As derived from the previously described conceptual model of financial capacity, the SCIFC assesses performance at the domain and global levels. Based on the interview, clinicians make capacity judgments (capable, marginally capable, incapable) for each of eight domains and for overall financial capacity. Older adults across the dementia spectrum demonstrate progressive impairments in financial abilities as measured by the SCIFC. In a recent study that evaluated financial capacity in participants with normal aging, MCI, and mild to moderate AD (Marson et al., 2006) five physicians demonstrated very good agreement (80+%) in capacity judgments across almost all groups and SCIFC variables. Discrepancy in physicians' judgments for select domains and overall financial capacity was greatest for persons with mild AD relative to controls and persons with MCI (Marson et al., 2006). Moreover, the percentage agreement for overall financial capacity of persons with moderate AD was similar to control and MCI groups and significantly better than mild AD patients, suggesting that moderate AD patients present less ambiguity to clinicians than do mild AD patients in global determinations of financial capacity (Marson et al., 2006). Overall, the results of this study suggest that financial capacity in older adults with and without dementia can be reliably evaluated by clinicians using a brief, semi-structured interview such as the SCIFC (Marson et al., 2006).

Self- and Informant-Report Approaches

Psychologists commonly use observational rating scales to supplement and inform their clinical interview. Observational rating scales are typically completed by the patient (self-report) and/or another knowledgeable person such as a spouse, adult child, close friend, or other caregiver (informant report). These instruments require that the patient or his or her informant rate the patient's ability to perform basic self-care and complex instrumental activities at home and in the community. Respondents indicate whether the older adult patient can perform a series of activities with or without the assistance of another individual or a special device (Angel & Frisco, 2001). The number of activities in which the older adult needs assistance and the amount of help needed to complete each activity is used to calculate an index of functional disability (Angel & Frisco, 2001).

Functional disability is any restriction or inability to perform an activity in a manner consistent with the individual's particular stage of sociobiological or cognitive development (Demers et al., 2000; World Health Organization, 1980). Difficulty in performing one or more physical self-care or independent daily-living skills qualifies as functional disability (Marson & Hebert, 2006). Functional disability is associated with increased likelihood of nursing home placement and higher mortality rates among older adults (Angel & Frisco, 2001; Wiener, Hanley, Clark, & Von Nostrand, 1990). Furthermore, functionally impaired older adults report greater need for assistance, poorer health status, poorer health outcomes, and poorer quality of life than individuals who are able to perform tasks independently (Angel & Frisco, 2001).

Until recently, lack of conceptual models and direct performance measures of financial capacity forced clinicians to rely heavily on patient and family reports in evaluating financial abilities. However, some older adult populations, particularly dementia patients and nondemented hospitalized elders, have been found to overestimate their own functional abilities (Rubenstein, Schairer, Wieland, & Kane, 1984; Wadley, Harrell, & Marson, 2003; Wild & Cotrell, 2003). The tendency of dementia patients to overestimate their functional abilities has been linked to a lack of insight into their disorder and calls into question the accuracy of their self-reports (Kiyak, Teri, & Borson, 1994; Van Wielingen et al., 2004; Weinberger et al., 1992). In a study conducted by Wadley and colleagues (2003), 50% of patients with AD overestimated their current financial abilities relative to both caregiver report and objective performance, rating themselves on average as functioning independently in all domains of financial activity. A separate study conducted by Van Wielingen and colleagues (2004) found that lack of awareness regarding financial difficulties was directly related to the complexity of the financial task being performed. In particular, individuals with mild AD were less aware of difficulties pertaining to more complex financial items, whereas moderate dementia patients lacked awareness of financial abilities irrespective of task complexity (Van Wielingen et al., 2004). The lack of insight into current financial abilities is an aspect of the overall anosognosia regarding functional change that is common to AD (Tabert et al., 2002; Wadley et al., 2003).

Due to inaccuracies in self-report common among older adults, clinicians typically rely on information provided by a caregiver or other knowledgeable informant. Caregivers and proxy informants observe the functional behavior of patients within the home environment on a daily basis and are believed to be in the best position to accurately rate their functional abilities (Loewenstein & Mogosky, 1999). Furthermore, because caregivers observe behavior across time and settings, they may provide more stable estimates of patients' functional skills and limitations (Loewenstein & Mogosky, 1999). Results of objective performance-based measures may fluctuate as a function of the patient's motivation, cognition, and behavior (DeBettignies, Mahurin, Roderick, & Pirozzolo, 1993; Loewenstein & Mogosky, 1999).

Recent evidence indicates that caregivers (spouse and adult children) of AD patients also misjudge patients' general functional abilities and their specific financial capacities. Although caregivers more often underestimate general functional abilities in patients with AD (Zanetti, Geroldi, Frisoni, Bianchetti, & Trabucchi, 1999), they have been found to overestimate patients' functional abilities in some circumstances (Loewenstein et al., 2001). Specifically, caregivers overestimated the functional abilities of AD patients with high Mini Mental Status Examination (MMSE) scores relative to their performance on a direct assessment of functional status (Loewenstein et al., 1989). Recent research suggests that financial skills and abilities of patients with AD may be particularly susceptible to misjudgment by caregivers. In a comparative study involving a performance-based measure of functional abilities and a corresponding observational rating scale, Loewenstein and colleagues (2001) found that caregivers overestimated the ability of AD patients to identify and count currency and to make change for a purchase. Patterns of caregiver misestimation also emerged in a separate study that specifically examined the construct of financial capacity (Wadley et al., 2003). Whereas caregivers *overestimated* patients' abilities to perform more elementary financial activities such as cash transactions, they tended to *underestimate* patients' abilities on more complex areas such as financial conceptual knowledge and checkbook management. Interestingly, caregivers in this study were equally likely to overestimate as underestimate a patient's ability to pay bills. Patterns of misestimation among caregivers has been linked not only to patient cognition but also to fluctuations in caregivers' mood, their perceived level of burden, and their use of denial as an adaptive mechanism (DeBettignies et al., 1993; Ippen, Olin, & Schneider, 1999; Sager et al., 1992).

These studies suggest caution about the use of informant report in clinical assessment of financial capacity in dementia and underscore the need for direct assessment methods to compliment existing interview and self- and informant-report approaches (Wadley et al., 2003). However, self- and caregiver/informant ratings are still commonly used because of their minimal cost and relative ease and brevity of administration and scoring (Angel & Frisco, 2001; Loewenstein & Mogosky, 1999). Two separate self- and informant-report measures have recently been designed to specifically and comprehensively assess financial capacity in normal older adults and dementia patients; these are the Current Financial Capacity Form (Wadley et al., 2003) and the Measure of Awareness of Financial Skills (Cramer et al., 2004).

Current Financial Capacity Form

The Current Financial Capacity Form (CFCF) provides observational ratings of a patient's current capacity to function independently on the same conceptual tasks, domains, and global variables previously described in the conceptual model of financial capacity (Marson, 2001; Wadley et al., 2003). With each revision of the conceptual model, corresponding changes have been made to the CFCF. The current version (CFCF-9) provides observational ratings for 18 specific financial tasks and nine broader domains of financial activity as well as two indices of global financial performance. Observational ratings are trichotomous: The patient is currently able to perform financial tasks and activities independently (2 points), only with assistance (1 point), or not at all even with assistance (0 points). Self-report and informant-report versions of the CFCF are available.

Unlike performance-based measures that assess financial capacity in artificial settings, such as clinics and laboratories, the CFCF appraises financial capacity over time in everyday settings using a behavioral observation approach. As such, the strength of the CFCF lies in its potential ecological validity. However, as described previously, the risk of bias and error in self and informant appraisal of financial functioning represents a possible weakness of the CFCF (Marson, 2001). These risks are more evident for dementia patients and their caregivers (Wadley et al., 2003). Wadley and colleagues (2003) found that AD patients and caregivers demonstrated high levels of disagreement on the CFCF. In contrast, healthy normal older adult controls and their caregivers demonstrated high levels of consistency, stability, and accuracy in CFCF ratings (Wadley et al., 2003). More specifically, control ratings did not differ from control informant ratings for individual domains of the CFCF or overall. Stability for CFCF ratings was excellent across a 1-month period for both controls and their informants, achieving ≥ 98% exact rating agreement. Based on control and control-informant data, the reliability and validity of the CFCF appears to be excellent (Wadley et al., 2003).

Research involving the CFCF provides strong evidence that, based on a psychometric performance criterion (the Financial Capacity Instrument), the accuracy of self- and informant-report regarding financial abilities is compromised in the context of dementia and caregiving, well above the level of inaccuracy found in older adult controls and control informants (Loewenstein et al., 2001). Therefore, clinicians should exercise caution in basing capacity determinations of dementia patients on patient or caregiver report.

Measure of Awareness of Financial Skills

Most measures that assess financial capacity focus on an individual's ability to perform tasks independently. However, competence does not rest solely on an individual's ability to perform tasks but also on his or her capacity to recognize performance deficits and to obtain help where difficulties arise (Van Wielingen et al., 2004). As previously noted, persons with AD often lack insight into their disorder and its resultant functional deficits. Cramer and colleagues (2004) designed the Measure of Awareness of Financial Skills (MAFS) to assess awareness of financial skills in persons with dementia.

The MAFS compares patient self-report to informants' ratings of patient disability and uses this information to quantify patients' awareness of financial deficits. The patient questionnaire and parallel informant version consist of 34 items. Respondents are asked to rate the degree of difficulty the patient experiences in performing specific financial tasks (16 items) and how much assistance he or she gets in performing these tasks (16 items). Specific financial tasks addressed in the MAFS include: identifying and counting coins and currency, completing cash transactions, writing a check, balancing a checkbook, handling day-today spending, managing investments, living within an income, completing taxes, and comprehending and paying bills. Respondents also rate the patient's overall financial capacity (1 item) as well as the likelihood that the patient may experience negative consequences as a result of financial mismanagement (1 item). All items are scored on a 4-point scale ranging from "no difficulty/no assistance needed/very capable" (0 points) to "completely unable/someone else does it entirely/minimally capable" (4 points). Total scores for patient and informant questionnaires range from 0 to 102. The discrepancy in total scores for patient and informant questionnaires serves as an index of the patient's unawareness of financial difficulties. The MAFS also utilizes a brief 6-item performance-based measure adapted from the Direct Assessment of Functional Status (DAFS; Loewenstein et al., 2001) to supplement patient and informant questionnaires (Cramer et al., 2004). However, these six tasks do not adequately parallel items on the self and informant questionnaires. Noticeably absent from the performance-based measure are more complex tasks that are difficult to assess in clinical and laboratory settings (i.e., doing taxes).

Preliminary research has demonstrated that the MAFS reliably and validly discriminates between healthy older adult controls and dementia patients in regard to financial capacity (Cramer et al., 2004; Van Wielingen et al., 2004). Dementia patients were found to demonstrate impaired awareness of financial difficulties relative to both informant-report and performance-based components of the MAFS, and this discrepancy was related to dementia severity, task complexity, and level of executive dysfunction (Cramer et al., 2004; Van Wielingen et al., 2004). Moreover, a comparison of informant questionnaire and performance-based components of the MAFS provided further evidence that dementia caregivers tend to overestimate the financial abilities of their patients (Cramer et al., 2004). Therefore, like the CFCF, the MAFS is subject to potential bias and error common to self- and informant-based approaches of capacity assessment. Despite these limitations, the MAFS makes a unique contribution to our understanding of financial capacity loss in dementia by defining capacity not in terms of actual performance, but by patients' recognition of the financial tasks they can and cannot perform. Awareness of financial deficits allows patients to access help, when needed, while maintaining independence in performing tasks for which they remain aware and capable of performing (Van Wielingen et al., 2004).

Brief Performance-Based Measures

In contrast to self- and informant-rating scales, performance-based functional assessment measures require that older adults actually perform a series of standardized tasks relevant to everyday living (Angel & Frisco, 2001). Typically these tasks range from basic self-care skills (or activities of daily living [ADLs]; i.e., eating, grooming, dressing) to more complex IADLs (i.e., using a telephone, meal preparation, managing medications). Tasks are usually selected based on their adaptability for administration in clinical or laboratory settings.

Performance-based measures gauge actual abilities equivalent to those performed in the home environment in a way that is psychometrically objective, quantifiable, repeatable, and norm referenced. As such, they are not affected by the subjective bias, lack of insight, and/or denial that is inherent to self- and proxy-report measures (Karagiozis, Gray, Sacco, Shapiro, & Kawas, 1998; Loewenstein et al., 2001; Tabert et al., 2002; Wadley et al., 2003). For these reasons, performance-based measures of everyday functioning can significantly inform and augment self- and informant-based measures of functional decline (Loewenstein & Mogosky, 1999; Wadley et al., 2003) as well as supplement clinical interviews, which also rely heavily on informant report.

Over the past 2 decades, numerous brief performance-based functional assessment measures have been developed to assess older adults and persons with dementia (Ashley et al., 2001; Leckey & Beatty, 2002; Loewenstein et al., 1989; Mahurin et al., 1991; Willis et al., 1998). These measures were designed to evaluate a broad spectrum of independent living skills and usually contain an insufficient number of items to assess financial capacity (Wadley et al., 2003). Moreover, they differ considerably in the specific financial skills and abilities that they assess. However, these measures represent the first formal attempt to measure, even briefly, financial skills and abilities and have contributed substantially to our knowledge regarding financial performance of older adults.

Some researchers question the degree to which brief performance-based assessment measures detect subtler functional deficits in MCI and very mild AD (Loewenstein & Mogosky, 1999). This concern stems, in part, from the insensitivity of some performance-based tasks to detect subtle performance deficits (Griffith et al., 2003; Loewenstein & Mogosky, 1999; Marson & Briggs, 2001). For instance, individuals with MCI and very mild AD may remain unimpaired in their ability to identify and count coins and currency. In contrast, measures that assess more cognitively demanding financial tasks, such as using a bank statement, have detected subtle impairments in MCI and very mild AD (Griffith et al., 2003; Marson et al., 2000). The Financial Capacity Instrument developed by Marson and colleagues (2000) requires a more specific and systematic approach to assessing financial capacity and is discussed in greater detail in the next section.

Financial Capacity Instrument

The Financial Capacity Instrument (FCI; Marson et al., 2000) is a standardized psychometric instrument designed to assess financial performance in older adults and persons with AD according to the previously described conceptual model of financial capacity. The FCI consists of standardized tasks of various difficulty levels organized into domains of financial activity. The current version of the FCI assesses nine domains, 18 tasks, and has two overall scores (Griffith et al., 2003).

The FCI-9 possesses a detailed scoring system (Marson et al., 2000). Each FCI task consists of standardized, behaviorally anchored, quantitatively scored test items (Marson et al., 2000). The FCI scoring system assigns scores weighted in relationship to the relative importance of the item within task to the financial function of community-dwelling older adults. The use of standardized prompts and scoring anchors are incorporated into tasks to facilitate the validity, reliability, and interpretability of scores. On many items, spontaneous recall questions are supplemented with recognition format questions so that partial credit is available to patients with prominent amnesia or expressive aphasia. Tasks are summed to obtain domain and overall capacity scores. The FCI also assigns individual capacity outcomes using different cut-score systems (Marson et al., 2000); thus, a patient may be categorized as capable, marginally capable, or incapable of performing certain financial activities.

The FCI has demonstrated good levels of reliability, particularly at the domain level (Marson et al., 2000; Marson, 2001). Good to excellent internal, test/retest, and interrater reliabilities were achieved for prior versions of the FCI (i.e., FCI-6 and FCI-8) at the domain level using small samples of older adult controls and AD patients (Marson et al., 2000). Task-level internal and test/retest reliabilities for prior versions of the FCI were more uneven (ranging from adequate to excellent) and reflected reduced task range and statistical artifact rather than a systematic lack of relationship (Marson, 2001). The current FCI-9 reflects revisions based on these reliability findings.

Neuropsychological Testing: A Secondary Approach to Financial Capacity Assessment

Neuropsychological testing involves the measurement of specific cognitive abilities and does not provide a direct assessment of everyday functional performance. In this way, it differs from the previously described methods of financial capacity assessment. Therefore, despite its clinical utility, neuropsychological testing is recommended as a supplement to financial capacity assessment. However, in recent years, the profession of neuropsychology has placed increasing emphasis on understanding the cognitive structure underlying everyday task performance with the intent of better predicting the nature and extent of functional impairment resulting from brain injury (Chelune & Moehle, 1986; Lemsky, 2000). Neuropsychologists are now called on not only to assess cognitive deficits, but also to identify their impact on everyday functional abilities, which are of immediate consequence to the individual patient, his or her family, and the treatment team. The degree to which neuropsychology can successfully address these evolving clinical needs is based on its ability to yield useful and valid information directly relevant to issues of everyday living (Chelune & Moehle, 1986).

A considerable body of research has examined the relationship between cognitive abilities and functional performance. Scores on various standardized psychometric measures of intelligence, attention, executive function, memory, and global cognitive functioning have been found to be significantly correlated with functional capacities such as basic self-care, IADLs, and academic achievement as well as vocational attainment and performance (Grigsby, Kaye, Baxter, Shetterly, & Hamman, 1998; Heaton & Pendelton, 1981; Lichtenberg & Nanna, 1994; Nadler, Richardson, Malloy, Marran, & Hostetler-Brinson, 1993; Norton, Malloy, & Salloway, 2001). Various cognitive domains have also been linked to higher order functions such as financial capacity, medical decision making, medication management, and driving (Duchek, Hunt, Ball, Buckles, & Morris, 1997; Griffith et al., 2003; Lundberg et al., 1997; Marson, Cody, Ingram, & Harrell, 1995; Marson, Ingram, et al., 1995; Okonkwo et al., 2006; Park, 1999).

Neuropsychological studies represent an important approach to understanding loss of financial capacity in dementia (Marson, 2001). Such studies can reveal neurocognitive changes in AD and other dementias associated with loss of different financial abilities, and may thereby establish clinical markers of financial incapacity. Several studies looking at IADL performance in dementia patients found a significant relationship between measures of executive functioning and items related to money management skills (Grigsby et al., 1998; Nadler et al., 1993). However, these studies were limited in the number and complexity of financial items assessed. A separate study conducted by Marson, Sawrie, Stalvey, McInturff, and Harrell (1998) identified neuropsychological predictors of financial capacity using the aforementioned FCI-6. Performance by AD patients on the FCI-6 domains demonstrated significant relationships with specific neurocognitive functions commonly compromised in dementia. Measures of simple executive function, semantic memory, verbal abstraction, attention, and receptive language emerged as key predictors of AD patient performance on a range of domains tapping important everyday financial activities (Marson, 2001). Research therefore suggests that multiple cognitive functions are associated with loss of financial abilities in AD patients (Marson et al., 1998). However, many neurocognitive measures tap multiple cognitive functions, complicating specific linkages between neurocognitive change and specific declines in financial capacity.

Although cognition has been found to inform the development and exercise of financial capacity (Griffith et al., 2003; Marson et al., 2000), it remains both conceptually and analytically distinct from it (Marson & Hebert, 2006). Difficulties in financial performance may occur without corresponding cognitive deficits. For instance, the inability to write checks may result from debilitating arthritis or severe tremors rather than cognitive impairment. The particular cognitive abilities that support financial capacity as well as the level of cognitive impairment necessary for declines in financial performance have only recently been explored and are not yet well understood (Griffith et al., 2003; Marson et al., 2000; Okonkwo et al., 2006). Therefore, although cognitive test performance is clearly related to financial capacity, decisions to limit an individual's financial autonomy should not be based solely, or even primarily on neuropsychological test performance. Rather, clinicians should rely primarily on capacity-specific information, using neuropsychological data as supporting evidence, in rendering judgments regarding an individual's financial capacity (Marson & Hebert, 2006).

RESEARCH ON FINANCIAL CAPACITY IN ALZHEIMER'S DISEASE AND MILD COGNITIVE IMPAIRMENT

Financial capacity represents a cognitively complex set of functional abilities that is particularly vulnerable to the effects of AD and related dementias (Marson et al., 2000). Subtle declines in complex financial skills and abilities emerge in preclinical stages of AD and continue in mild to moderate AD, resulting in increasingly impaired performance of simple as well as complex financial tasks (Griffith et al., 2003; Marson et al., 2000; Okonkwo et al., 2006). Therefore, clinicians must be sensitive to money management difficulties in persons with AD and MCI (Wadley et al., 2003).

Until recently, few empirical studies of financial capacity have been conducted (Cramer et al., 2004; Crowe, Mahoney, & Jackson, 2004; Griffith et al., 2003; Marson & Briggs, 2001; Marson et al., 2000; Okonkwo et al., 2006; Van Wielingen et al., 2004). The scarcity of clinical research in this area is likely due in part to a lack of a conceptual model and standardized assessment instruments specific to financial capacity. As previously described, the FCI was specifically designed by our group to assess performance of older adults at the task, domain, and global levels of the financial conceptual model.

Psychometric Study of Financial Capacity in Alzheimer's Disease

In an initial study, a sample of 23 older control subjects and 53 AD patients (30 with mild dementia, and 23 with moderate dementia) were administered the FCI-6 (Marson et al., 2000). The FCI-6 consists of six broad domains of financial activity and 14 specific financial tasks (Marson et al., 2000). As shown in Table 11.2, mild AD patients performed equivalently with control subjects on Domain 1 (basic monetary skills), but significantly below control subjects on the other five domains of financial activity. In regard to FCI tasks, mild AD patients performed equivalently with controls on simple tasks such as naming and counting coins/currency, understanding parts of a checkbook, and detecting risk of mail fraud. However, the performance of mild AD patients on more complex tasks (e.g., defining and applying financial concepts, obtaining change for vending machine use, writing a check and recording transactions in a checkbook register, understanding and using a bank statement, and making an investment decision) fell significantly below control participants. In contrast, moderate AD patients performed significantly below controls and mild AD patients on all financial domains and tasks (Marson & Briggs, 2001; Marson et al., 2000).

This initial study represented the first empirical effort to investigate loss of financial capacity in patients with AD (Marson & Briggs, 2001). The findings suggest that significant impairment of financial capacity emerges in early AD. Mild AD patients appear to experience deficits in

Table 11.2   Group Comparison of FCI-6 Domain and Task Performance

Domain/ Task Level	Score Range	Controls [n = 23] M (SD)	Mild AD [n = 30] M[a] (SD)	Moderate AD [n = 20] M (SD)
Domain 1 Basic Monetary Skills	0–79	77.9[b] (1.9)	75.5 (3.5)	57.9 (16.3)
Task 1a Naming coins/ currency	0–30	30.0[b] (0.0)	30.0 (0.0)	26.7 (4.7)
Task 1b Coin/currency relationships	0–37	36.0[b] (1.8)	34.0 (3.0)	22.7 (9.2)
Task 1c Counting coins/ currency	0–12	11.9[a] (0.3)	11.5 (0.8)	8.6 (3.8)
Domain 2 Financial Concepts	0–41	35.5[b,c] (2.7)	29.6 (5.4)	19.1 (6.3)
Task 2a Defining concepts	0–16	13.0[b,c] (1.9)	9.7 (2.9)	7.1 (2.7)
Task 2b Applying concepts	0–25	22.5[b,c] (1.4)	19.9 (3.6)	12.0 (4.6)
Domain 3 Cash Transactions	0–48	46.2[b,c] (2.7)	38.6 (8.5)	22.2 (10.1)
Task 3a 1-item purchase	0–16	15.3[b] (2.5)	14.4 (3.2)	8.6 (4.9)
Task 3b 3-item purchase	0–16	15.2[b,c] (1.3)	10.7 (5.0)	4.6 (3.3)
Task 3c Change/vending machine	0–16	15.7[b,c] (0.6)	13.6 (2.8)	9.0 (4.1)
Domain 4 Checkbook/Register	0–62	60.2[b,c] (2.1)	50.7 (8.0)	33.3 (16.1)
Task 4a Understanding checkbook	0–32	30.7[b] (1.5)	27.9 (3.1)	20.6 (7.6)
Task 4b Using checkbook	0–30	29.5[b,c] (1.5)	22.8 (6.1)	12.2 (9.1)
Domain 5 Bank Statement	0–40	37.4[b,c] (2.2)	28.6 (7.6)	14.9 (7.2)
Task 5a Understanding bank statement	0–22	19.7[b,c] (2.1)	15.0 (4.1)	8.0 (3.6)
Task 5b Using bank statement	0–18	17.7[b,c] (0.9)	13.6 (4.3)	6.9 (4.1)
Domain 6 Financial Judgment	0–37	30.0[b,c] (3.0)	20.8 (5.4)	10.7 (5.1)
Task 6a Detecting fraud risk	0–10	8.6[b] (2.0)	7.8 (2.2)	6.9 (2.8)
Task 6b Investment decision	0–27	21.4[b,c] (2.1)	13.0 (4.4)	5.3 (3.5)

[a]Mild AD mean differs from moderate AD mean (*p* < .01). [b]Normal control mean differs from moderate AD mean using LSD post-hoc test (*p* < .01). [c]Normal control mean differs from mild AD mean (*p* < .01).

Source: "Assessing Financial Capacity in Patients with Alzheimer's Disease: A Conceptual Model and Prototype Instrument," by D. C. Marson et al., 2000, *Archives of Neurology, 57,* p. 880. Copyright 1995 by the American Medical Association. Reprinted with permission.

complex financial abilities (tasks), and some level of impairment in almost all financial activities (domains). Moderate AD patients appear to experience loss of both simple and complex financial abilities and sustain severe impairment across all financial activities. Based on these initial findings, we proposed two preliminary clinical guidelines for assessment of financial capacity in patients with mild and moderate AD (Marson et al., 2000):

1. *Mild AD patients* are at significant risk for impairment in most financial activities, in particular complex activities like checkbook and bank statement management. Areas of preserved autonomous financial activity should be carefully evaluated and monitored.
2. *Moderate AD patients* are at great risk for loss of all financial activities. Although each AD patient must be considered individually, it is likely that most moderate AD patients will be unable to manage their financial affairs. (p. 883)

Psychometric Study of Financial Capacity in Mild Cognitive Impairment

In a subsequent study, our group also examined financial capacity in patients with amnestic MCI (Griffith et al., 2003). The term MCI denotes a transitional period between normal cognitive aging and dementia (Morris et al., 2001; Petersen, Doody, et al., 2001; Peterson, Stevens, et al., 2001) and has otherwise been characterized as a preclinical or prodromal phase of AD (Collie & Maruff, 2000; Morris, 1993). Diagnostic criteria for MCI currently include subjective complaints of memory loss, objective impairment on memory testing, normal performance overall on general cognitive tests, and generally preserved ADLs (Petersen, Stevens, et al., 2001). The criterion that patients with MCI do not show any functional change has recently been challenged. Emerging evidence demonstrates that individuals with MCI do experience changes in everyday function prior to dementia diagnosis (Daly et al., 2000; Morris et al., 2001; Ritchie, Atero, & Touchon, 2001; Touchon & Ritchie, 1999).

To investigate functional change in MCI, the FCI-9 (see Table 11.3) was administered to 21 older control subjects, 21 patients with amnestic

Table 11.3 Group Comparisons of FCI-9 Domain and Task Performance

Domain/ Task Level	Score Range	Controls [n = 21] M (SD)	MCI Patients [n = 21] M (SD)	AD Patients [n = 22] M (SD)	P (2-tailed)	Post-hoc p < .05
Basic Monetary Skills	0–48	45.2 (3.5)	44.3 (3.7)	41.0 (6.3)	.010	CM > A
Naming coins/currency	0–8	7.9 (0.3)	7.8 (0.4)	7.6 (0.7)	.050	C > A
Coins/currency relationships	0–28	24.9 (3.4)	24.8 (3.5)	22.0 (5.5)	.044	—
Counting coins/money	0–12	12.0 (0.2)	11.7 (0.5)	11.5 (1.2)	.119	—
Financial Concepts	0–40	36.9 (3.2)	33.1 (4.7)	27.6 (7.5)	.001	C > M > A
Understanding concepts	0–15	13.8 (1.2)	12.9 (1.8)	11.2 (2.6)	.001	CM > A
Applying concepts	0–25	23.1 (2.4)	20.2 (3.6)	16.4 (5.3)	.001	C > M > A
Cash Transactions	0–30	27.0 (3.4)	24.8 (3.6)	20.6 (5.9)	.001	CM > A
One-item transaction	0–6	6.0 (0.0)	5.8 (0.6)	5.5 (1.1)	.044	C > A
Multi-item transaction	0–7	6.1 (1.9)	5.7 (1.8)	4.5 (2.4)	.037	C > A
Vending machine	0–9	8.6 (0.9)	8.0 (1.4)	5.6 (1.9)	.001	CM > A
Tipping	0–8	6.3 (1.7)	5.4 (1.5)	5.1 (2.1)	.068	—
Checkbook Management	0–54	53.2 (1.5)	50.6 (2.9)	42.9 (8.0)	.001	CM > A
Understanding checkbook	0–24	23.5 (0.8)	22.8 (1.5)	21.2 (2.5)	.001	CM > A
Using checkbook	0–30	29.6 (1.4)	27.9 (2.2)	21.7 (6.0)	.001	CM > A
Bank Statement Management	0–38	35.2 (2.7)	29.9 (5.6)	23.3 (8.3)	.001	C > M > A
Understanding bank statement	0–18	16.2 (1.6)	13.4 (2.7)	10.6 (3.9)	.001	C > M > A
Using bank statement	0–20	19.1 (1.5)	16.5 (4.0)	12.7 (4.9)	.001	C > M > A

Financial Judgment	0–26	25.6 (1.2)	23.2 (3.7)	23.5 (3.5)	.029	—
Mail fraud	0–8	8.0 (0.0)	7.3 (1.3)	7.1 (1.6)	.045	—
Telephone fraud	0–18	17.6 (1.2)	15.9 (3.0)	16.4 (2.3)	.051	—
Bill Payment	0–46	43.7 (3.3)	38.4 (6.2)	28.3 (9.6)	.001	C > M > A
Understanding bills	0–6	5.9 (0.4)	5.1 (1.2)	4.7 (1.6)	.006	C > MA
Identifying/prioritizing bills	0–13	12.6 (0.6)	12.3 (1.1)	10.9 (1.7)	.001	CM > A
Preparing bills for mailing	0–27	25.1 (3.3)	20.4 (6.1)	12.7 (8.4)	.001	C > M > A
Assets and Estate Arrangements[a]	0–20	18.1 (1.6)	17.4 (2.6)	16.2 (2.8)	.068	—
Investment Decision Making[b]	0–17	13.9 (2.9)	12.4 (2.3)	9.2 (3.5)	.001	CM > A
FCI Total Score (Domains 1–7)	0–282	266.8 (13.2)	243.8 (21.7)	207.2 (38.0)	.001	C > M > A
FCI Total Score (Domains 1–8)[a]	0–302	282.1 (14.1)	264.0 (17.8)	223.8 (39.9)	.001	CM > A

Note: C > A = Control mean is greater than AD mean; C > M > A = Control mean is greater than MCI mean and AD mean, and MCI mean is greater than AD mean; C > MA = Control mean is greater than MCI and AD means; CM > A = Control and MCI means are greater than AD mean.

[a]Control = 15, MCI = 13, AD = 21. [b]Control = 21, MCI = 19, AD = 18.

Source: "Impaired Financial Abilities in Mild Cognitive Impairment: A Direct Assessment Approach," by H.R. Griffith et al., 2003, *Neurology, 60*(3), p. 450. Copyright 2003, American Academy of Neurology. Reprinted with permission.

MCI, and 22 patients with mild AD (Griffith et al., 2003). The groups were well matched on demographic variables of education, gender, race, and socioeconomic status (Griffith et al., 2003). At the domain level, the MCI group performed significantly below control subjects in regard to financial conceptual knowledge (Domain 2), checkbook management (Domain 4), bank statement management (Domain 5), financial judgment (Domain 6), and bill payment (Domain 7). There were no domains on which the MCI group performed better than control participants. However, the MCI group performed significantly better than mild AD patients on all financial domains with the exception of Domain 8 (knowledge of personal assets and estate arrangements).

At the task level, control subjects performed significantly better than the MCI group on tasks of applying financial concepts (i.e., selecting interest rates or preparing taxes), understanding and using a bank statement, and understanding bills and preparing bills for mailing (Griffith et al., 2003). Again there were no tasks on which the MCI group performed better than controls. The MCI group, in turn, demonstrated significantly higher scores than the AD group on tasks of understanding and applying financial concepts, using a vending machine, understanding and using a checkbook, understanding and using a bank statement, prioritizing bills, and preparing bills for mailing.

For overall financial capacity (Domains 1 to 7), control participants performed significantly better than MCI and AD participants, and MCI participants performed significantly better than AD participants. Using a direct assessment approach, we found that patients with amnestic MCI demonstrated significant, albeit mild, declines on some (but not all) financial abilities compared to age, education, gender, and racially matched normal controls. These results strongly suggest that decline in financial abilities is an aspect of functional change in MCI (Griffith et al., 2003).

Summary of Financial Capacity Research

In summary, these two studies support the value of the conceptual model and the FCI as new approaches for assessing financial capacity in patients with neurodegenerative disease. The FCI represents a potential advance in functional assessment in dementia (Moye, 2003). Because it involves a wide range of cognitively demanding financial tasks, the FCI has demonstrated sensitivity in detecting subtle performance changes in mild AD and MCI that might otherwise go undetected by conventional IADL performance measures and observer rating forms.

CONCLUSION

Financial capacity is a cognitively complex set of skills and abilities critical to the independent functioning of older adults in our society. Most if not all community dwelling older adults regularly engage in some form of financial activity. Thus, financial capacity represents a useful construct for examining the interrelationship between cognitive and functional change in normal aging and dementia. With the aging of society, clinical assessment of financial capacity has become increasingly important (Marson, 2001). Older adults as a whole are disproportionately targets of financial and other types of consumer fraud ("Woman Out," 1996; Nerenberg, 1996). Loss of higher order functional abilities like financial capacity is a defining diagnostic feature of AD and related dementias (American Psychological Association, 1994; McKhann et al., 1984). Dementia patients and their families often suffer challenges and hardships related to loss of financial abilities (Marson et al., 2000). In some cases, financial mismanagement (i.e., failure to pay bills) and poor financial judgment (i.e., susceptibility to mail or telephone scams) of persons with AD result in financial exploitation or unintentional self-impoverishment (Marson, 2001). Financial incapacity in AD may also have post mortem consequences, particularly when a will is contested on the grounds that the testator lacked sufficient knowledge of his or her financial assets at the time that the will was executed (Marson & Hebert, 2005). Early clinical detection of impaired financial abilities helps protect the economic resources as well as the emotional well-being of dementia patients and their families (Marson et al., 2000). However, we still know surprisingly little about impairment or loss of financial capacity in dementia patients and persons undergoing normal cognitive aging (Willis, 1996). This lack of knowledge is in part due to a lack of a conceptual model and standardized instruments for assessing financial capacity as well as an absence of formal training in financial capacity assessment (Marson, 2001).

In this chapter, we have provided a conceptual overview of financial capacity, described current approaches for assessing financial capacity (including clinical interview, self- and informant-rating scales, performance-based measures, and neuropsychological testing), and summarized literature linking cognitive and functional change in aging and dementia. Although much work remains to be done in terms of conceptualizing financial capacity as a construct and in developing clinically useful methods of assessment, the information provided here should provide a thorough introduction to the topic of financial capacity and contribute to a basic clinical and scientific understanding of the process by which financial skills and abilities erode and are lost in AD.

REFERENCES

American Psychiatric Association. (1994). *Diagnostic and statistical manual of mental disorders* (4th ed.). Washington, DC: Author.

Angel, R. J., & Frisco, M. L. (2001). Self-assessments of health and functional capacity among older adults. *Journal of Mental Health and Aging, 7*(1), 119–135.

Ashley, M. J., Persel, C. S., & Clark, M. C. (2001). Validation of an independent living scale for post-acute rehabilitation applications. *Brain Injury, 15,* 435–442.

Chelune, G. J., & Moehle, K. A. (1986). Neuropsychological assessment and everyday functioning. In D. Welding & A. M. Horton Jr. (Eds.), *The neuropsychology handbook: Behavioral and clinical perspectives* (pp. 489–525). New York: Springer.

Collie, A., & Maruff, P. (2000). The neuropsychology of preclinical Alzheimer's disease and mild cognitive impairment. *Neuroscience and Biobehavioral Reviews, 24,* 365–374.

Cramer, K., Tuokko, H. A., Mateer, C. A., & Hultsch, D. F. (2004). Measuring awareness of financial skills: Reliability and validity of a new measure. *Aging and Mental Health, 8*(2), 161–171.

Crowe, S. F., Mahoney, K., & Jackson, M. (2004). Predicting competency in automated machine use in an acquired brain injury population using neuropsychological measures. *Archives of Clinical Neuropsychology, 19,* 673–691.

Daly, E., Zaitchik, D., Copeland, M., Schmahmann, J., Gunther, J., & Albert, M. (2000). Predicting conversion to Alzheimer's disease using standardized clinical information. *Archives of Neurology, 57,* 675–680.

DeBettignies, B. H., Mahurin, R. K., Roderick, K., & Pirozzolo, F. J. (1993). Functional status in Alzheimer's disease and multi-infarct dementia: A comparison of patient performance and caregiver report. *Clinical Gerontologist, 12*(4), 31–49.

Demers, L., Oremus, M., Perrault, A., Champoux, N., & Wolfson, C. (2000). Review of outcome measurement instruments in Alzheimer's disease drug trials: Psychometric properties of functional and quality of life scales. *Journal of Geriatric Psychiatry and Neurology, 13,* 170–180.

Drachman, D., & Swearer, J. (1993). Driving and Alzheimer's disease: The risk of crashes. *Neurology, 43,* 2448–2456.

Duchek, J., Hunt, L., Ball, K., Buckles, V., & Morris, C. M. (1997). The role of selective attention in driving and dementia of the Alzheimer's type. *Alzheimer's Disease and Associated Disorders, 11*(1), 48–56.

Griffith, H. R., Belue, K., Sicola, A., Krzywanski, S., Zamrini, E., Harrell, L. E., et al. (2003). Impaired financial abilities in mild cognitive impairment: A direct assessment approach. *Neurology, 60*(3), 449–457.

Grigsby, J., Kaye, K., Baxter, J., Shetterly, S. M., & Hamman, R. F. (1998). Executive cognitive abilities and functional status among community-dwelling older persons in the San Luis Valley Health and Aging Study. *Journal of the American Geriatrics Society, 46,* 590–596.

Grisso, T. (Ed.). (2003). *Evaluating competencies: Forensic assessments and instruments* (2nd ed.). New York: Kluwer Academic/Plenum Press.

Heaton, R. K., & Pendleton, M. G. (1981). Use of neuropsychological tests to predict adult patients' everyday functioning. *Journal of Consulting and Clinical Psychology, 64,* 121–129.

Hebert, K., Martin-Cook, K., Svetlik, D., & Weiner, M. F. (2002). Caregiver decision-making and driving: What we say versus what we do. *Clinical Gerontologist, 26*(1/2), 17–29.

Hunt, L., Murphy, C., Carr, D., Duchek, J., Buckles, V., & Morris, J. (1997). Reliability of the Washington University road test: A performance-based assessment for drivers with dementia of the Alzheimer type. *Archives of Neurology, 54,* 707–712.

Ippen, C. G., Olin, J. T., & Schneider, L. S. (1999). Can caregivers independently rate cognitive and behavioral symptoms in Alzheimer's disease patients? A longitudinal analysis. *American Journal of Geriatric Psychiatry, 7*, 321–330.

Karagiozis, H., Gray, S., Sacco, G., Shapiro, M., & Kawas, C. (1998). The Direct Assessment of Functional Abilities (DAFA): A comparison to an indirect measure of instrumental activities of daily living. *Gerontologist, 38*(1), 113–121.

Kiyak, H., Teri, L., & Borson, S. (1994). Physical and functional health assessment in normal aging and in Alzheimer's disease: Self reports versus family reports. *Gerontologist, 34*, 324–330.

Leckey, G. S., & Beatty, W. W. (2002). Predicting functional performance by patients with Alzheimer's disease using the Problems in Everyday Living (PEDL) Test: A preliminary study. *Journal of the International Neuropsychological Society, 8*, 48–57.

Lemsky, C. (2000). Neuropsychological assessment and treatment planning. In G. Groth-Marnat (Ed.), *Neuropsychological assessment in clinical practice: A guide to test interpretation and integration* (pp. 535–574). New York: Wiley.

Lichtenberg, P. A., & Nanna, M. (1994). The role of cognition in predicting activities of daily living and ambulation functioning in the oldest old rehabilitation patients. *Rehabilitation Psychology, 39*(5), 251–262.

Lieff, S., Maindonald, K., & Shulman, K. (1984). Issues in determining financial competence in the elderly. *Canadian Medical Association Journal, 130*, 1293–1296.

Loewenstein, D. A., Amigo, E., Duara, R., Guterman, A., Hurwitz, D., Berkowitz, N., et al. (1989). A new scale for the assessment of functional status in Alzheimer's disease and related disorders. *Journals of Gerontology, 44*(4), P114–P121.

Loewenstein, D. A., Arguelles, S., Bravo, M., Freeman, R. Q., Arguelles, T., Acevedo, A., et al. (2001). Caregivers' judgments of the functional abilities of the Alzheimer's disease patient: A comparison of proxy reports and objective measures. *Journal of Gerontology: Psychological Sciences, 56B*(2), P78–P84.

Loewenstein, D. A., & Mogosky, B. J. (1999). The functional assessment of the older adult patient. In P. A. Lichtenberg (Ed.), *Handbook of assessment in clinical gerontology* (pp. 529–554). New York: Wiley.

Lundberg, C., Johnasson, K., Ball, K., Bjerre, B., Blomqvist, C., Braekhus, A., et al. (1997). Dementia and driving: An attempt at consensus. *Alzheimer's Disease and Associated Disorders, 11*(1), 28–37.

Mahurin, R. K., DeBettignies, B. H., & Pirozzolo, F. J. (1991). Structured assessment of independent living skills: Preliminary report of a performance measure of functional abilities in dementia. *Journals of Gerontology, 46*(2), P58–P66.

Marson, D. C. (2001). Loss of financial competency in dementia: Conceptual and empirical approaches. *Aging, Neuropsychology, and Cognition, 8*(3), 164–181.

Marson, D. C., & Briggs, S. D. (2001). Assessing competency in Alzheimer's disease: Treatment consent capacity and financial capacity. In S. Gauthier & J. Cummings (Eds.), *Alzheimer's disease and related disorders annual, 2001* (pp. 1–28). London: Dunitz.

Marson, D. C., Cody, H. A., Ingram, K. K., & Harrell, L. E. (1995). Neuropsychologic predictors of competency in Alzheimer's disease using a rational reasons legal standard. *Archives of Neurology, 52*, 955–959.

Marson, D. C., & Hebert, K. R. (2005). Assessing civil competencies in older adults with dementia: Consent capacity, financial capacity, and testamentary capacity. In G. Larrabee (Ed.), *Forensic neuropsychology* (pp. 334–377). New York: Oxford University Press.

Marson, D. C., & Hebert, K. R. (2006). Functional assessment. In D. K. Attix & K. Welsh-Bohmer (Eds.), *Geriatric neuropsychology: Assessment and intervention* (pp. 158–197). New York: Guilford Press.

Marson, D. C., Huthwaite, J., & Hebert, K. (2004). Testamentary capacity and undue influence in the elderly: A jurisprudent therapy perspective. *Law and Psychology Review, 28*, 71–96.

Marson, D. C., Ingram, K. K., Cody, H. A., & Harrell, L. E. (1995). Assessing competency of patients with Alzheimer's disease under different legal standards. *Archives of Neurology, 52*, 949–954.

Marson, D. C., Martin, R., Griffith, R., Wadley, V., Belue, K., Snyder, S., et al. (2006, July). *Clinical assessment of financial capacity in Alzheimer's disease.* Paper presented at the 10th International Conference on Alzheimer's Disease, Madrid, Spain.

Marson, D. C., McInturff, B., Hawkins, L., Bartolucci, A., & Harrell, L. E. (1997). Consistency of physician judgments of capacity to consent in mild Alzheimer's disease. *Journal of the American Geriatrics Society, 45*, 453–457.

Marson, D. C., Sawrie, S. M., Snyder, S., McInturff, B., Stalvey, T., Boothe, A., et al. (2000). Assessing financial capacity in patients with Alzheimer's disease: A conceptual model and prototype instrument. *Archives of Neurology, 57*, 877–884.

Marson, D. C., Sawrie, S. M., Stalvey, T., McInturff, B., & Harrell, L. (1998, February). *Neuropsychological correlates of declining financial capacity in patients with Alzheimer's disease.* Platform presentation at the 26th annual meeting of the International Neuropsychological Society, Honolulu, HA. [Abstract published in *Journal of the International Neuropsychological Society, 4*(37).]

McKay, M. (1989). Financial and personal competency in the elderly: The position of the Canadian Psychiatric Association. *Canadian Journal of Psychiatry, 34,* 829–832.

McKhann, G., Drachman, D., Folstein, M., Katzman, R., Price, D., & Stadlan, E. (1984). Clinical diagnosis of Alzheimer's disease: Report of the NINCDS-ADRDA work group under the auspices of the Department of Health and Human Services Task Force on Alzheimer's disease. *Neurology, 34,* 939–944.

Morris, J. (1993). The Clinical Dementia Rating Scale (CDR): Current version and scoring rules. *Neurology, 43,* 2412–2414.

Morris, J., Storandt, M., Miller, P., McKeel, D., Price, J., Rubin, E., et al. (2001). Mild cognitive impairment represents early stage Alzheimer's disease. *Archives of Neurology, 58,* 397–405.

Moye, J. (2003). Guardianship and conservatorship. In T. Grisso (Ed.), *Evaluating competencies: Forensic assessments and instruments* (pp. 309–389). New York: Kluwer Academic/Plenum Press.

Nadler, J. D., Richardson, E. D., Malloy, P. F., Marran, M. E., & Hostetler-Brinson, M. E. (1993). The ability of the Dementia Rating Scale to predict everyday functioning. *Archives of Clinical Neuropsychology, 8,* 449–460.

Nerenberg, L. (1996). *Financial abuse of the elderly.* Washington, DC: National Center on Elder Abuse.

Norton, L. E., Malloy, P. F., & Salloway, S. (2001). The impact of behavioral symptoms on activities of daily living in patients with dementia. *American Journal of Geriatric Psychiatry, 9*(1), 41–48.

Okonkwo, O. C., Wadley, V. G., Griffith, H. R., Ball, K., & Marson, D. C. (2006). Cognitive correlates of financial abilities in mild cognitive impairment. *Journal of the American Geriatric Society, 54,* 1745–1750.

Overman, W., & Stoudemire, A. (1988). Guidelines for legal and financial counseling of Alzheimer's disease patients and their families. *American Journal of Psychiatry, 145,* 1495–1500.

Park, D. (1999). Cognition, processing resources, and self-report. In N. Schwarz, D. C. Park, B. Knaüper, & S. Sudman (Eds.), *Cognition, aging, and self-reports* (pp. 45–69). Philadelphia, PA: Psychology Press.

Petersen, R., Doody, R., Kurz, A., Mohs, R., Morris, J., Rabins, P., et al. (2001). Current concepts in mild cognitive impairment. *Archives of Neurology, 58*, 1985–1992.

Petersen, R., Stevens, J., Ganguli, M., Tangalos, E., Cummings, J., & DeKosky, S. (2001). Practice parameter: Early detection of dementia—Mild cognitive impairment (an evidence based review) (Report of the Quality Standards Committee of the American Academy of Neurology). *Neurology, 56*, 1133–1142.

Ritchie, K., Atero, S., & Touchon, J. (2001). Classification criteria for mild cognitive impairment: A population based validation study. *Neurology, 56*, 37–42.

Rubenstein, L. Z., Schairer, C., Wieland, G. D., & Kane, R. (1984). Systematic biases in functional assessment of elderly adults: Effects of different data sources. *Journal of Gerontology, 39*(6), 686–691.

Sager, M. A., Dunham, N. C., Schwantes, A., Mecum, L., Halverson, K., & Harlowe, D. (1992). Measurement of activities of daily living in hospitalized elderly: A comparison of self-report and performance-based methods. *Journal of the American Geriatrics Society, 40*, 457–462.

Spar, J. E., & Garb, A. (1992). Assessing competency to make a will. *American Journal of Psychiatry, 149*, 169–174.

Tabert, M., Albert, S., Borukhova-Milov, L., Camacho, Y., Pelton, G., Lui, X., et al. (2002). Functional deficits in patients with mild cognitive impairment: Prediction of AD. *Neurology, 58*, 758–764.

Toffoli, N., & Herrmann, N. (1993). Determination of financial competence in consultation-liaison psychiatry. *Canadian Journal of Psychiatry, 38*, 595–598.

Touchon, J., & Ritchie, K. (1999). Prodromal cognitive disorder in Alzheimer's disease. *International Journal of Geriatric Psychiatry, 14*, 556–563.

Van Wielingen, L. E., Tuokko, H. A., Cramer, K., Mateer, C. A., & Hultsch, D. F. (2004). Awareness of financial skills in dementia. *Aging and Mental Health, 8*(4), 374–380.

Wadley, V. G., Harrell, L. E., & Marson, D. C. (2003). Self- and informant report of financial abilities in patients with Alzheimer's disease: Reliable and valid? *Journal of the American Geriatrics Society, 51*, 1621–1626.

Weinberger, M., Samsa, G. P., Schmader, K., Greenberg, S. M., Carr, D. B., Wildman, D. S., et al. (1992). Comparing proxy and patients' perceptions of patients' functional status: Results from a geriatric outpatient clinic. *Journal of the American Geriatrics Society, 40*, 585–588.

Wiener, J. M., Hanley, R. J., Clark, R., & Van Nostrand, J. F. (1990). Measuring activities of daily living: Comparisons across national surveys. *Journal of Gerontology: Social Sciences, 45*(6), S229–S237.

Wild, K. V., & Cotrell, V. (2003). Identifying driving impairment in Alzheimer's disease: A comparison of self and observer reports versus driving evaluation. *Alzheimer's Disease and Associated Disorders, 17*(1), 27–34.

Willis, S. L. (1996). Everyday cognitive competence in elderly persons: Conceptual issues and empirical findings. *Gerontologist, 36,* 595–601.

Willis, S. L., Allen-Burge, R., Dolan, M. M., Bertrand, R. M., Yesavage, J., & Taylor, J. L. (1998). Everyday problem solving among individuals with Alzheimer's disease. *Gerontologist, 38*(5), 569–577.

Woman out of $5,300 in two cons. (1996, March 3). *Birmingham News,* p. 15-A.

World Health Organization. (1980). *International classification of impairment, disabilities, and handicaps.* Geneva, Switzerland: Author.

Zanetti, O., Geroldi, C., Frisoni, G. A., Bianchetti, A., & Trabucchi, M. (1999). Contrasting results between caregiver's report and direct assessment of activities of daily living in patients affected by mild and very mild dementia: The contribution of the caregiver's personal characteristics. *Journal of the American Geriatrics Society, 47*(2), 196–202.

12

Clinical Interventions for Decision Making with Impaired Persons

SARA HONN QUALLS

Cognitive impairment in later life is typically a degenerative condition that leads to changes in decision-making ability over time. Dementias are by nature progressive, irreversible diseases of the brain that impair cognition and functioning in daily life (American Psychiatric Association, 2000). Physical conditions that produce long-term cognitive impairment due to adverse impact on the central nervous system also show increasing impact on decision-making capacity over time (see descriptions in Kaye & Grigsby, Chapter 3, this volume). Even the focal impact of head injury or stroke often leads to broad, diffuse deterioration over time (Schofield et al., 1997).

The various trajectories of declining cognitive abilities typically evoke restrictive actions by persons whose concern about safety leads them to restrict decision-making opportunity or authority. Many players (including the wide range of those described in Qualls, Chapter 5, this volume) take informal actions along the course of a trajectory of decline, most of which function as discrete decisions to restrict choice. A daughter or physician or attorney who charges an older adult to restrict driving to local neighborhoods or daytime has made one such restrictive choice. A husband's decision to restrict his wife's access to the couple's checkbook when she has written checks to unknown persons or paid the same bill multiple times is also an informal choice that occurs far outside the legal system to restrict decision-making activity. The purpose of this chapter is to offer a framework and several strategies for intervening to assist persons with diminishing cognitive capacity in an effort to avoid or postpone loss of legal rights through guardianship or conservatorship.

ASYNCHRONOUS TIMING OF INTERVENTION AND COGNITIVE DECLINE

Even the most well-meaning persons who choose to restrict another adult's decision-making activity typically struggle with those choices. Choice-restricting interventions are quite challenging to players in the daily dramas of declining cognition for several reasons that are grounded in the asynchronous timing of activity restriction and cognitive decline.

Cognitive decline is usually insidious with very ambiguous consequences for daily functioning (Reisberg, Ferris, de Leon, & Crook, 1982). Observers of the decline are often confused about the specific points at which declining cognition warrants intervention by others (Knopman, Donohoe, & Gutterman, 2000). Family members of persons who are ultimately diagnosed with dementia recall signs that occurred several years prior to the point that they decided that something was wrong, and over a year elapsed between that decision point and the time when action was taken (Knopman et al., 2000). The interpersonal cost of the ambiguity in cognitive decline is notable in couples and families as they struggle to shore up the functioning of the declining person while determining when restrictive decisions need to be made (Blieszner, Roberto, & Wilcox, 2007; Qualls, 2003).

The trajectory of decline rarely overlaps perfectly onto the trajectory of restrictive intervention, leaving families feeling guilty for creating risk by intervening too late or creating offense by intervening too early. Consider the varied trajectories of decline for the three women depicted in Figure 12.1. As background, Mrs. Jones and Ms. Tanaka are both diagnosed with Alzheimer's disease whereas Mrs. Montoya's trajectory of

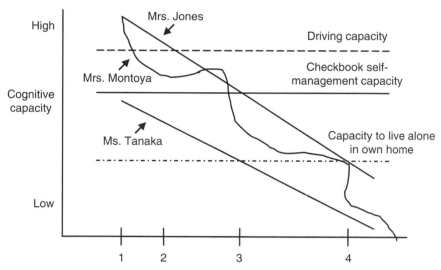

Figure 12.1   Trajectories of Cognitive Ability, Task Requirements, and Restrictive Interventions at Four Points in Time

decline shows the cumulative effects of mild cardiovascular incidents (strokes). However, Mrs. Jones and Mrs. Montoya have identical functioning at Time 1, whereas Ms. Tanaka is at a considerably lower level of cognitive function at the time of diagnosis.

The graph illustrates the disconnection between the continuous process of decline and the discrete impact of behavioral restrictions. Between two points in time, cognitive abilities are changing continuously whereas decisions about intervention are inevitably discrete. As a consequence, when their respective families make decisions about stepping in to restrict driving, they are likely to feel guilty (most people do) because their decisions are not perfectly mapped onto the functional ability of any of these three women.

Compare the functioning of each woman at Time 1 with the hypothetical line for defining cognitive capacity for safe driving that runs horizontally at the top of Figure 12.1. Mrs. Jones actually would have been able to drive safely until Time 2, whereas Mrs. Montoya was about to decline rapidly enough that her capacity would make her unsafe to keep driving. Ms. Tanaka's network was remiss in not protecting her and her community from her unsafe driving prior to Time 1 if she lacked cognitive skills needed to drive. By Time 2, the level of capacity and actions to restrict driving are synchronous for all three women. However, Ms. Tanaka is still at risk in the domain of finances where she is below capacity to manage her checkbook and bills safely. At Time 3, Mrs. Jones has just reached the point where she is unable to manage her checkbook whereas Mrs. Montoya reached that level of cognitive deterioration sooner, and Mrs. Tanaka is functioning far below the level needed to be safe. Obviously, the conditions for having capacity to drive are neither universal nor as easily defined as the illustration suggests. Indeed, Chapter 1 of this volume uses variations in driving regulations across states as an illustration of the challenges in this field. Furthermore, individuals vary in the level of cognitive capacity needed for different domains of function based on their ability to apply compensatory skills, environmental supports, and other naturally occurring interventions. Yet, the principles illustrated in Figure 12.1 are key to our ability to understand when and how to intervene in support of autonomy or safety.

Interventions to support autonomy can be designed when the information about an individual's capacity is compared with the resources needed to function in a particular domain. Although much of the focus of this book is on assessment of decision-making capacity to determine when to restrict rights functionally or legally, the information from a cognitive assessment is critical to assist members of the informal networks in designing interventions that support independence. Compensatory strategies may be enacted by the individual with declining cognition or by concerned others. Rarely is information about cognitive decline provided to formal or informal networks with specific suggestions for interventions to support independence.

PRINCIPLES TO GUIDE INFORMAL DECISIONS

Informal decisions to intervene on behalf of a cognitively declining adult should consider the four principles that are described in this section. The first two principles are based on ethical standards that are written into policy for the care of persons with disabilities, and the latter two are principles to guide the structure and timing of interventions.

Least Restrictive Environment

All persons with disabilities have been granted the right to live in the least restrictive environment since the Americans with Disabilities Act with judicial sanction of enforcement outlined in the recent U.S. Supreme Court's *Olmstead* decision. This principle is now the legal standard, founded on the ethical principle of autonomy and the nearly universal value of support for quality of life. Additionally, we affirm this principle as humans and treat it as a personal imperative in our own lives.

The right to live in the least restrictive environment exists for individuals with cognitive impairment just as it does for persons with physical disabilities, requiring us to be vigilant and creative in assessing capacity, risk, and opportunity for intervention.

Balance, Autonomy, and Safety

Three primary ethical principles that are often in conflict during decisions related to older adults with cognitive impairment are: support for autonomy, beneficence to those in need, and justice in allocation of support for quality of life. Families struggle throughout the life cycle with maintaining a balance among these principles during each stage of family development.

A primary function of families is to support the individual development of children to reach maturity to maintain the genetic line. Although the pressure to protect offspring is powerful, the long-term protection of the genetic line requires training to support full autonomous functioning. Human parents face this dilemma daily as they determine what children need to learn to become fully autonomous, while ensuring a safe environment in which to learn it. The warp and woof of the parental tapestry is visible in simple decisions such as whether to allow a child to learn to do tricks on a skateboard, shop independently, drive to a nearby town alone, or attend college away from parental oversight.

The balance of support for autonomy and safety is also evident in later life when Mrs. Jones' husband and adult children struggle with decisions about restricting her activities against her will. The effects of dementias later in life and neurological immaturity of teenagers are similar in that they result in poor insight into the limits of capacity. Anosognosia is the inability to recognize the presence, scope, or implications of impairments on daily functioning. Often families, therefore, are not only struggling with decisions about supporting both autonomy and safety, but must do so in the face of the patient's defensive argument that others are viewing his or her capacity inaccurately.

Periods of transition in individual development are particularly challenging because they force changes in family members' frameworks and strategies for balancing the inevitable competing forces in support of autonomy and beneficence (Minuchin, 1974). Adolescence is defined by this struggle as parents attempt to provide the ideal level of support for autonomy while stepping in with beneficent activity in support of safety. Similarly, late life deterioration in cognition requires families and other informal networks to view their helping behavior in the context of the necessity to support both safety and autonomy. Personality and family dynamics both influence the urge to err on one side or the other of that delicate balance. Risk takers may appeal to ethical support for autonomy more quickly than those whose definition of a good person emphasizes beneficent protection of family from harm.

The principle of justice in allocation of support for the quality of life across society's members is evident in conflict as individuals vie for resources within families in each stage of the family life cycle. The demands created by an infant restrict the autonomy of the parent to be beneficent toward the vulnerable infant. The restrictive effects of parenting on individual development have been detailed by Guttman (1987), who defined the phase of the family life cycle as the "chronic parental emergency" that sacrifices parents' individual development for child development. Later, parents may rebalance justice within the family by demanding room and board when that same child returns home to live while launching her career after college graduation. Filial maturity exemplifies another shift in the balance as adult children donate energy to parental care in lieu of their own individual development (Nydegger, 1991).

Person-Environment Fit

The concept of person-environment fit claims that optimal outcomes occur when a person's capacities are optimally supported and challenged by the environment (Lawton & Nahemow, 1973; Scheidt & Windley, 2006). Figure 12.2 illustrates how the relationship between competence and environmental press contributes to affect and behavioral functionality. Persons with low competence, who are placed in an environment with moderate or strong challenges (i.e., press), lack the behavioral repertoire to adapt, which leads to maladaptive behavior and negative affect. Alternatively, extremely weak environmental press (e.g., isolation in a padded cell) generates negative affect and maladaptive behavior in almost everyone. The ideal person-environment fit is believed to occur when competence and environmental press are well matched, leading to optimal performance and positive affect (for critical review of empirical support for this framework, see Scheidt & Windley, 2006).

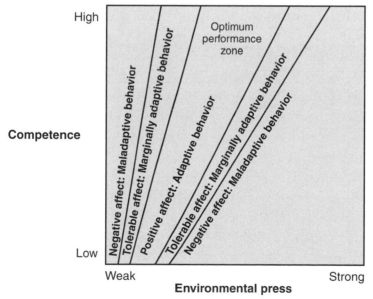

Figure 12.2   Relationship between Competence and Environmental Press.
Source: "Ecology and the Aging Process" (pp. 619–673), by M. P. Lawton and L. Nahemow, in *The Psychology of Adult Development and Aging,* C. Eisdorfer and M. P. Lawton (Eds.), 1973, Washington, DC: American Psychological Association.

When applied to persons with cognitive impairments, the principle of person-environment fit illuminates the role of environments in affecting decision-making capacity, a striking reframe for capacity, which is typically presumed to be a function only of the person. However, if placed in an understimulating or overstimulating environment, all of us can show maladaptive behavior. Evaluation of a cognitively impaired individual's capacity to function independently requires assessment of possible environmental changes that enhance the fit to increase adaptive behavior that is based on decisions. The environment plays a key role in shaping an individual's ability to perform instrumental activities of daily living (IADLs) or activities of daily living (ADLs), which are often the critical factors in challenges to a person's legal autonomy (Day, Carreon, & Stump, 2000; Gitlin & Gwyther, 2003).

Support Dying as Well as Living

Elder care inevitably culminates in choices related to the timing and contexts of dying. Persons experiencing cognitive decline are less likely to die from the disease that impairs cognition than from other age-related illnesses that are as prevalent in cognitively impaired persons as in all other populations (e.g., heart disease, cancer, and stroke). However, persons with declining cognition are at risk for a particularly poor quality of life due to their inability to communicate their needs and preferences; to actively create environments, activities, and relationships that bring satisfaction; and to participate in choices about interventions for acute as well as chronic illnesses.

Families need to be informed of their rights to consider shaping the dying process through intervention strategies that focus on comfort rather than cure, including comfort or palliative care and hospice care (Institute of Medicine, 1997; Miller, Mor, Gage, & Coppola, 2001; National Institute of Health Consensus Development Program, 2004). Families must face a simple question: "when is it time?" The answer comes only when the family appreciates the continuum of life and death that becomes increasingly evident in advanced stages of cognitive decline. I sometimes shock families when I ask them to spin forward in time (and sometimes not even very far forward) to consider how they want their loved ones to die. Only after those values are articulated can we address the immediate questions about how to support living today. My intent is not to determine the timing or substance of decisions, but to offer a framework for conceptualizing the links between dying and living. Naming the issue of balancing their focus on processes of dying as well as living is a key intervention with caregivers.

INTERVENTIONS

Three categories of interventions that can help avoid or delay legal decisions about guardianship or conservatorship are described here. Some families use these interventions intuitively as they attempt to compensate for lost abilities. Other *players* (as defined in Chapter 5) can benefit from being shown specific intervention options. Unfortunately, little focus has been placed on disseminating interventions to the various players whose involvement shapes the lives of persons with declining cognitive abilities. This chapter can provide only a cursory overview of an emerging field, and thus concludes with a call for rapid development and testing of interventions for this vulnerable population.

Environmental Interventions

Based on the paradigm espoused by Lewin (1935), Lawton and others developed applied gerontology in the person-environment fit paradigm, leading naturally to research on environmental interventions that shape behavior (Lawton, Windley, & Byerts, 1982). Recently, gerontological researchers have renewed their interest in environmental interventions, now more broadly construed to encompass social, technological, and design implications (Wahl, Scheidt, & Windley, 2003). These interventions illustrate the range of designs intended to improve the autonomy of cognitively impaired persons through environmental interventions.

Assistive Technology

Assistive technology offers supportive tools to prompt behavior, monitor behavior, and provide feedback or guidance on behavior. Within a few years, assistive technologies are anticipated to be universal (i.e., no longer for the disabled) within the Western world because of their value in enhancing performance (Mollenkopf & Fozard, 2003). The past 2 decades have witnessed rapid cultural change in our views of technology, driven primarily by the ubiquitous cell phone and computer. Assistive technologies are designed to enhance or support cognitive abilities, thus offering powerful potential to benefit the lives of persons with cognitive disabilities.

A variety of technologies are now available to enhance memory functioning, ranging from low-tech solutions such as calendars and notepads to higher tech options such as electronic reminding devices (Scialfa & Fernie, 2006). Medication reminder systems are now available with features such as sound prompts, timed dispensing, sensitivity to pill removal from the dispenser, and monitoring of the user's indication of completion. Sensors can be installed to remind a user to turn off a stove after a particular period of time or to remind a caregiver to toilet a person. The technologies to deliver memory prompts are already available in most homes in the form of telephones or computers, and software applications appear daily to assist individuals and families.

Communication skills can also be enhanced with assistive technology (Charness, Park, & Sabel, 2001). Persons with expressive aphasia can use tools ranging from a letter board to computerized translation of eye movement. A former professor colleague who lives in a nursing home due to severe, degenerative multiple sclerosis recently completed a new edition of a textbook using a computer adapted to head and eye movement. A computer mouse can be modified for use by persons with significant tremors, and voice recognition allows visually impaired persons to benefit from the myriad of cognitive supports available from computers.

Monitoring devices may also enhance the safety of cognitively impaired persons, allowing them to retain more autonomy. Movement sensors can be installed in private homes to alert caregivers when patients wander into danger zones (e.g., nighttime wandering out the front door). Video monitoring allows families to monitor behavior from an office setting or to monitor the care provided by staff in a facility.

Assistive technology's importance in an individual's functioning matches its importance to the technology marketplace. Manufacturers invest in research and development to expand their marketplace; a trend that promises to generate rapidly expanding technologies useful to cognitively impaired persons. Mental health professionals can stay abreast of offerings by tracking web sites of trade organizations (e.g., Center for Aging Services Technologies, www.agingtech.org), research centers (e.g., Rehabilitation Engineering Research Center for the Advancement of Cognitive Technologies at the University of Colorado, www.rerc-act.org), and the rapidly exploding research literature in psychology and related disciplines such as rehabilitation and occupational therapy.

Environmental Design

Architectural design has been used for centuries to shape movement, support functioning, and challenge performance. The concept of universal design has gained visibility although it is certainly not universally accepted or used. In addition to universal design to support functioning of persons with physical disabilities (e.g., wider doorways, lower countertops, lever door handles), environmental design can be used to support the autonomy of persons with cognitive impairments (Iwarsson, 2004; Rowles, Oswald, & Hunter, 2003; Weisman, 2003).

Inappropriate behaviors of persons with dementia can be managed with behavioral interventions (for reviews, see Cohen-Mansfield, 2001 and Logsdon, McCurry, & Teri, 2007). For example, wandering behavior has been managed effectively for some persons with dementia using strategic placement of visual barriers, textured floors, and painted doorways (Hussian, 1986). Another simple example is the design of enclosed outdoor spaces contiguous with indoor spaces, encouraging active walking in persons whose proclivity to pace might generate social difficulties if others are bothered by their actions.

Design characteristics can function as prompts as well (Iwarsson, 2004; Weisman, 2003). As a simple example, many housing units designed for persons with dementia now mount shadowboxes with familiar pictures and objects next to each residence door to help impaired people identify their own rooms. Similarly, laminated placemats inlaid in dining room tables can assist residents in defining food territory, reducing conflict over food sharing.

Restricted Access Strategies

A recent *New York Times* article described the strategy used by the son of a man in his 90s whose stock market activities had changed in ways that put his assets at risk. Although he chose his stocks well, he had increased the frequency of trades to a level where fees were eroding his assets. The son worked with the father's stockbroker to restrict access to stocks that could be bought and sold with high frequency without economic penalty (i.e., no load stocks). A less savvy son might have taken over control of the stock portfolio, eliminating this source of competent behavior, joy, and meaning in his father's life.

Cognitive impairments sometimes produce problem behaviors only in restricted circumstances. Particular times of day, settings, or conditions may challenge a person past his or her capacity to adapt well. Restricted access to cooking, driving, financial management, or even neighborhood walks may be all that is needed to ensure safety for a person with compromised decision-making capacity. The least restrictive environments imperative pushes us to design interventions to restrict access at certain times or in certain contexts without impinging on the person's overall legal status, privileges, or rights that can be implemented without danger.

Enhanced Access Strategies

Underperformance of certain behaviors can compromise safety, suggesting the benefit of interventions designed to enhance access to certain behaviors. Food grazing options are used to enhance nutritional intake in persons who are unable to eat in a sit-down meal setting. Technologies that support social connections provide enhanced access to information or communication that a person might not be able to access independently. For example, a light that goes on in the home of a woman with dementia when her children turn on lights in their own home is a simple way of letting her know that family is available at home. She might not be able to read a clock or modulate her anxiety about whether they will return as promised, unless the cue for their return is familiar and simple to access.

Finally, the familiar injunction given to caregiving family members to tell a person with dementia what "to do" rather than what "not to do" is an example of an enhanced access strategy. Enhancing access to distracter activities can reduce the risk of dangerous behaviors. After breaking a glass, a cognitively impaired person feels the need to assist with cleanup but may not have judgment to participate safely. Caregivers who provide a distracter activity are enhancing access to safe behavior.

Family Interventions

Because they are intimately involved in the care of persons with cognitive impairments, family members are appropriate targets for interventions. To date, most caregiver interventions have focused on reducing the well-established risks to caregiver well-being with the long-term goal of delaying institutionalization of the care recipient. Most existing interventions reduce risks to the caregiver's well-being by enhancing his or her skill in handling the behavioral challenges caused by dementias, strengthening social support, and enhancing self-care. An exhaustive review of the caregiver literature is beyond the scope of this chapter. See Pinquart and Sorensen (2006) for a review of the impact of caregiver interventions, and Gallagher-Thompson and Coon (2007) for a review of evidence-based treatments for caregivers.

The purpose of including a chapter on interventions in this book, however, suggests another focus for family interventions: guiding families in how to support autonomy while ensuring safety and supporting justice within the family distribution of resources. The traditional focus on supporting caregiver well-being is one example of supporting justice in the distribution of resources. However, many existing caregiver interventions also can contribute to enhancing the autonomy of the care recipient while ensuring safety.

Education

Educational interventions that teach caregivers about the disease and care needs of the care recipient are effective relatively quick interventions (Sorensen, Pinquart, & Duberstein, 2002). Health psychology offers strong justification for ensuring that caregivers' understanding about illnesses is accurate and complete (Leventhal, Foster, & Leventhal,

2007; Qualls & Benight, 2007). Accurate understanding leads to appropriate attributions for problem behaviors and more helpful interventions. A common point of confusion regarding persons with cognitive impairment is the extent to which behavior is volitional versus uncontrollable (Knopman et al., 2000; Nichols & Martindale-Adams, 2006). Behaviors that are consistent with long-term personality disorders are particularly difficult to discriminate, leading families to readily make dispositional attributions, which imply volitional control. Deterioration of executive functioning, characteristic of frontal lobe decline, typically impairs initiation, which is interpreted by observers as depression or laziness (i.e., motivational in origin) rather than as a consequence of brain impairment.

Ideally, education is offered to caregivers at a specific level that interprets the cognitive impairments of the particular care recipient beyond the level available in a support group's general education about a diagnostic class (e.g., Alzheimer's disease). Neuropsychological test reports offer rich data on cognitive abilities and impairments that can educate caregivers about the particular behavioral challenges and strengths of an individual. Table 12.1 presents one form of functional guide developed at the Colorado University Aging Center to translate data from a neuropsychological report for a woman to her family members who were struggling with decisions about placement. Family members reported the following useful characteristics of the format:

- Clear statements about behavioral challenges that would result from documented impairments.
- Suggestions for adapting the environment and communication strategies.
- Background on the diagnostic class (in this case, dementia) in lay language, including general statements about prognosis.
- Information about caregiver experiences.
- Statements about particular safety issues to monitor.

Many clinicians at our center have commented that families respond to this guide with tears as they absorb information about the disease and

Table 12.1 Guide to Functional Changes Based on Neuropsychological Test Data

Patient: Mr. Smith
Caregiver: Mrs. Smith
Date: 2-1-07

Domain of Cognitive Function	Skill Deficits and Behavior Challenges	Implications for Daily Life and Strategies to Assist
Executive function Judgment, ability to plan, organize, and strategize *Mild impairment*	The patient has difficulty: –Making plans and informed judgments. –Formulating solutions to everyday problems and correcting mistakes. –Processing complex information or multiple inputs presented simultaneously. –Being in a room with high rates of activity. The patient may be impulsive; he may say and do things that seem uncharacteristic. He may also withdraw socially to manage the sensory overload. *Anosognosia:* He is **not** aware of the scope of his cognitive decline even though he recognizes that he has some deficits and feels embarrassed about them.	Use prompts to help him initiate activities rather than trying to motivate him. Structure his environment so he does not need to organize objects or tasks by: –Presenting only those items he really needs to see or hear when he is doing a task. –Presenting objects one at a time for complex tasks such as bathing or hobbies. Engage him in planning and decision making at the level of his values and preferences rather than in the details (e.g., for trips, family gatherings, financial decisions). Keep the environmental stress to a minimum by: –Selecting public environments with low stimulation (e.g., restaurants). –Providing opportunities for him to observe busy family gatherings from the sidelines. Family and caregiver need to learn new ways to respond to unusual behavior to maintain interpersonal peace. The people in the environment

(continued)

285

Table 12.1 (Continued)

Domain of Cognitive Function	Skill Deficits and Behavior Challenges	Implications for Daily Life and Strategies to Assist
		will be the ones who manage changes in personality or attitude at this point in the illness because he will not be able to be flexible or creative.
		Risks: Without assistance the patient is likely to ignore hygiene, medication regimens, nutrition, or doctor's appointments.
Initiation	Patient difficulty in starting activity appears to others as passivity, depression, or laziness.	Structure all activities with 1-stage commands to lead him through the action sequence without requiring him to plan or remember what comes next.
Ability to act on a plan/get started on an activity	Patient inability to anticipate, plan, or sequence events underlies this problem.	Provide a regular schedule that includes necessary activities as the priority.
Mild to moderate impairment		Avoid using motivational speech as the only prompt to initiate action; engage the person in behaving differently by just starting the activity with him.
		Environments with built-in activity stimulation are ideal as long as they are not too stimulating.
Disinhibition	Patient may say or do things that are uncharacteristic of prior personality, including socially inappropriate actions in public settings (e.g., undressing, critical remarks).	Avoid efforts to correct him or expect him to learn what is appropriate because learning what is right does not keep him from engaging in inappropriate behavior.
Loss of control of inappropriate comments and behaviors		As needed, prepare friends and family for the possibility that inappropriate behavior can happen, so that his social contacts can comfortably redirect his attention from the inappropriate action.
Mild impairment		

Mental calculations Ability to do math/arithmetic *Mild impairment*	Patient has difficulty paying bills or managing finances independently.	Arrange for a finance support person to take over responsibility for managing daily finances as well as long-term financial planning. Restrict access to large sums of money to reduce possibility of exploitation or fraud (e.g., credit cards and bank accounts). Provide contact with money, as needed, in small sums to support independence and the patient's identity as an adult.
Abstract reasoning Ability to think flexibly, creatively, and to solve problems *Mild to moderate impairment*	Mr. Smith responds to abstract tasks with vague responses, likely to cover his inability to provide reasoned responses.	Structure the environment to restrict his need to use abstract reasoning and problem solving. Engage him in decisions primarily by presenting options for selection in multiple-choice format *and* by encouraging him to state preferences and values.
Shifting cognitive set Ability to hold and manipulate multiple lines of information *Mild to moderate impairment*	Mr. Smith focuses on one topic at a time and may get *stuck* perseverating on one point when the conversation has passed that topic.	Provide clear verbal signals when the topic has changed. Redirect him if he remains stuck on a previous topic. Understand that he truly cannot hold multiple pieces of information in his mind at one time, and so cannot participate fully in the details of complex decisions. His ability to function as a collaborative decision maker with Mrs. Smith will be extremely limited because he cannot manipulate multiple pieces of information about their household, finances, health care, or other factors simultaneously in his mind.

(continued)

287

Table 12.1 (*Continued*)

Domain of Cognitive Function	Skill Deficits and Behavior Challenges	Implications for Daily Life and Strategies to Assist
Verbal memory Ability to recall information immediately after hearing it and over time *Severe impairment*	Mr. Smith cannot consistently hold information for even a few minutes.	Use written memory prompts as much as is useful to him without overstimulating him with visual details to process. Recognize that information he provides is not based on his memory but on the way his mind fills in the gaps of what he cannot remember. Make sure that a reliable historian is available at all doctor visits.
Verbal processing Ability to understand and respond to verbal information *Mild impairment*	Mr. Smith can understand language quite well, and generates smooth speech that sounds quite normal on the surface. He relies increasingly on vague information to cover for his memory deficits, and fills in the blanks of his memory with verbal descriptions that are not necessarily true but have no mal-intent.	Use simplified speech without talking down to him as if he was a child. Avoid complex sentence structures that would overtax his memory and processing ability. Engage him in conversation normally, encouraging his involvement but not relying on him to recount events accurately. Expect verbal skills to fluctuate across days and within a day. Support his sense of competence in this area by engaging him in conversations and leading him through reminiscence topics in which he is likely to be relatively competent.
Visual processing Ability to judge distance, see contrast, navigate effectively, recall visual detail, and analyze and correctly process visual stimuli *Mild to moderate impairment*	Mr. Smith has the ability to see and process visual information but is limited in working with it because of his difficulties with planning, sequencing, and initiation.	Structure his environment with prompts and supportive stimuli that will help him respond more effectively to visual information. Limit visual inputs to reduce overstimulation.

Attention/concentration Ability to focus and follow speech, a story, to be alert of surroundings *Mild impairment*	Mr. Smith shows good attention and concentration on simple tasks but is unable to hold information long enough to manipulate it. He fatigues with sustained attention and concentration demands.	As needed, prompt him in the relationships between parts and wholes (e.g., relationship between utensils on the table and the task of serving a meal). Pace activities to maximize his involvement prior to fatigue. Present tasks in 1-stage commands that do not require memory or manipulation of multiple pieces of information.
Information processing Ability to take in necessary information, comprehend it and formulate a response *Mild to moderate impairment*	Mr. Smith shows considerable difficulty holding and manipulating information to respond.	Provide 24-hour supervision because of his difficulties, responding to any dangerous situation; recognize that he would be unlikely to respond reliably to fire or health hazards (e.g., he may know to dial 911 but in distress not remember how to operate the telephone). Limit involvement in decisions to the level noted previously.
Language ability Ability to communicate effectively, ability to understand and respond to information, specifically verbal information *Mild impairment*	Mr. Smith is reasonably articulate and able to express thoughts. He responds at a normal pace to simple verbal information. He has severe difficulty remembering words, and mild difficulty generating names of objects, etc. He can accurately track conversation and is comfortable joining or exiting conversation in a variety of settings.	

(continued)

Table 12.1 (Continued)

Domain of Cognitive Function	Skill Deficits and Behavior Challenges	Implications for Daily Life and Strategies to Assist
Daily functioning *Moderate impairment*	The patient likely has significant impairment in instrumental activities of daily living (i.e., skills and behaviors necessary to survive independently—cleaning the house, using transportation, managing finances, safety, communication, and shopping). The patient likely also has some impairment in activities of daily living including grooming, eating, dressing, toileting, bathing, mobility, and transferring.	The patient is a safety risk if left on his own. He is at risk for exploitation and needs to be protected by those who have the patient's best interest in mind. He needs structure to keep on task and engaged during the day, otherwise he will only sit around. Finding the right balance of stimulating activity that does not overwhelm the patient will be a challenge. The patient needs to be cued and assisted to complete almost all ADLs and IADLs and to maintain adequate nutrition and hydration. Even cueing does not always ensure that a task will be completed, and the caregiver will likely be forced to provide hands-on care directly to the patient or to hire skilled care

Source: "Caregiver Family Therapy," by S. H. Qualls, in *Handbook of Emotional Disorders in Older Adults*, B. Knight and K. Laidlaw (Eds.), in press, Oxford: Oxford University Press. Reprinted with permission.

impairment that previously was bound up in abstract labels that offered them little guidance. Consistently, this type of information has been greeted with deep gratitude and comments about how this is the first time they were given something truly useful.

More important than the clinician's gratification at hearing such comments, is the very real message that much of the information available to caregivers of persons with cognitive impairments does not go far enough. As the primary partners in care, caregivers need very specific information about the level of impairment *today*, the safety risks to monitor, and interventions that can empower both care recipient and caregiver to live as autonomously and richly as possible.

Social Support

Family caregivers who perceive adequate social network support evidence less impact of stress than those who feel unsupported (Aneshensel, Pearlin, Mullan, Zarit, & Whitlatch, 1995). Interventions to enhance support range from support group attendance to technological devices that facilitate communication with the network (Schulz et al., 2003; Sorensen, Pinquart, & Duberstein, 2002). Even interventions that assist caregivers in determining the boundaries to the level of contact and assistance they need to provide are useful (Scharlach, 1987).

An emerging theme in the literature is that no single support network characteristic predicts caregiver outcomes. Instead, individual caregivers need to determine the form of social support that generates the strongest sense of support for that particular person. Assessment of precaregiving status social support structures and meanings is a useful step in determining the type of support most likely to be perceived as useful. We find it helpful to map a family genogram and a social network diagram (e.g., Antonucci, Akiyama, & Lansford, 1998) as a way of identifying the sources of social support that have been useful pre- and postcaregiving *and* to highlight opportunities for building support. Not surprisingly, research now documents that more social contact is not necessarily better because of the aversive nature of some interactions (Malone-Beach & Zarit, 1995; Smith & Goodnow, 1999). Thoughtful assessment and planning of meaningful interaction helps guide caregivers into social contact that feels supportive.

In the U.S. culture, many family caregivers are hesitant to ask for help, so interventions should presume that identification of potential sources of support is not sufficient. Interventions also need to address resistance to seeking support. Often, care recipients complain about respite care options or day care, resisting unfamiliar people or schedules. Caregivers can benefit from coaching on how to bypass resistance. For example, caregivers need to be coached in how to respond to care recipients' typical comments such as, "I don't need to go be with people like that, I'm fine at home" or "You are just trying to get rid of me." Comments such as these are so painful to a loving caregiver that a planned intervention can be abandoned before the care recipient has a chance to try it or adapt to it. Furthermore, some great ideas just don't work. The same family that received the guide shown in Table 12.1 decided to use day care to give the spousal caregiver a break. Despite daily coaching on strategies for engaging him, however, his resistance was sufficient that after a week of attempts, the caregiver was encouraged to try a different respite strategy.

Caregivers with premorbid personality disorders often find it challenging to feel supported, regardless of caregiving status (Olin, Schneider, & Kaser-Boyd, 1996). Prior to caregiving, their personality kept them from meaningful, intimate relationships. With the added burden of caregiving, many communicate almost solely about the trials of daily life, with the expected result of a shrinking network. Formal providers or structured respite care can provide some relief from the daily burdens while demonstrating support, even if no intimate communication occurs between supporter and caregiver. Persons with personality disorders lack insight into the aversive role of constant complaint about caregiving, so therapeutic coaching may be needed to teach them how to restrain the urge to focus on caregiving stresses during social interaction.

Problem Solving

Behavior problems are nearly universal among persons with cognitive impairment. Sometimes, the problem behavior is the person's best solution to a problem; unfortunately, the solution causes problems for others. For example, a man with dementia frequently urinated in a window sill at home, much to his wife's consternation. He had found a receptacle, just not one that his wife found acceptable. Viewed from his vantage point, the problem was not indiscriminant urination, but determining which receptacle was appropriate. Behavior problems may be the most distressing aspect of caregiving, and thus, a common cause of institutionalization or other restrictive intervention.

Interventions using assistive technology and environmental design, as described previously, are often remarkably simple to do, many times with remarkable enhancement of behavioral competence. Not all individuals can remain independent throughout the course of a dementia, for example, but many can be empowered to live in their desired setting with supportive interventions to compensate for their impairments. Monitoring, prompting, and altering access are common strategies for solving behavior problems in ways that enhance a person's decision-making autonomy.

Evidence-based psychosocial interventions for behavior problem management offer a range of options for reducing the frequency, intensity, or impact of behavior problems (Logsdon et al., 2007). Interventions with the most empirical support for their efficacy are those that identify and modify antecedents or consequences of behavior problems, assist caregivers with increasing the rate of incompatible behaviors such as pleasant events, along with individualized problem-solving approaches to behavior problems.

Decision-Making Structures

The decisions made by caregivers to restrict decision-making authority are among the most stressful aspects of loving someone with a cognitive impairment. Caregivers report that they were aware of the need to restrict driving or to change residences long before they acted, primarily because the process of intervening was so distressing (Nichols & Martindale-Adams, 2006). Given the lack of insight that is characteristic of persons with cognitive impairment, caregivers rightly assume that the care recipient will resist restrictive decisions and often will feel offended or betrayed by the caregiver.

Caregiver Family Therapy is one new approach developed specifically to assist families in restructuring to meet the needs of a person with cognitive impairment (Qualls, 2003, in press). The three primary steps in this therapy are: (1) naming the problem, (2) restructuring the family, and (3) balancing structures to meet the needs of all family members. The tasks involved in naming the problem are described previously: guiding the family to gather thorough assessment data and then disseminating information about the etiology, prognosis, and functional implications of the impairment to all relevant players. Restructuring the family involves assisting the family members in defining their values related to aging and care, defining the tasks that need to be accomplished (e.g., restricting driving, monitoring medications), exploring alternative strategies that can be used to accomplish those tasks, and negotiating role transitions. The person with impairment may be included in some or all of the discussions, based on their capacity to contribute to and benefit from the discussions. In many families, the person with impairments is able to participate at a minimum in the discussion of values and often in choices about surrogate decision makers. Again, the goal of family interventions is to empower autonomy as much as possible, while ensuring safety *and* balancing support for development of all family members. A more thorough discussion of the process of renegotiating family structures is available elsewhere (Qualls, 1999, in press).

CONCLUSION

Mental health professionals have significant roles in the care of persons with impaired decision-making capacity that extend beyond assessment to include interventions. The legal and ethical principles that guide our care of persons with cognitive impairment direct us to attempt interventions before restricting legal or functional rights. Although not well organized to guide professionals, a growing research literature offers evidence of the potency of interventions to enhance decision-making capacity through assistive technology, environmental design, and family interventions. The time has come to focus efforts on organizing the information into a systematic framework within which we can test the power of interventions to benefit individual caregivers of persons whose decision-making capacity is compromised.

REFERENCES

American Psychiatric Association. (2000). *Diagnostic and statistical manual of mental disorders* (4th ed., text rev.). Washington, DC: Author.

Aneshensel, C., Pearlin, L. I., Mullan, J. T., Zarit, S. H., & Whitlatch, C. J. (1995). *Profiles in caregiving: The unexpected career.* New York: Academic Press.

Antonucci, T. C., Akiyama, H., & Lansford, J. E. (1998). Negative effects of close social relations. *Family Relations, 47,* 379–384.

Blieszner, R., Roberto, K. A., & Wilcox, K. L. (2007). Dimensions of ambiguous loss in couples coping with mild cognitive impairment. *Family Relations, 56,* 196–209.

Charness, N., Park, C., & Sabel, A. (Eds.). (2001). *Communication, technology, and aging: Opportunities and challenges for the future.* New York: Springer.

Cohen-Mansfield, J. (2001). Nonpharmacologic interventions for inappropriate behaviors in dementia: A review, summary, and critique. *American Journal of Geriatric Psychiatry, 9,* 361–381.

Day, K., Carreon, D., & Stump, C. (2000). The therapeutic design of environments for people with dementia: A review of the empirical research. *Gerontologist, 40,* 397–416.

Gallagher-Thompson, D., & Coon, D. W. (2007). Evidence-based psychological treatments for distress in family caregivers of older adults. *Psychology and Aging, 22,* 37–51.

Gitlin, L., & Gwyther, L. (2003). In-home interventions: Helping caregivers where they live. In D. Coon, D. Gallagher-Thompson, & L. Thompson (Eds.), *Innovative interventions to reduce caregiver distress: A clinical guide* (pp. 139–160). New York: Springer.

Guttman, D. L. (1987). *Reclaimed powers: Toward a new psychology of men and women in later life.* New York: Basic Books.

Hussian, R. A. (1986). Severe behavioral problems. In L. Teri & P. M. Lewinsohn (Eds.), *Geropsychological assessment and treatment* (pp. 121–144). New York: Springer.

Institute of Medicine. (1997). M. J. Field & C. K. Cassel (Eds.), *Approaching death: Improving care at the end of life.* Washington, DC: National Academy Press.

Iwarsson, S. (2004). Assessing the fit between older people and their physical home environments: An occupational therapy research perspective. In

H.-W. Wahl, R. J. Scheidt, & P. G. Windley (Eds.), *Annual review of gerontology and geriatrics: Vol. 23. Aging in context—Sociophysical environments* (pp. 85–109). New York: Springer.

Knopman, D., Donohoe, J. A., & Gutterman, E. M. (2000). Patterns of care in the early stages of Alzheimer's disease: Impediments to timely diagnosis. *Journal of the American Geriatrics Society, 48,* 300–304.

Lawton, M. P., & Nahemow, L. (1973). Ecology and the aging process. In C. Eisdorfer & M. P. Lawton (Eds.), *The psychology of adult development and aging* (pp. 619–673). Washington, DC: American Psychological Association.

Lawton, M. P., Windley, P., & Byerts, T. (1982). *Aging and environment: Theoretical approaches.* New York: Springer.

Leventhal, H., Forster, R., & Leventhal, E. (2007). Self-regulation of health threats, affect, and the self: Lessons from older adults. In C. M. Aldwin, C. L. Park, & A. Spiro (Eds.), *Handbook of health psychology and aging* (pp. 341–366). New York: Guilford Press.

Lewin, K. (1935). *A dynamic theory of personality.* New York: McGraw-Hill.

Logsdon, R. G., McCurry, S. M., & Teri, L. (2007). Evidence-based psychological treatments for disruptive behaviors in individuals with dementia. *Psychology and Aging, 22,* 28–36.

Malone-Beach, E. E., & Zarit, S. H. (1995). Dimensions of social support and social conflict as predictors of caregiver depression. *International Psychogeriatrics, 7,* 25–38.

Miller, S. C., Mor, V., Gage, B., & Coppola, K. (2001). Hospice and its role in improving end-of-life care. In M. P. Lawton (Ed.), *Annual review of gerontology and geriatrics: The end of life—Scientific and social issues* (Vol. 20, pp. 193–223). New York: Springer.

Minuchin, S. (1974). *Families and family therapy.* Cambridge, MA: Harvard University Press.

Mollenkopf, H., & Fozard, J. L. (2003). Technology and the good life: Challenges for current and future generations of aging people. In H.-W. Wahl, R. J. Scheidt, & P. G. Windley (Eds.), *Annual review of gerontology and geriatrics: Vol. 23. Aging in context—Sociophysical environments* (pp. 250–279). New York: Springer.

National Institute of Health Consensus Development Program. (2004). *National Institutes of Health State-of-the-Science Conference statement on improving end-of-life care.* Retrieved June 2, 2007, from www.consensus.nih .gov/2004/2004EndofLifeCareSOS024html.htm.

Nichols, L. O., & Martindale-Adams, J. (2006). The decisive moment: Caregivers' recognition of dementia. *Clinical Gerontologist, 30,* 39–52.

Nydegger, C. N. (1991). The development of paternal and filial maturity. In K. Pillemer & K. McCartney (Eds.), *Parent-child relations throughout life* (pp. 93–112). Hillsdale, NJ: Erlbaum.

Olin, J. T., Schneider, L. S., & Kaser-Boyd, N. (1996). Associating personality pathology with emotional distress in caregivers of patients with Alzheimer's disease. *Journal of Clinical Geropsychology, 2,* 93–101.

Pinquart, M., & Sorensen, S. (2006). Helping caregivers of persons with dementia: Which interventions work and how large are their effects? *International Psychogeriatrics, 18,* 577–595.

Qualls, S. H. (1999). Realizing power in intergenerational family hierarchies: Family reorganization when older adults decline. In M. Duffy (Ed.), *Handbook of counseling and psychotherapy with older adults* (pp. 228–241). New York: Wiley.

Qualls, S. H. (2003). Aging and cognitive impairment. In D. K. Snyder & M. A. Whisman (Eds.), *Treating difficult couples: Managing emotional, behavioral, and health problems in couples therapy* (pp. 370–391). New York: Guilford Press.

Qualls, S. H. (in press). Caregiver family therapy. In B. Knight & K. Laidlaw (Eds.), *Handbook of emotional disorders in older adults.* Oxford: Oxford University Press.

Qualls, S. H., & Benight, C. B. (2007). The role of clinical health geropsychology in the health care of older adults. In C. M. Aldwin, C. L. Park, & A. Spiro (Eds.), *Handbook of health psychology and aging* (pp. 367–389). New York: Guilford Press.

Reisberg, B., Ferris, S. H., de Leon, M. J., & Crook, T. (1982). The Global Deterioration Scale for the assessment of primary degenerative dementia. *American Journal of Psychiatry, 139,* 1136–1139.

Rowles, G. D., Oswald, F., & Hunter, E. G. (2003). Interior living environments in old age. In H.-W. Wahl, R. J. Scheidt, & P. G. Windley (Eds.), *Annual review of gerontology and geriatrics: Vol. 23. Aging in context—Sociophysical environments* (pp. 167–194). New York: Springer.

Scharlach, A. E. (1987). Relieving feelings of strain among women with elderly mothers. *Psychology and Aging, 2,* 9–13.

Scheidt, R. J., & Windley, P. G. (2006). Environmental gerontology: Progress in the post-Lawton era. In J. E. Birren & K. W. Schaie (Eds.), *Handbook of the psychology of aging* (6th ed., pp. 105–125). Burlington, MA: Elsevier Academic Press.

Schofield, P. W., Tang, M., Marder, K., Bell, K., Dooneief, G., Chun, M., et al. (1997). Alzheimer's disease after remote head injury: An incidence study. *Journal of Neurology, Neurosurgery, and Psychiatry, 62,* 119–124.

Schulz, R., Burgio, L., Burns, R., Eisdorfer, C., Gallagher-Thompson, D., Gitlin, L. N., et al. (2003). Resources for Enhancing Alzheimer's Caregiver Health (REACH): Overview, site-specific outcomes, and future directions. *Gerontologist, 43,* 514–520.

Scialfa, C. T., & Fernie, G. R. (2006). Adaptive technology. In J. E. Birren & K. W. Schaie (Eds.), *Handbook of the psychology of aging* (6th ed., pp. 425–441). Burlington, MA: Elsevier Academic Press.

Smith, J., & Goodnow, J. J. (1999). Unasked-for support and unsolicited advice: Age and the quality of social experience. *Psychology and Aging, 14,* 108–121.

Sorensen, S., Pinquart, M., & Duberstein, P. (2003). How effective are interventions with caregivers: An updated meta-analysis. *Gerontologist, 42,* 356–372.

Wahl, H.-W., Scheidt, R. J., & Windley, P. G. (Eds.). (2003). *Annual review of gerontology and geriatrics: Vol. 23. Aging in context—Sociophysical environments.* New York: Springer.

Weisman, G. (2003). Creating places for people with dementia: An action research perspective. In K. W. Schaie, H.-W. Wahl, H. Mollenkopf, & F. Oswald (Eds.), *Aging independently: Living arrangements and mobility* (pp. 162–173). New York: Springer.

13

The Business of Geropsychology: Billing and Preparing Legal Reports and Testimony

KATHRYN KAYE AND MICHAEL KENNY

Frequently, geropsychologists are contacted by professionals in the medical and legal fields and asked to assess the mental and decisional capacity of an older adult. Geropsychologists' extensive training and experience in assessment, which involves aspects of neuropsychology and rehabilitation neuropsychology, places them in a unique position to evaluate the capacity of elderly individuals who typically have a mix of complex medical, neurological, and psychiatric conditions. Legal work is simultaneously frustrating, intellectually stimulating, and (potentially) financially rewarding. Forensic evaluation is not for the faint of heart, nor is it a suitable choice for individuals who have an aversion to detail or a low tolerance for ambiguity. High levels of stress are to be expected when you are deposed or required to testify in court. For example, neuropsychological and psychological tests, procedures, and results often are challenged in the courtroom by opposing attorneys; your credentials and credibility may be questioned; and your carefully considered and confidently stated responses may be short-circuited or artfully twisted by a savvy attorney until what you said is not what you meant.

On a more positive note, engagement in the legal system can lead to improved services for older adults who are mentally incapacitated and thereby in need of assistance. The geropsychologist has a unique opportunity to impart knowledge regarding the cognitive changes associated with normal aging as well as information about various forms of dementia and delirium. As an expert witness, he or she serves in the combined roles of investigator, teacher, and performer. Though appealing in several ways, the seriousness of these roles cannot be overstated because the geropsychologist's opinions may have grave consequences for an elderly person whose autonomy may be lost or limited, whose finances may be strained, and/or whose family may suffer as a result.

The business of establishing and maintaining a practice in geropsychology is a challenging endeavor, even for those who are fortunate enough to enter the field with training in business management. To date, guidelines for business practices have been scarce, variable in quality and scope, and occasionally unreliable; and many experienced psychologists will admit to a few minor (and occasionally major) pitfalls along the way. The purpose of this chapter is to provide basic guidelines for individuals just entering the field or for professionals seeking more knowledge about legal work and the business aspects of private practice.

ESSENTIALS FOR FORENSIC GEROPSYCHOLOGISTS

In addition to expertise in clinical psychology and training and experience in geriatric neuropsychology, the forensic geropsychologist must: (a) be aware of his or her personal and professional strengths and weaknesses, (b) understand the laws regarding mental and decisional capacity, and (c) be familiar with the legal system as well as courtroom etiquette and procedures. Comprehensive knowledge of the different types of capacity (decisional capacity/informed consent for medical treatment, contractual capacity, donative capacity, testamentary capacity, ability to managing finances, care for oneself independently, continue to drive, etc.) is necessary as well. Detailed explanations of capacity types are available in other chapters of this volume.

GETTING STARTED

A preliminary step in setting up a geropsychology practice involves consultation with established professionals in the field. Many of these individuals have learned about the business through trial and error. If you are just starting out and are fortunate enough to spend some time with one of them, you most likely will learn a few valuable lessons that may enable you to avoid or at least minimize some common mistakes.

NETWORKING

Networking is important, especially if you have not had the advantage of being trained or employed in a medical or legal setting. Attending and possibly participating in legal, ethical, medical, and/or psychiatric conferences are strongly recommended. In addition to the general wealth of information often provided at such events, you may be able to determine which services are most needed by the elderly, and as a result, discover a special niche that will enable you to stand out from other psychologists who are just entering the field. Referrals often are initiated by professionals in these settings as well. Keep in mind that many different professionals are potential referral sources, so you should avoid focusing your attention on a single group.

THE MAZE OF MEDICARE BILLING

To best serve older adults, geropsychologists must be willing to accept their primary insurance, which typically is Medicare. Although it is possible to establish a practice that relies solely on legal fees, evaluations that are purely clinical offer not only rich clinical insight, but also important opportunities to work with and learn from geriatricians, internists, neurologists, nurses, rehabilitation therapists, social workers, and case managers, all of whom can be important resources as well as potential sources for referrals to your practice.

Medicare, and many third party insurers, will not pay for evaluations in which capacity is the sole or primary referral issue. In order for the service to be billable to Medicare, the evaluation must be deemed *medically* necessary. Definitions of *medical necessity* unfortunately are varied and not always definitive. Elements that appear most frequently include provision of services that are consistent with accepted standards of practice and will benefit the patient through prevention, diagnosis, and/or treatment of an illness or symptoms. We encourage you to become familiar with professional and local standards of practice for determination of medical necessity and search APA (Holloway, 2003) and Medicare web sites (such as those listed at the end of this chapter) for updates.

We have found that much of the stress associated with Medicare billing can be minimized if you hire an experienced billing service. The billing contractor should know the ins and outs of Medicare billing and be willing to find answers to your reimbursement-related questions as well as tirelessly resubmit payment requests that have been denied. Patience and persistence are useful, if not critical, qualities.

Medicare reimbursement is more likely when an elderly person is referred to you by a physician who wishes to know the extent of a patient's impairment, the diagnosis, and the implications for treatment, living environment, or driving, *after which*, based on your assessment, legal proceedings may be initiated. Such cases should be approached in a clinical manner unless you have made a commitment in advance to provide specific information to the court regarding the patient's need for guardianship or conservatorship.

You should obtain as much information as possible before you accept the referral, after which you will be better able to decide the most appropriate way to handle billing. If a family member requests that you bill Medicare for a capacity evaluation, you should inform him or her that Medicare probably will refuse to pay for the evaluation and ask the patient to sign a waiver. Remember that even though a family member has requested your services, if the patient chooses not to consent to an evaluation, you must respect his or her wishes and delay the examination until an authorized party signs a consent form. (More information regarding this issue is provided later in the chapter.) In rare instances, you may determine that you cannot examine the patient. A straightforward approach from the outset is best. In our experience, you will be less likely to encounter patient refusal at an evaluation session if you have obtained information ahead of time from the referral source.

BILLING THE COURT

There will be occasions when you will be asked to assess the capacity of an elderly person who has no insurance coverage or money with which to pay for an examination. In these cases, if the evaluation is court referred, the state will pay a specified amount for the evaluation. You will send your bill to the patient's court-appointed attorney or *guardian ad litem*, who will submit it to the appropriate agent or agency for payment. In most cases, although you will receive only the allotted amount, payment is forwarded to you promptly.

SERVING AS AN EXPERT WITNESS

An expert witness is a professional who, based on his or her education and experience, is hired to provide an opinion that is formed through review of information contained in case materials, medical records, direct interviews or interviews performed by other professionals, and depositions of persons involved in the case (see also Chapter 6). As an expert, you may be asked to review and comment on the work of another mental health professional, and you should be prepared to provide an honest and unbiased opinion of that work. In many cases, you will evaluate an older individual directly and attempt to identify and clarify (in a report and often in court) critical issues regarding the examinee's capacity. You also may interview the elderly person's family, friends, and/or business acquaintances. In the majority of cases, you will do all of the above.

When you are asked to provide information as a consultant or expert witness, you are entering into a business arrangement in which your time and services are purchased. You should have a written professional fee agreement that clearly states your standard fees and rates for different services (records review, travel, phone consultation, transportation time, and cancellation requirements). A retainer, to be paid by the law firm *before* you spend a large amount of time on the case, is strongly advised.

Keep in mind that your fee agreement is a contract and not a guarantee. Unfortunately, there may be times when you will not be paid for your work. One way to avoid this is to withhold your report until payment has been received. Although this action may ensure that you will receive some portion of your fee, additional billing for the case will be necessary if you later are deposed or asked to testify in court.

ACCEPTING CASES

The initial contact with an attorney is usually by phone. The attorney will ask whether you are available to serve as a consultant or expert witness for a particular case and often will provide a brief summary of the issues. You should clarify the following:

- *What are the specific referral question(s)?* Your goal at this point is to determine whether the questions seem reasonable (e.g., answerable) and whether you are qualified to address them. You should not, for example, be asked to determine whether someone actually has exerted undue influence against another (usually older) individual. This is a legal determination. You *can*, however, state an opinion as to whether the person you have evaluated appears to have been, or continues to be, vulnerable to undue influence. You also may state an opinion regarding whether an examinee is able to understand and sign documents or make a will (testamentary capacity).
- *Whom does the attorney represent?* Listen carefully to the attorney's response to this question. You may choose not to become involved in a case in which a lawsuit is likely or in which family members have broken laws or are embroiled in other types of litigation. Consider your level of expertise and willingness to become entangled in such cases, especially early in your career. Although your reasons for declining a referral will vary depending on the unique facts of the case, we have found that an honest, straightforward response is preferable and most likely to result in future referrals from the same attorney.

- *Is there a conflict of interest?* Do you know the client, a member of his or her family, or his or her friends? Are you a friend of the referring/retaining attorney or of another mental health professional who has been hired by the opposing attorney? If there are close personal relationships of any kind, you should decline to accept the referral.

- *Is there a temporary or emergency guardian? Guardian ad litem? Power of attorney?* You will need answers to these questions for a variety of reasons, including identification of a person who may be authorized to sign a consent form if there are concerns that the examinee cannot understand its contents. It is your responsibility to obtain this information and be sure that a consent form is properly signed before an examination is initiated.

- *Who will be responsible for your payment?* You must clarify whether the responsible party will be the law firm or the client the firm is representing. In most if not all cases, you should bill the law firm rather than the person the attorney represents. Some attorneys will be reluctant to assume responsibility for payment of your fees, but you should discuss this issue with them until you are comfortable that you will be reimbursed for your work. (There is greater risk of nonpayment if the attorney's client is expected to pay you directly.)

- *What are the time constraints for the evaluation, and has a court date already been scheduled?* You must be certain that you can meet a deadline previously established. If you believe that you cannot complete a thorough evaluation by an established date, you should ask whether the court date could be moved forward. If not, you must decline the referral.

- *If you are being asked to provide a neuropsychological examination, can the person be examined at your office, or must he or she be assessed at another location?* If you must see the patient in another setting, you should obtain information regarding the type of setting, its exact location, the examinee's availability, whether someone will be present to introduce you, and so on. In some cases, an older person's home may not be a safe environment for you due to

the patient's potential for violent behavior or to the possible presence of a dangerous (angry or psychotic) family member.

- *What is the examinee's understanding of the purpose of the evaluation, and is he or she likely to cooperate?*
- *Who is directly involved in the case, and where are the known conflicts (e.g., immediate family members, close friends, distant relatives,
  dueling attorneys)?*
- *What documents will be made available to you, and what additional
  information will you need to obtain?* For example, you may request
  records from prior psychiatric or medical hospitalizations, arrests
  or investigations of alcohol-related incidents or motor vehicle accidents, incidents of domestic violence, or referrals to Adult Protective Services for suspected neglect or elder abuse. Be persistent
  and thorough.
- *Does the hiring attorney make statements indicating that he or she as-
  sumes that you will give the opinion he or she prefers?* If so, you could
  find yourself in the ethically unacceptable position of hired gun.
  You should not accept the case.
- *Is your role that of consultant as opposed to expert witness?* If you are
  a consultant, you are merely providing an opinion to the retaining attorney, and your conclusions will not be disclosed to the
  other side. In many cases, you will first serve as a consultant, and
  if the attorney determines that your conclusions are beneficial to
  his or her client, your status will be changed to expert witness. At
  that point, your report or any information on which you have
  based your opinion will be disclosable to the opposing attorney,
  and you likely will be required to testify in deposition and or
  court.
- *Do you have ethical concerns of **any kind**?* (Rather than be involved in the case, would you prefer to retreat to a third world
  country? If this is your reaction, say no to the referral.)

MOVING AHEAD

If, after talking with the referring attorney, you decide to proceed, you
may request that the attorney mail or fax to you a written summary of

the major issues in the case. He or she may refuse to do this unless you have made at least a verbal commitment to accept the case; however, you have a right to request a summary. Such documents must be maintained in a strictly confidential manner.

If you decide to accept the referral, you will be asked to submit a curriculum vita that, unless you are being hired as a consultant only, will be viewed by all parties involved and will be sent to the court. You also should submit a fee agreement as described previously. Your agreement should be clear and specific, and you should insist that it be signed and dated by the referring attorney and/or party responsible for your payment. We recommend against reviewing documents until the agreement has been signed, but you should include a statement in your agreement indicating that your total fee will cover all the work you have done on the case *before as well as after* the fee agreement is finalized.

YOUR ROLE AS AN EXPERT WITNESS

In typical clinical cases, psychologists work closely with their clients or patients in an attempt to help them in various ways while protecting their confidentiality. The expert witness, in contrast, strives for objectivity and honesty in the absence of confidentiality. The expert is not an advocate for the examinee or the retaining attorney; he or she merely provides an opinion. Psychologists who are new to forensic work may find this to be a difficult concept, and at times even experienced professionals are challenged by this position. Keep in mind that an expert witness is not hired to be an advocate of any party in the case. The attorney advocates for the client(s) who hired him or her.

The psychologist should explain his or her role to the examinee before proceeding with an evaluation, and as previously stated, a written consent form should be read and signed by the examinee. These tasks are particularly difficult when you are asked to assess an older person who is too impaired to comprehend the explanation of your role or the purpose of the evaluation, or to read or understand the information provided to him or her in written form. In some instances, you may decide not to proceed with the evaluation; in others, you may attempt to obtain consent for assessment from a temporary guardian, a guardian ad litem, the examinee's attorney, or a durable power of attorney. If a guardian or the court insists on an examination, but the person to be examined refuses to cooperate, you may choose to write a brief statement (usually directed to the referring attorney) describing your attempts to evaluate and the person's refusal to proceed. Obviously, you cannot formally test a person who is uncooperative; however, we have encountered very few individuals who refuse all portions of an examination. In all cases, you should have written authorization before you begin to directly examine a person for forensic purposes.

THE CONSENT FORM

Your consent form as an expert witness is different from the standard form for clinical work. (A sample form is included in the Theodore Blau's *Forensic Documentation Sourcebook*, listed in the references at the end of this chapter.) The forensic consent form should contain at least the following information:

- Explanation that the examination is not intended for treatment purposes and the information you obtain from it will not remain confidential. You should state that as part of your evaluation you will interview other individuals, review records, and so on, and prepare a report that will be provided to the referring attorney and eventually the court.
- Indication that multiple sessions for interview or testing may be necessary. More than one session is recommended unless there are time or geographical constraints.
- A statement indicating that the outcome of the assessment and its impact on the case cannot be predicted.

THE EXAMINATION REPORT

In addition to sources of referral and background legal information, your report should contain a list of all the individuals, medical records, and other documents used in reaching your conclusions. Most of the following topics should be marked by separate headings that facilitate rapid scanning of the findings in your report:

- Personal history (birth, development, education, occupational history, etc.).
- Neurologic and psychiatric history in family and examinee, including information regarding previous and current alcohol or drug use.
- Medical history, including a list of prescription and over-the-counter medications.
- Sensory functioning.
- Behavioral observations.
- List of assessment instruments and procedures.
- Results of functional assessment performed by you or by another professional such as a social worker, occupational therapist, or physical therapist.
- Details of formal neuropsychological assessment: level of arousal, orientation, information processing speed and capacity, language skills, executive cognitive skills and ability to regulate behavior, movement, visuospatial and perceptual skills, memory, abstract reasoning, judgment, problem solving, mood, affect, presence or absence of hallucinations or delusions, and personality.
- Description of his or her performance on various tests along with comparisons with normative data based on the examinee's age and level of education and implications of related deficits.
- Specific examples of the patient/examinee's behavior during the evaluation, including significant comments he or she has made during the session.

Major issues on which you will focus in forming an opinion:

- The examinee's comprehension of the situation or conditions leading to referral and potential legal intervention.
- Awareness of available choices and their risks and benefits and the consequences of making or avoiding relevant decisions.

- Consistency of responses to questions regarding reasoning and insight.
- Methods of reasoning regarding the current issues and situation as well as in hypothetical situations.
- The examinee's values and preferences (you may confirm these with collaterals).
- The examinee's understanding of the significance of his or her deficits and their potential or current impact on his or her health, safety, financial affairs, ability to drive, and so on. (Remember that memory and basic understanding can be present without the ability to consider actively the consequences of a choice or action.) The examinee may be aware of his or her problems at times but deny or underestimate them at others. Less frequently, he or she may underestimate his or her actual level of functioning.
- Finally, your opinion, stated concisely and in language that laypersons will understand, regarding the person's capacity, strengths and weaknesses, and if requested, the type of protection or assistance required.

FORENSIC ASSESSMENT SOURCES

In your role as a clinician, you generally will rely on statements made by your client or patient. In contrast, in forensic work you will rely on many other sources, obtaining as much data as possible on which to base your conclusions. If you are unable to gain access to certain documents that you believe would be helpful in forming your opinion, you should note this in your report. Working with the material that is available, you must analyze information from each source, comparing and contrasting the impressions of others and the statements made in direct interview with the patient/examinee, in addition to interpreting examination results. Areas of uncertainty and discrepancy are inevitable, and you should include statements about them in your report along with conclusions based on a higher degree of probability. Express not only aspects of an opinion about which you feel confident, but also include areas for which information is limited or absent. You also may choose to include references to literature and research results that support your conclusions, especially if recent studies are available. (Familiarity with literature that contradicts your opinions is useful as well.)

RELEASING THE REPORT

In forensic cases, you will release the report only to the retaining attorney, who will then release it to other attorneys involved in the case. You also may discuss your findings with the retaining attorney. You are not required to, nor should you, discuss the results of your assessment with family members, friends and acquaintances of the patient/examinee. If you have evaluated a patient at the request of a family member or physician, you will release information (with the patient's signed consent) to the individual who made the referral. In the latter case, you may discuss the results of the case with the examinee, if he or she desires, or with the individuals who have been authorized to receive the report.

KEY ISSUES IN CAPACITY ASSESSMENT

Remember that mental capacity is not an abstract concept. Instead, it is *decision* or *action specific;* that is, a person's ability to **do** something, such as live independently, handle finances, prepare a will, and so on. Your referral questions should be specific, and your response to those questions should be specific as well. You may need to reassess the examinee if there are reasons to suspect the presence of a reversible factor such as illness, fatigue, or sensory deficits that may have impacted the test results and could result in a significant fluctuation in mental status.

An examinee may perform poorly on formal assessment due to anxiety, depression, sensory deficits, fatigue, sleep deprivation, physical pain, medical illness, medication side effects, or apathy associated with executive dyscontrol. Many daily activities are learned and performed procedurally, and thus may not be significantly affected by certain types of declarative memory loss that are detected easily on formal testing. Also, due to the structure inherent in the assessment session, an examinee's test results may suggest that he or she is capable of a higher level of functioning than is the case in a less structured setting. Psychometric tests are effective yet imperfect measures of real-life abilities; therefore, functional decline may not be readily determined from test data alone.

Remember also that the final decision regarding *competency* is a legal one. Your opinions will add information to assist in the determination of competency (a legal term), but they will not constitute a judicial decision. Ideally, as an independent examiner or expert witness, you will provide substantial, clear, thoughtful and relevant information that can be reviewed and understood by people who have not been trained in your field. The judge, and sometimes a jury, will deliberate, weigh the evidence, and ultimately render a decision.

COURT APPEARANCE

If you have completed an assessment of an older person's capacity in specific areas and have submitted a report, you may not be asked to testify in court unless there is strong opposition to your findings. You should write your report in such a way that your appearance in court is rarely necessary because the report can stand on its own. Nevertheless, you should be prepared to go to court if requested by the retaining attorney or if you receive a subpoena.

A deposition is a legal proceeding, conducted with specific rules, for the purpose of preserving the testimony of a witness for use in court. Opposing attorneys will take your deposition to determine what you know about the case. They will look for evidence favorable to their side and attempt to commit you to statements under oath. They may seek ways to discredit your testimony or get you to make conflicting statements. Minor moments of discomfort on your part are practically inevitable. The following guidelines for navigating depositions and court testimony may minimize your distress:

- Your deposition, as well as your testimony in court, will be taken under oath; therefore, your first duty is to tell the truth even if it hurts the retaining attorney's case. You should avoid vague statements and technical jargon and be as accurate as possible.
- Never volunteer information, even though you may wish to be helpful or explain something in more detail, unless a yes or no answer

truly is insufficient. If you believe that a brief response is insufficient and that further information is needed, you may be permitted to elaborate; however, you should proceed with care. When testifying in court, there may be times when an attorney will cut you off or the judge will not permit you to elaborate on a response.

- Do not answer a question until you are sure you understand what is being asked. Ask for clarification if a question is ambiguous or confusing. If you receive a response that remains unclear, ask again. You may paraphrase the attorney's question to determine whether you have understood it correctly. Beware of hypothetical questions.
- Think, be patient, and take your time. Take as much time as you need, but remember that delayed responses to nearly every question may raise concern regarding your confidence as a witness. If you make a statement that you later believe to be incorrect, you have a right to correct it, even at a later point during your deposition or testimony.
- It is all right to say you don't know. It also is acceptable to say you cannot remember if indeed you can't.
- Try not to become angry. When you are angry, you are more likely to make a mistake. Opposing attorneys may attempt to intimidate you or make you angry during cross-examination. Refuse to allow them to do this.
- If you are given a document to read, take your time and read it carefully before making a comment.
- Before appearing for deposition or testimony, check with the retaining attorney to determine which documents you should bring with you. In most cases, you should bring nothing. In some cases, you must bring everything that contributed to your conclusions.

CASE EXAMPLES

The case vignettes and tips that follow address a number of the issues discussed previously as well as some that have not yet been discussed. These vignettes are designed to illustrate critical issues and raise vital questions you may be asked to address in your role as a consultant in capacity and other forensic cases. They are not intended to illuminate an exhaustive list of ethical and legal issues, but are intended to increase awareness of some of the potentially thorny situations that may arise. Case descriptions are brief, with minimal clinical information, as we wish to shift the focus from diagnostic case formulations to systems issues, broad case subjects, and pertinent assessment questions.

The purpose of general cognitive and neuropsychological assessments continues to evolve. Originally they were intended to help localize cerebral lesions and differentially diagnose abnormal conditions in the central nervous system. More recently, the emphasis has been shifting toward identification of functional cognitive and behavioral strengths and weaknesses. This trend relies on a premise that neuropsychological tests are ecologically valid; that is, that the domains they purport to assess actually predict functioning in the real world. Only if this is the case can a neuropsychologist make reasonable prognostic statements about the patient/examinee. For a more in-depth discussion of ecological validity, the reader may wish to refer to Chaytor & Schmitter-Edgecombe (2003).

Your learning should be ongoing, and exceptions will arise in nearly every new case. Read on, and have an interesting journey.

> There is absolutely no substitute for a genuine lack of preparation.
> —Fortune cookie wisdom

Case Example: Multifactorial Causality

The patient is a 67-year-old male with a long history of depression, traumatic brain injury from an alcohol-related motor vehicle accident 2 years previously, and a history of alcohol abuse. He has been sober for the past 7 months. The probate court is referring the patient for determination of the extent of his cognitive deficits and whether he can be his own decision maker.

- The tricky aspect of this case is that there are multiple contributing causal factors with varying degrees of relevance to the patient's current presentation.

- Questions and information needed to proceed:
  —Are there recent urinalyses to confirm sobriety?
  —Are there reversible medical or psychiatric conditions that could affect assessment results?
  —What role does alcohol play in the patient's life at this point?
  —Is he in treatment or has he recently completed treatment for alcohol abuse?
  —What was the nature and severity of his brain injury? (You should acquire and review hospital/medical records documenting evaluation and treatment of the injury, including patient and collateral reports of changes in functioning that followed.)
  —How did the patient come to the attention of the legal system?

 ## Case Example: Guardianship Tug-of-War

You are contacted by the daughter of an 80-year-old parent with the question of whether she can still make decisions on her own behalf. A brother also is involved, and attorneys represent both adult children. The siblings disagree about their mother's level of impairment. The daughter is seeking both guardianship and conservatorship. An estate is involved, and the daughter believes that her brother is motivated by money and may be exploiting the mother.

- The tricky aspect of this case involves understanding the motivation for the evaluation with multiple, conflicting parties involved.
- Questions and information needed to proceed:
  —The referral source (in this case, the daughter) is paying for the evaluation. You must be clear in your discussion with her that the mother is the client and as such has the right to confidentiality, including the decision as to whether or not to release the report. To clarify roles in such cases, you may ask the referring person to sign a collateral contract. This contract

explains that the information provided by the informant will be included in the report, provides the name of the person about whom the report is written, and details the respective rights of those involved.

—What are the bases of concern about the mother's functioning? You will need to verify reported details of these concerns and obtain collateral information from more than one source.

—Has the mother agreed to an evaluation? Can you determine whether any type of coercion was used to enlist her cooperation? Are other family members involved? What legal activity is pending?

—Is there a will and is it being contested? Is there evidence of exploitation? (This question may involve rendering an opinion, if possible, about if and how long the mother's capacity has been compromised.)

Case Example: Questionable Informant Capacity

A spouse is concerned about his 75-year-old wife's declining memory. He reports that she has been failing to recognize familiar faces, forgetting how to prepare meals, and is not taking medications. She reportedly has not been involved in managing the family's finances for the past several years. As you talk with the husband on the phone, you notice that his reporting is poorly organized, he has word finding problems, and his statements contain inconsistencies. He asks you to evaluate his wife's memory so that he can assume legal management of their financial affairs.

- The tricky aspect of this case is determining how to proceed when the referral source's reliability is questionable.
- Questions and information needed to proceed:
  —Could the informant benefit from an evaluation and how might this be discussed with him? You might talk with the informant about caregiver stress and how this could affect his own concen-

tration and memory. You then could discuss the appointment of a durable power of attorney to assist with financial decision making plus the usefulness of an evaluation of the informant.

—Can you talk directly with the informant's wife?

—Is the wife aware that she may be evaluated, and has she consented?

—If the wife is found to lack capacity, how will the report be used? This becomes especially complicated if her husband, the referral source, also has cognitive dysfunction and is expected to pay for the evaluation. Other family members, if any, should be interviewed if possible, and a protective agency and/or an individual with legal authority may need to be consulted.

—Are there safety issues, and is it possible to obtain reliable information regarding these from the informant or his wife?

—How can *medical necessity* be determined and documented?

Case Example: Confounding Physical Infirmities and Change in Capacity Status

A physician refers an 82-year-old woman who is wheelchair bound, oxygen dependent, diabetic, and wears glasses and hearing aids. She was evaluated 4 months earlier by a neuropsychologist colleague who found her to lack capacity; however, she was in a hospital for treatment of medical problems at that time and her family believes that she now has capacity. The referring physician administered a Mini Mental State Examination on which the patient scored 23 out of 30 possible points. Reports about the extent of her current cognitive deficits are inconsistent as to how much difficulty she is having with instrumental activities of daily living (IADLs). Her physician wants to know if she has some type of dementia, and her family wants to determine her mental capacity:

- The tricky aspects of this case involve appreciating and understanding the impact of multiple medical problems and sensory limitations on her cognitive abilities (both currently and on the previous neuropsychological evaluation) and determining if the referral questions are answerable.

- Questions to be asked and information needed to proceed:
  —Is the patient medically stable to the extent that she can tolerate an evaluation?
  —Is she compliant with her medications?
  —What information does the physician need, and do you need a more specific referral question?
  —How involved are the family members in the patient's daily life? How much IADL assistance are they providing? Can they provide accurate collateral information? Is there someone in the family who is a legal decision maker or who could become one if necessary?
  —What has changed since the last evaluation?
  —Pragmatics: Is food available to ensure stable blood sugar levels during an evaluation? Does the patient have sufficient supplemental oxygen to make it through a lengthy examination? Have wheelchair and transportation issues been addressed beforehand? What is the extent of the patient's sensory and perceptual limitations?
  —Can you review the initial neuropsychological report and hospital records to determine whether acute medical issues may have contributed to her impaired cognition? Are medical issues stabilized at this point?
  —What was the patient's level of functioning prior to her hospitalization 4 months ago? Was she declining prior to that time?

We conclude this section by providing additional common assessment issues that merit consideration when clinical evaluations are particularly complex:

- When assessing capacity, always consider limited guardianship.
- Consider consulting Adult Protective Services if the patient is in danger or if urgent medical or psychiatric treatment is needed.

- Keep in mind that assessment instruments may not be (and usually are not) good predictors of a person's ability to manage IADLs with some degree of assistance. Be prepared to state an opinion as to how much assistance a patient may need to insure that he or she can function safely in the current living environment.
- Always address discrepancies in informal reports of a patient's functional and cognitive status.
- When available, review previous evaluations and include comparisons in your report.
- Make sure you obtain information about the patient's medical problems and medication so you will be aware of any reversible or treatable conditions that may exist.

CONCLUSION

This overview of the business of geropsychology focuses on provision of services geared toward assessment of mental and decisional capacity. The area is broad, and much of the information that we have presented in an abbreviated form can be found in more detail in other chapters of this volume or in attached references. The issues and suggestions included in the case vignettes are culled from our experience with referrals in the state of Colorado. We encourage you to become familiar with your individual state statutes and regulations, which may differ in certain respects. Definitive answers to all questions regarding clinical and legal challenges are beyond the scope of the chapter, but it is our hope that you have acquired some valuable reference points for initiating and maintaining dialogues with colleagues and other professionals involved in the care and assessment of older adults.

SUGGESTED READING

Agronin, M. (2004). *Dementia: Practical guides in psychiatry.* Philadelphia: Lippincott Williams & Wilkins.

Babitsky, S., & Mangraviti, J. (1999). *How to excel during depositions: Techniques for experts that work.* Falmouth, MA: SEAK.

Bieliauskas, L. (1996). Practical approaches to ecological validity of neuropsychological measures in the elderly. In R. Sbordone & C. Long (Eds.), *Ecological validity of neuropsychological testing* (pp. 261–281). Delray Beach, FL: St. Lucie Press.

Brodsky, S. (1991). *Testifying in court: Guidelines and maxims for the expert witness.* Washington, DC: American Psychological Association.

Brodsky, S. (1999). *The expert expert witness: More maxims and guidelines for testifying in court.* Washington, DC: American Psychological Association.

Centers for Medicare and Medicaid Services web site. www.cms.hhs.gov.

Chaytor, N., Schmitter-Edgecomb, M., & Burr, R. (2006). Improving the ecological validity of executive functioning assessment. *Archives of Clinical Neuropsychology, 217–227.*

Department of Veterans Affairs. (1997). *Assessment of competency and capacity of the older adult: A practice guideline for psychologists.* Milwaukee, WI: National Center for Cost Containment.

Farias, S., Harrell, E., Neumann, C., & Houtz, A. (2003). The relationship between neuropsychological performance and daily functioning in individuals with Alzheimer's disease: Ecological validity of neuropsychological tests. *Archives of Clinical Neuropsychology, 655–672.*

Green, J. (2000). *Neuropsychological evaluation of the older adult.* San Diego, CA: Academic Press.

Grisso, T. (1986). *Evaluating competencies: Forensic assessments and instruments.* New York: Plenum Press.

Grisso, T. (1994). Clinical assessment for legal competence of older adults. In M. Sotrandt & G. VandenBos (Eds.), *Neuropsychological assessment of dementia and depression in older adults: A clinician's guide* (pp. 119–139). Washington, DC: American Psychological Association.

Gutheil, T. (1998). *The psychiatrist as expert witness.* Washington, DC: American Psychiatric Press.

Gutheil, T., & Simon, R. (2002). *Mastering forensic psychiatric practice: Advanced strategies for the expert witness.* Washington, DC: American Psychiatric Press.

Lubert, S. (1998). *Expert testimony: A guide for expert witnesses and the lawyers who examine them.* South Bend, IN: National Institute of Trial Advocacy.

National Academy of Neuropsychology. (2001). *Professional issues: Billing and reimbursement.* Retrieved May 27, 2006, from www.nanonline.org/content/text/prof/billing.shtm.

National Academy of Neuropsychology. (2003). *Independent and court-ordered forensic neuropsychological examinations*. Retrieved May 27, 2006, from http://nanonline.org.paio/IME.shtm.

Shapiro, D. (1984). *Psychological evaluation and expert testimony: A practical guide to forensic work*. New York: Van Nostrand-Reinhold.

Spar, J. (2000). Competency and related issues. In C. Coffey & J. Cummings (Eds.), *Textbook of geriatric neuropsychiatry* (pp. 945–963). Washington, DC: American Psychiatric Press.

Spooner, D., & Pachana, N. (2006, May). Ecological validity in neuropsychological assessment: A case for greater consideration in research with neurologically intact populations. *Archives of Clinical Neuropsychology, 21*(4), 327–337.

Sweet, J., Grote, C., & van Gorp, W. (2002). Ethical issues in forensic neuropsychology. In S. Bush & M. Drexler (Eds.), *Ethical issues in clinical neuropsychology* (pp. 103–133). Lisse, The Netherlands: Swets & Zeitlinger.

Tuokko, H., & Hadjistavropoulos, T. (1998). *An assessment guide to geriatric neuropsychology*. London: Erlbaum.

Wood, S., & Kubik, J. (2005). Presenting the complex client in court: Practical issues related to the assessment of capacity. *Rehabilitation Psychology, 50*, 201–206.

REFERENCES

Blau, T. (1999). *The forensic documentation sourcebook*. New York: Wiley.

Chaytor, N., & Schmitter-Edgecombe, M. (2003). The ecological validity of neuropsychological tests: A review of the literature on everyday cognitive skills. *Neuropsychology Review, 13*, 181–197.

Holloway, J. (2003). Getting paid under Medicare. *APA Online*. Retrieved May 27, 2006, from www.apa.org/monitor/may03/medicare.html.

Epilogue

MICHAEL A. SMYER

We go to the foothills
To think about growing
Old.
Who decides, how can they decide,
How to rise to the risks of age.
The change in altitude and latitude
Leaves me dizzy
Over the prospect of the
Downhill run to the
Garden of the Gods.

—*Michael Smyer*

Consider the case of David introduced in Chapter 1.

Case Example: Hospice Request

David had been diagnosed with melanoma 2 years ago. At first, it looked like the surgery had been successful. But then the cancer reemerged and the news was sobering: stage 4. His doctor was direct and deliberate: "You have at most a year to live. You should put your affairs in order."

The doctor had been an optimist. Now 9 months later David was receiving hospice care at home. He knew that the end was near. As a religious person, he was not afraid of death. In fact, his religious devotion gave him a great deal of comfort. But he was worried about those whom he would leave behind, in particular Jane. David had been part of Jane's life for 19 years, ever since he married Jane's mother, Barbara. Although David and Barbara were now divorced. David had been a fatherly presence for Jane, a consistent source of support and encouragement. David had two biological children—Jane's half-brother, Dan, and another daughter, Pat. Pat and David had been estranged for several years; he refused to see her during his time in hospice.

During the week before his death, David called his lawyer: "I need your help. I want to adopt Jane, and I want to change my will. I want to write Jane into the will and I want to eliminate Pat from any inheritance." Does David have the capacity to make this set of decisions?

This volume was designed to provide mental health professionals with conceptual frameworks, background information, and a knowledge base for involvement in the process of assessing older adults' decision-making capacities. If we were successful, you will now approach David's case with different, more discerning questions than when you first opened this volume.

Kurt Lewin's (1935, 1951) summary—Behavior is a function of the Person and the Environment or $B = f(P/E)$—provided the ecological framework that was the basis of this volume. Along those lines, decision-making capacity is a function of the interaction of the individual's functioning and the social, cultural, and legal environment. This ecological framework also provides the structure for this Epilogue.

THE PERSON

We began this collection with an overview of recent conceptualizations of older adults' decision-making capacity (Smyer, Chapter 1, this volume). The first chapter introduced the legal frameworks that shape mental health professionals' involvement in decision-making assessment. The first chapter also introduced the *legal fiction* of a person's decision-making capacity, and the state-by-state variations in that fiction.

The next three chapters introduced the cognitive changes associated with normal aging and with medical conditions and dementia. Foster and her colleagues (Chapter 2, this volume) provided a summary of data indicating that decline in most cognitive domains (with the exception of crystallized intelligence) begins in adulthood and demonstrates a progressive decline across the life span. This pattern becomes the benchmark against which to gauge an individual's current functioning. Foster et al. also reminded us that 10% to 30% of those 60 and older may be classified into a category of cognitive impairment without dementia—what they term a "hidden epidemic."

The Patient Self-Determination Act (PSDA) requires that patients be informed about their rights to determine treatment processes (including the termination of treatment). Often this requirement occurs at the very time that medical conditions and medications offer a significant challenge to patients' decision-making capacity (Dellasega, Frank, & Smyer, 1996). Kaye and Grigsby (Chapter 3, this volume) focused on a range of medical and physiological variables that may influence older adults' cognitive status. Infection, endocrine disorders, a variety of diseases (e.g., cardiovascular, chronic obstructive pulmonary disease, electrolyte imbalances) and vitamin deficiencies may affect an older person's cognitive functioning. In addition, medications (including chemotherapy) may have individual and combined deleterious cognitive effects.

Wood and Tanius (Chapter 4, this volume) tackled one of the most clinically salient issues: the impact of dementia on decision-making abilities. They provided a review of the current neuroscience of decision making, including the role of both cortical and subcortical regions. They also highlighted older adults' increased reliance on System 1 (affective) rather than System 2 (deliberative) processes in decision making. When they turned to the impact of dementias on decision making, Wood and Tanius warned that three elements affect the specific effects of a dementia: the clinical population in question, the brain regions impaired by the disorder, and the presentation (early versus late) of the disease. They urged that we combine cognitive, behavioral, and functional perspectives to determine specific decision-making capabilities.

Moye (Chapter 8, this volume) provided a comprehensive framework for integrating these elements. She noted that an effective assessment and intervention process must integrate knowledge of the person's functioning in several key areas: medical functioning, cognition, functional capacity, personal values and preferences, risk of harm, and potential means to enhance capacity.

THE ENVIRONMENT

The older person's familial, social, legal, and cultural contexts shape the process of assessing decision-making capacity. These contexts provide the environment for raising questions about an older person's capacities, shaping both the framing and answering of the questions.

Qualls (Chapter 5, this volume) focused on the key roles that family members play in both the informal and formal processes of assessing older adults' decision making. Family members are often the first to raise questions about capacity. Also, agency staff members often turn to them for an informal assessment. At the same time, however, they often have direct and indirect stakes in the outcomes of the assessment process. Qualls offered advice for mental health professionals who are called on to mediate various roles for family members and others in the informal network.

Qualls (Chapter 12, this volume) also sketched the roles that staff from various agencies may play in assessing older adults' decision-making capacity. Mental health professionals may find themselves conferring with colleagues in the legal, housing, health care, and social service arenas because older adults' challenges often cut across traditional agency or service-delivery boundaries. To be effective requires understanding the context of each setting and the formal and informal ties that can provide a supportive context for older adults' decisions.

Marshall, Seal, and Vanatta-Perry (Chapter 6, this volume) described the legal environment that mental health practitioners and families must respond to in determining an older adult's decision-making capacity. They highlighted two key questions that the court and its officers try to answer: Does the older person meet the definition of an incapacitated person? If so, who should be appointed as guardian and/or conservator? Answering both of these questions requires an appreciation of the rules, regulations, and skills that determine the role of each of the legal players.

Karel (Chapter 7, this volume) reminded us that cultural attitudes, beliefs, and practices provide a powerful environmental context for all aspects of medical decision making. Cultural elements influence how problems are framed, how solutions are considered, and who is involved in the process. Karel used truth telling and end-of-life care issues to illustrate these important lessons.

Kaye and Kenny (Chapter 13, this volume) reminded us that the fiscal demands of practice are another important part of the environment of decision-making assessments. From Medicare billing to client networks to report structure and content—Kaye and Kenny outlined the complex set of relationships that mental health professionals must maintain to be effective.

BEHAVIOR

Three chapters focused on specific elements of behavioral assessment: neuropsychological assessment, medical consent and independent living, and assessment of financial capacity. For many older adults, determining how they will receive treatment and how their finances will be distributed are two key decisions they will face in later life.

Wood (Chapter 9, this volume) highlighted the distinctive contribution that neuropsychological evaluation makes in describing behavioral patterns of strengths and weakness. Wood stressed that the optimal clinician combines a keen understanding of clinical practice standards with an understanding of legal standards and cognitive disorders of the elderly.

Moye and Braun (Chapter 10, this volume) focused on assessing medical consent and independent living capacity. These are essential behavioral areas that bring older adults and their families into the legal context. In the medical area, they emphasized the importance of assessing the older adult's values and clarity of communication with a spokesperson (if one is available).

Hebert and Marson (Chapter 11, this volume) provided a conceptual model for assessing financial capacity. They stressed that a comprehensive approach includes three elements: (1) specific financial tasks and abilities, (2) broader domains of financial activities, and (3) overall financial capacity. They also reviewed four approaches for assessing these elements (clinical interview, rating scales, performance-based measures, and neuropsychological approaches).

CONCLUSION

Later life is often a time of challenge for older adults and their families. They must respond to changing abilities and increasing demands for decision making regarding health care and financial matters.

Mental health professionals can play an important role in assessing older adults' decision-making capacity. To do so requires a comprehensive knowledge of normal age-related changes in cognition, disease-related changes in decision making, and domain-specific functioning. It also requires close collaborations with lawyers and judges to assure that each jurisdiction's definitions of capacity are adhered to while developing appropriate options for older adults and their families.

Issues of capacity are becoming increasingly important as our society ages. Decisions about medical care, transfer of property, and end-of-life decision making are becoming more common. Our hope is that this collection will enable mental health professionals to play an important role in these decisions.

REFERENCES

Dellasega, C., Frank, L., & Smyer, M. A. (1996). Medical decision-making capacity in elderly hospitalized patients. *Journal of Ethics, Law, and Aging, 2*(2), 65–74.
Lewin, K. (1935). *A dynamic theory of personality.* New York: McGraw-Hill.
Lewin, K. (1951). *Field theory in social science.* New York: McGraw-Hill.

Author Index

Subject Index